Christian Parenting ANSWERS

A reference book
for parents of children ages 0 to 5.

 From the pages of
Christian Parenting Today magazine

Christian Parenting Books is an imprint of
Chariot Family Publishing, a division of
David C. Cook Publishing Co., Elgin, Illinois 60120
David C. Cook Publishing Co., Paris, Ontario
Nova Distribution Ltd., Eastbourne, England

Christian Parenting Today Magazine
P.O. Box 36630, Colorado Springs, CO 80936-3663 (800) 238-2221

CHRISTIAN PARENTING ANSWERS
© 1994 David C. Cook Publishing Co.

Scripture references are from the Holy Bible, New International Version, © 1973,
1978, 1984, International Bible Society. Used by permission of Zondervan Bible
Publishers.

Cover design by Walljasper Design
Text design by Colin Miller
Cover photograph by Bill Gale Photography, Inc., Minneapolis, MN
Model by New Faces Models & Talent, Inc., Minneapolis, MN
General Editor Debra Evans
Text Editor Erin McMahan

First Printing, 1994
Printed in the United States of America
98 97 96 95 94 5 4 3 2 1

Library of Congress Cataloging-in-Publication Data
Applied for

ISBN 0-7814-0182-8

Christian Parenting ANSWERS

Table of Contents

Chapter One
Before Baby Arrives

Chapter Two
The First Days of Life

Chapter Three

Now You're Mom and Dad

Chapter Four

Babycare Basics

Chapter Five

Feeding Your Baby

Chapter Six

Bonding With Baby

Chapter Seven

Uniquely Created

Chapter Eight

Passages

Chapter Nine
Testing Times

Chapter Ten
Toddler Safety

Chapter Eleven
Early Childhood Health

Chapter Twelve
Nutrition and Dental Care

Chapter Thirteen
Play-and-Learn Ideas

Chapter Fourteen
Common Concerns

Chapter Fifteen

Learning New Skills

Chapter Sixteen

Parenting Your Preschooler

Chapter Seventeen

Growing in God

Foreword

I remember what a wise older parent told me when our first baby was born. Seven simple words, none more than five letters long. Yet they're filled with a great and simple profoundness about what it means to be a parent: "Your life will never be the same."

I don't know if he meant the words in a good way or a bad way. But if you're honest and you're like me, you know for sure that the words are completely and utterly true—in both good and bad ways.

Most of us who are parents now were strolling quite happily through the honeymoon phase of our lives when suddenly—boom!—the news came, "We're expecting!" And after that, the boom-type news that goes along with being a parent seems to occur with greater and greater frequency. Pregnancy, childbirth, choosing a pediatrician, caring for a newborn, bonding, postpartum depression, sleepless nights, breast-feeding vs. bottlefeeding, diaper rash, teething—boom! boom! boom! boom!—and your baby isn't even 6 months old yet!

No wonder you'll find a lot of parenting books on bookstore shelves. And now here's another one. But we're hoping that you'll notice that this book is just a bit different from the others. Nearly everything in these pages has appeared in the pages of *Christian Parenting Today* magazine. That means that although Debra Evans served as the general editor of this book, the content reflects the parenting ideas of many experts—just take a look at all the names in the table of contents. And beyond this collection of diverse people, the chapters have had the touch of the editors of *Christian Parenting Today,* who have cast careful eyes along the way to make sure that each word is there to help meet your parenting needs.

Of course, everyone is committed to communicating fresh truths based on what the Bible says about parenting and relationships.

The magazine-style format of this book gives busy parents another benefit—short, easy-to-read but packed-with-information chapters that you can digest in bite-sized chunks.

Debra Evans and all of the contributors to this book deserve a lot of thanks for their writings through the years, and for their dedication to helping Christian parents meet their needs. This book also benefited greatly from the contributions of several current and former members of CPT's staff: David Kopp, our former editorial director, who rallied and railed to get this book published; Erin McMahan, CPT's assistant editor, who did a lot of brainstorming and editing work; and Colin Miller, CPT's associate editor, who spent countless hours putting everyone else's work together into a great final product.

Like many of our magazine's readers who have saved every issue of CPT for reference, you'll probably find a easy-to-reach place for this book. And as your child grows through the early years of life, you'll find yourself referring to these pages again and again and offering to lend it to friends (then wishing you had it back and suggesting they buy their own copy).

Whether you're a new parent or an experienced pro just using *Christian Parenting Answers* for occasional reference, congratulations! You've got the world's most important job—being a parent. Remember, "Your life will never be the same" And you wouldn't want it any other way!

Brad Lewis, Editor
Christian Parenting Today magazine

Editor's Introduction

Becoming parents is an experience unlike any other. It's an exhilarating event, challenging crisis, and amazing achievement all at once, a fork in the road that brings many different changes that are impossible to ignore. "There were two and now there's a third human being, a new spirit, finished and complete, unlike the handiwork of man; a new thought and a new love," wrote 19th-century Russian author Fedor Dostoevski. "It's positively frightening . . . . And there's nothing grander in the world."

It's natural to think that your parenting experience starts with your baby's arrival. But a closer look confirms what recent research and the Bible tell us: the shaping of your child's life began long before birth, even before conception took place. A number of things are already influencing who your baby is—and is still becoming. As a psalm of David tells us, "All the days ordained for me were written in your book before one of them came to be" (Ps. 139:16).

The months of pregnancy and years of early childhood will benefit greatly from your willingness to learn about childbearing and parenting both prior to greeting your little one for the first time and after your baby is born. *Christian Parenting Answers* has been put together to help you meet that need, whether you're right in the midst of preparing yourself—spiritually, emotionally, physically—for the task of parenting, or are now beyond the birth and well into the day to day responsibilities of caring for your child.

We believe that parenting is important. The birth or adoption of a child is a major event in the life of a family, and because some segments of our society devalue parenting and childhood, we want to offer you a feast of support, encouragement and useful tips. The menu of options supplied here, written by a wide variety of Christian parents and professionals, is designed to be digested slowly as you take what you need, when you need it, and leave the rest for later.

We don't guarantee that you'll like everything we say. People's tastes vary, as do parents' styles and their beliefs about raising children. We know you will use your own judgment to decide which ideas and suggestions will be helpful to you.

If you're feeling some anxiety about your new life, that's OK. According to renowned pediatrician T. Berry Brazelton, "The feelings of being overwhelmed, of feeling anxious, of not knowing what is best, of caring too much, of being inexperienced and inadequate are universal ones for all parents. In fact, the amount of anxiety that a new parent experiences may parallel just how much he or she cares about doing well by that baby." (*On Becoming a Family: The Growth of Attachment,* Dela-courte Press).

Over time, these feelings will subside as you grow in wisdom and ability as a parent. Nothing can substitute for the daily on-the-job training required of mothers and fathers on their parenting journey. But the companionship of friends helps to make the going easier. In this book, it's our hope that you'll find a few friends in us, as our words extend beyond these pages and into your life.

Thank you for inviting us to join you on your grand adventure.

Debra Evans,
general editor

CHAPTER ONE

―≈―

Before Baby Arrives

―≈―

Chapter One ────────────────────────────

The Expectant Mom

by Debra Evans

Deep within your body, securely nestled in your womb, your child is growing. From the moment of conception, your baby's life has begun to unfold according to God's perfect plan.

Our Creator's design for fetal growth and development is incredibly intricate, woven together in a beautiful way through many minute details. The physiological aspects of pregnancy—the various changes your body began to go through the instant your child was conceived—are amazing. Did you know, for example, that as an embryo, your baby started secreting a substance to prepare your breasts for lactation *before* implantation took place? Or that your entire immune system was initially suppressed to avoid mounting a biological assault on your little one?

While many of the processes linked to your pregnancy escape unnoticed, other changes in your body eventually become unmistakable: the increase in your respiratory rate, which supplies extra oxygen to your uterus and the baby; a slowing down of digestive processes, often resulting in heartburn and constipation; hormone shifts resulting in skin softness, breast fullness and complexion changes. As you've experienced these physical changes, you may have noticed your heart changing as well.

As you prepare for your baby's entry into the outside world, you may feel weak, tired, frustrated or frightened at times. That's OK. It isn't unusual to feel pulled in many different directions by friends, family and

───── ∼ ─────

It's positively frightening. . . . And there's nothing grander in the world.

Fedor Dostoevski,
on becoming a parent

───── ∼ ─────

21

society. Being a Christian doesn't automatically confer some sort of "super-humanity" on believers that exempts us from experiencing a wide range of emotions. Instead, it means that our emotional strength rests upon our reliance on God's unfailing love and acceptance. *Nothing* can separate us from his love. Learning to trust God with your arms wide open will help you embrace his love for you anew each day.

Being human makes it easy to hug our fears and concerns close to ourselves rather than trust God with our wayward hearts. It takes real effort to depend on our heavenly Father to meet our needs. We must *choose* to walk with him day by day. This pregnancy, your upcoming birth experience, and mothering this little one will provide you with almost unlimited opportunities for spiritual growth, enabling you to become increasingly aware that God's Word is *true*. Know that the Lord's grace will always be sufficient for you as you draw near to him with a sincere heart, even when things happen that you weren't planning on. In all circumstances, the comfort of the Holy Spirit will be present to sustain you.

Although your due date may seem a long way off, the coming months will give you time to prepare for your baby's arrival. This period of waiting can be both fruitful and fulfilling as you move closer in time to that incredible moment when you hold your precious child in your arms. Between now and then, take advantage of this opportunity to get ready for mothering.

These next several months will give you time to prepare and plan for your baby's birth in much the same way that your engagement gave you a chance to get ready for your wedding. There are a number of things to consider as you plan to make this birth as safe and as special as possible: Where will the event take place? Who will attend as your birth attendant and support team? What things are important to you and your husband in terms of promoting your values and beliefs during birth and the immediate recovery period? Numerous books, classes, maternal-child health advocates and childbirth organizations offer information for your consideration and education. Take advantage of these resources!

Protect your pregnancy by eating well, getting plenty of rest, exercising sensibly, and avoiding exposure to harmful substances, such as cigarette smoke and alcohol, in any amounts. Your pregnancy is not a disease or an illness, but a physiological state that is wonderfully "normal"! In spite of how complicated this entire process seems, God's design for labor and birth is not geared for frequent complications. Your body is capable of accomplishing amazing tasks during pregnancy and childbirth, especially if you take care of yourself wisely. Also, encourage your husband to assume a greater degree of responsibility for the birth by including him in your prenatal care and education.

Most of all, enjoy these months of intimate sharing with your developing baby. Dream! Go for long walks! Sing lullabies! Marvel as your belly shifts and sways while your baby somersaults! Pregnancy isn't just a time of waiting and hoping. It's a time for participating in the exuberant joy of creation. These will be remarkable, memorable months worth enjoying and experiencing to the fullest.

The Expectant Dad

by William Sears

Though God has blessed mothers with the privilege of carrying, birthing and nourishing a baby, he has also given us Christian fathers a vital role in the pregnancy, birth, and care of our children.

Perhaps outsiders appreciate an expectant mother's feelings more than her spouse's because hers are more obvious. But a dad also has personal adjustments to make during his wife's pregnancy that merit much prayer and consultation.

One of the earliest father feelings you will have is a pride in your masculinity and fertility. This can be normal and healthy, similar to the pride that comes with any accomplishment. To help keep this pride in Christian perspective, thank God for the pregnancy, and acknowledge him as the ultimate Creator of life.

Your other feelings may be less positive: As the reality of another mouth to feed sinks in, increased responsibilities may weigh heavily on you. It's unfortunate that we have to consider the subject of money at all, but economic worries are unquestionably among the earliest concerns of any new father. Like many fathers, you may exaggerate this worry way out of proportion. For example, you may worry about how you are going to educate your child, even before he is born. In addition to the dependency of the new life, your wife may highly depend on you throughout the pregnancy. You might begin to question your abilities to father your baby and "mother" your wife.

Some men actually experience pregnancy-like symptoms during their wives' pregnancies; this may reflect a subconscious desire to take part in their wives' physical condition. Other fathers consider pregnancy a necessary nuisance that will eventually yield a baby. If the latter is your attitude, you may tend to focus on your baby's arrival, subconsciously ignoring the pregnancy *and* the mother. This tendency will probably be overruled by your wife's constant physical and emotional changes, which will serve as a reminder of the reality of the family pregnancy.

Rewards of Sharing the Pregnancy

A number of benefits result when you willingly support your wife throughout the process of pregnancy, birth, and recovery:

• Your compassion for and understanding of your wife's sexuality deepen.

• The intimate, exclusive bond shared through the act of love which created your child will widen to include you in the birth of your child as well.

• Your sense of attachment to your wife and baby will become more real as you participate in your baby's life from his first breath.

• Your involvement in caring for your wife during childbirth actively conveys love and concern for your family, reinforcing a sense of "oneness" and belonging to each other.

Toward the end of the pregnancy, you might have ambivalent feelings about how your baby will affect your marital relationship. The following tips can help you handle these uneasy father feelings:

• Take stock of your situation. As your preborn baby matures, so will you. Your wife's pregnancy may be a time for you to ripen spiritually and become a more mature man. Pregnancy can be inventory time in the fathering business—a time to sit back and define your priorities. It is a time to account for where you have been and where you are going.

Specifically, take an in-depth look at how you are walking with God and how you are walking with your wife. Is your marital relationship God-centered? This is a prerequisite for God-centered parenting.

Are you sensitive to your wife's needs during her pregnancy? As described in Ephesians 5:25, one of the greatest ways you can prepare yourself for loving your child is to continue loving her mother. Does your job assume priority over your marital relationship? It is important to put your *marriage* before your job so that later you know how to put your *fathering* before your job.

• Get involved in the pregnancy. The earlier you become involved in the family pregnancy, the more involved you will be throughout the pregnancy and the years of child-rearing to come. Involve yourself with the choices you and your wife will make early in the pregnancy: which doctor, which hospital, which birthing environment, and so on. Accompany your wife on her visits to the obstetrician. Involvement increases knowledge of what is going on; knowledge can help prevent shying away from these decisions.

• Attend Christian-led childbirth classes. A father's involvement in childbirth is one of the major focuses of these classes. In many instances, fathers actually benefit as much as, if not more than, mothers.

• Help prepare the nest. Assist your wife in the traditionally motherly task of getting ready for the baby. Accompany your wife on shopping trips, and help prepare and decorate the nursery. Respect your wife's nesting instinct. If major changes in your lifestyle—moving to a new house or changing jobs—are necessary, don't make these changes in the last months of the pregnancy.

• Pray daily that God will give you wisdom to be a father and husband according to his divine plan. The following Scripture verses may help you overcome your uneasy father feelings: Ephesians 5:25 and 6:4; Colossians 3:19, 21; Philippians 4:19. Applying these verses to your own live can help you become a God-centered Christian father.

Prenatal Bonding:
Talking with Your Unborn Child

by V. Gilbert Beers

Have you ever heard of a Pregaphone? It was new to me when I saw the ad. The picture told the whole story—a pregnant woman with a telephone in hand. The wire from the phone went to a little cup attached to her telltale abdomen. She was talking to her unborn child.

Two women wrote to me before I saw the Pregaphone, telling me they had a habit of reading books I had written to their unborn children.

Why would anyone read to unborn children? They won't smile or laugh, at least that we can see. Nor can we see them point or cuddle. Certainly they won't ask questions. So why bother?

The two mothers who wrote gave the same reason: They spoke of "vibes" between a mother and her unborn child. One asked, "If vibes between mother and unborn child are so important, why not send Christian vibes—songs, stories and talk?"

Why not?

I believe we underestimate the power of relationships built during the nine months of pregnancy. God knew that time frame was not merely for the fetus to develop physically, but for a child to develop as *a child* within a friendly environment. Can you think of a more friendly environment than a mother's womb—unless the mother and her circumstance turn it into a hostile environment?

Recognizing *who* inhabits that friendly environment of the mother's womb is the foundation on which vital relationships are built during pregnancy. I say "who" because our attitude toward the unborn child as a child is the basic rationale for building a relationship during pregnancy.

During a pregnancy, God is at work in a daily, continuing act of creation. During our five pregnancies, my wife and I felt a deep sense of awe in our three-way creation—hers, mine and the Creator's. We found it helpful to think of our unborn baby not merely as a person, but as a person of great value. This was our future son or daughter—no, our *present* son or daughter—in a quiet, private stage of growth.

Don't be embarrassed or ashamed to talk to your unborn child, even though you haven't yet seen his face. There is something special going on—a building of relationships that none of us fully understands. But somehow we know it is happening.

Nutrition in Pregnancy: Table for (Almost) Two

by Pamela Smith

Not long after becoming pregnant, a morning-sick and information-overloaded Heidi sat before me saying, "Pam, consider me 'nutritionally illiterate.' I know there's a lot of information out there about how to eat right, but I just never bothered with it. Now I'm pregnant, and I know I have to eat better. I just don't have a clue how."

No maternal instinct was going to draw Heidi to a good diet. She needed some firm directions.

If you're like Heidi, finding yourself pregnant but lost in the world of nutrition—this is for you! Once you begin to eat well, you will begin to feel well. Right away, you will have the advantage of seeing a big difference in your energy level, your stamina, your skin, hair, nails and eyes. Every aspect of your baby's life will be affected by nutrition that starts long before birth. Current research shows that your baby's resistance to infection *for the first 18 years of life* is strengthened by good nutrition in the womb.

Six essential nutrients form the foundation of a healthy life: protein, carbohydrates, vitamins, minerals, water and even fat (in limited amounts). Pregnancy intensifies your body's need of these. You do require more *calories* during pregnancy—but only 15 to 20 percent more. You don't need to double your normal intake just because you're "eating for two." However, your *vitamin and mineral needs* can jump as much as 100 percent. It's quality, not quantity, your baby needs. Your best bet is not to count calories, but to focus on eating nutritious foods at the right times, in the right balance.

The typical person living life in the fast lane subsists on a diet that is high in fat, sodium and sugar, and generally low in protein, calcium and vitamins A and C. This is *not* the recipe for a healthy pregnancy. The key is to replace erratic, sporadic eating with small meals and smart snacks evenly spaced throughout the day. The following guidelines will permit your body to make better use of nutrients and will provide you with more energy.

Never skip breakfast. Breakfast still is the most important meal of your day. If you want to start your day with a boundless energy level, your metabolism in high gear, and proteins actively building your and your baby's new cells, then eat breakfast.

Don't make the mistake of skipping breakfast because you're queasy—skipping will make it worse. Eat breakfast soon after you get up (within the first half hour of arising).

Since time often seems to be short for many women, I recommend these breakfast ideas: a slice of whole-wheat bread topped with natural peanut butter and banana slices, broiled; a breakfast parfait with layers of plain, low-fat yogurt, Grape-Nuts and fresh fruit, sprinkled with cinnamon; whole-wheat french toast made with egg whites and skim milk, topped with sugarless fresh-fruit preserves. If you're really in a hurry, try a fresh-fruit and skim-milk shake, cheese toast and fruit, or yogurt with a muffin.

Power snack. Continue to eat "mini-meals" throughout each day, about every three hours. Healthy and wise snacking is like consistently throwing wood on a fire to keep it burning well. Snacking will result in more energy, proper weight gain, and a constant source of nutrients for your baby. It will also help prevent nausea and fatigue.

Make snacks into power combos of *energy-giving carbohydrates* (whole-grain breads, rolls, English muffins and bagels, low-fat crackers and frozen waffles) and *power proteins* (low-fat cheeses, lean meats, yogurt, cottage cheese, skim milk, tofu, cooked beans, tuna and salmon).

Your need for protein increases greatly during pregnancy. The brain-cell development of your baby depends on your protein intake. Protein boosts your metabolism, building body muscles and nerve tissue, and provides for growth of the placenta and uterus. It serves to keep body fluids in balance (excessive swelling and fluid retention is often caused by inadequate protein) and makes beautiful hair, skin and nails for your baby.

Women need at least 70 grams of protein a day during pregnancy. Generally, one ounce of meat contains about seven grams of protein. Be sure to take in protein in small, evenly distributed amounts. Protein is not stored, so it must be replenished frequently. It also needs to be eaten with energy-giving carbohydrates to protect the protein from being wasted as a less-efficient source of energy.

Choose your proteins wisely. By choosing the low-fat versions of protein foods, you will get all of their goodness without the risks of a high-fat diet.

Why High Calcium Foods?

Eating enough high-calcium food is particularly crucial in the last three months of pregnancy when your baby's bone formation takes place at an accelerated rate. You need at least 1,200 milligrams of calcium each day to cover this need. This can easily be obtained by eating four to five servings selected from among these high-calcium foods each day (amount of one serving):

milk or yogurt (1 cup)
cheese (1½ ounces)
ricotta cheese (½ cup)
salmon, water-packed (⅔ cup)
collard or turnip greens (1 cup)
broccoli (2 cups)
dried beans, cooked (2½ cups)
calcium-processed tofu or fortified soy milk (1 cup)

What about minerals? The minerals you need during pregnancy are calcium, iron, zinc and sodium. In general, we eat too much sodium and not enough of the other three.

At one time, health-care professionals recommended that pregnant women cut back on salt, which can cause fluid retention. This is no longer recommended, and moderate salt use is acceptable and encouraged. Mild swelling of the ankles and feet is considered normal during pregnancy, and assuring adequate protein and fluid intake is often a more critical move to manage swelling.

Zinc is an important mineral for fetal growth and development. You need 15 milligrams per day, but this amount is easily obtained by eating adequate protein.

If you do not eat adequate food sources of calcium to supply your baby's skeletal needs, your baby will draw from your reserves, threatening the strength of your bones. Inadequate calcium intake can result in sleeplessness, irritability, muscle cramps, uterine pain and eventual osteoporosis.

Similarly, if you don't take in enough iron each day, your baby will draw from your reserves and leave you iron-deficient and anemic. You will tire easily and be more susceptible to infections. Your baby will be more prone to anemia in the first year of life.

Because a pregnancy also requires much iron, your physician will probably prescribe a supplement. The most efficiently absorbed forms of iron are ferrous gluconate and ferrous fumerate. Even if you are taking an iron supplement, you should include food sources of iron, especially: red meats, dried apricots, prunes, prune juice, dried beans and whole grains. In addition:

• Eat fruits high in vitamin C (citrus, strawberries and pineapple) and vegetables from the cabbage family (broccoli, cabbage and cauliflower) at your meals and snacks. (Vitamin C increases your absorption of iron.)

• Avoid drinking tea, colas and coffee with your meals. These contain tannic acid, which hinders your absorption of iron. Drink water instead.

What about vitamins? The best way to assure your vitamin intake is to eat whole-grain carbohydrates whenever possible and choose meals full of a variety of brightly colored fruits and vegetables.

Generally, the more vivid the color the fruit or veggie is, the higher in essential nutrients it will be for you and your baby. That deep orange-red color of carrots, sweet potatoes, apricots, cantaloupe and strawberries is a sign of their vitamin A content. Dark green, leafy vegetables like greens, spinach, romaine lettuce, broccoli and brussels sprouts are also loaded with an extra bonus: They are *the* source of folic acid, a "must have" in pregnancy.

Folic acid is the vitamin hero. It is critical for protein metabolism, particularly in periods of rapid growth. The need for folic acid nearly doubles during pregnancy to 400 milligrams per day, so a supplement is usually recommended.

No matter what stage of pregnancy you may be in, applying these principles immediately will have big payoffs. I see many of my pregnant patients for the first time just a few weeks before delivery. I commonly hear their frustration, maybe a little guilt and fear, that they have not been eating well throughout their pregnancy.

I do my best to displace those negative feelings—our bodies are wonderfully made. Any positive nutrition change now will still bring rewards. If there have been deficiencies in your diet during the past few months, your body will begin to compensate for them, using the good nutrition now being received to fill in the gaps. Remember, you have been created as the perfect host for your baby. Your body freely gives to whatever your baby's needs may be.

Remedies for Pregnancy Discomforts
by Pamela Smith

• Waking well. The exact cause of morning sickness is unknown. What *is* known is that it's not restricted to mornings. An even, frequent intake of low-fat proteins balanced with carbohydrates throughout the day will help keep your blood sugars stable and help prevent the queasiness before it hits.

Start before you even get out of bed. Have some crackers that you can eat at your bedside before you get up. If possible, lie still for 10 to 15 minutes. When you get up, drink a cool, soft juice (like white grape or apple-cranberry) with a small balanced breakfast. Continue to eat every two hours all through the day and evening, including a night snack. Drink water *after* meals and snacks, not on an empty stomach. Don't wait to eat until you're hungry and weak.

• Cooling heartburn. Heartburn is caused by hormonal changes and the pressure of the back pushing against the gastric area. It can be aggravated by citrus juice, tomato sauces, caffeine, pickled foods, chili powder, pepper and peppermint candy. Prevent discomfort by avoiding these irritants and by eating often to keep your gastric juices neutralized.

• Curing constipation. Hormonal changes and the pressure of the baby upon the gastrointestinal (GI) tract cause digestion to slow, resulting in constipation and gas formation. You can help your GI tract to speed things up by adding fiber, water and exercise to your new lifestyle.

Be sure to get plenty of whole-grain carbohydrates, specifically unprocessed wheat bran, fresh fruits and leafy vegetables. Be sure to drink adequate water (eight to 12 ounces after each meal and snack). Daily exercise will also help keep the digestive tract moving. A mere 15-minute walk each day will do you good.

• Sleeping sweetly. If you find yourself waking up during the night or sleeping restlessly, change your bedtime snack to one that will keep your blood-sugar levels more even as you sleep. This will help you prevent that lighter state of sleep where you acutely notice baby aerobics, full bladders and general discomfort. An ideal snack is a whole-grain cereal with skim milk or yogurt. Also, try to drink most of your daily water requirement before and through dinner, not afterward.

Prenatal Weight Gain: General Guidelines

by Patricia Rushford

Like most moms-to-be, you've probably been deluged with advice and theories about weight gain. Even "experts" differ. How do you know what to believe?

Overall health is more important than weight gain. Up until recently, the medical profession recommended that pregnant women gain no more than 25 to 32 pounds. But according to a study by Abrams and Parker, of the University of California at San Francisco, these figures may be too conservative. They analyzed records of 4,674 women at the university hospital who experienced "good pregnancy outcomes" (meaning no apparent problems, a healthy baby, normal vaginal delivery and no maternal diabetes or hypertension). Most of the women gained between 22 and 46 pounds (about 20 percent gained more than 40).

Too little weight gain is as concerning as too much. Severe bouts of nausea and vomiting that prevent adequate nutrition must be closely monitored by your doctor. Dieting during pregnancy is also unwise, since it can deprive your baby of essential nutrients. If you were overweight before you became pregnant, work with your doctor to keep excess weight at a minimum while still making healthy choices.

The 1990 recommendations from the U.S. National Institute of Medicine suggest that most women gain between 25 and 35 pounds throughout the pregnancy. If you were underweight before pregnancy, you should gain a little more (28 to 35 pounds), and if you were overweight, a little less (18 to 25 pounds). The pattern of weight gain is at least as important as the total amount. The goal is a slow, steady gain: approximately four to five

What Makes Up the Weight
A healthy weight gain is not made up of fat alone, but of specific body changes. For example, a 25-pound weight gain at delivery would consist of:

Your baby: 7½ pounds
Increased size of breasts and uterus: 4 to 5 pounds
Placenta: 1½ pounds
Amniotic fluid: 2 pounds
Extra blood volume: 3 pounds
Energy reserves: 6 to 7 pounds

31

pounds during the first three months and three to four pounds during each of the remaining six months.

Most doctors now agree there is no "ideal" weight gain for pregnant women. Of greater importance is knowing what you can do to stay healthy and have a healthy baby.

Avoid fatty foods. To keep fat intake to a minimum, limit red meats. Meat provides some nutrition, but it is also high in cholesterol and fat. Though your need for iron is exceptionally high during pregnancy, there are plenty of other iron-rich sources: raisins, grains, legumes, dried fruits, soybean and tofu products and green, leafy vegetables.

Exercise. Exercise should be regular, not intermittent. Pregnancy is not the time to take up a new, strenuous form of activity. Avoid major workout sessions and jarring movements. Recommended activities include walking, swimming and low-impact aerobics. Check with your doctor prior to undertaking any exercise program.

The key word in all of this is moderation. Eat appropriately when you are hungry; drink water and nutrient-dense liquids when you're thirsty. Take walks, have fun, and make plans for your new arrival.

Finding Your Birth Attendant

by Debra Evans

In our culture today, there is no one "right" way to give birth. Expectant parents usually can choose who will be their birth attendant, who will accompany the mom through labor, and what can be done to make their baby's birth special.

Prenatal care primarily involves three people: the mother, her preborn child and the maternity-care provider. The baby's father also plays a key role by supporting lifestyle changes to promote his family's well-being.

This three-step selection process increases the likelihood that you'll find the birth attendant who can best meet your health-care needs:

1. Consider who is available in your area. Begin your search by checking with your health insurance company to determine the extent of your maternity benefits. If applicable, obtain a list of approved providers in your HMO or physicians' network. Find out which of the following providers accept your insurance and think about who you might prefer to see:

Midwife: Typically a woman, a midwife specializes in the art and practice of assisting women during the normal processes of pregnancy, childbirth and breastfeeding. Midwives work with physicians, who supply medical backup if complications arise. A *nurse-midwife* is a registered nurse and graduate of an approved training program who has passed a certification exam. Traditional, or *"lay," midwives* learn the art of midwifery by self-study programs, tutorial training, experiential observation and "hands-on" apprenticeship. They are licensed in some states; in others, their practice of midwifery is either illegal or not regulated by law. As birth attendants, midwives are different from physicians because they spend significantly more time with their clients during prenatal exams and remain with women throughout labor.

Family practitioner: A family-practice physician is either a licensed medical doctor (M.D.) or doctor of osteopathy (D.O.) who has graduated from an approved medical school and has often completed an additional three-year residency training program. Family practitioners are qualified to treat a variety of birth complications, but they cannot perform Cesarean surgery. Many family practitioners use fewer routine obstetrical interventions and are more conservative concerning the use of anesthetics. They also offer expectant couples the advantage of being able to meet the entire family's medical needs.

Obstetrician-gynecologist: An OB-GYN is also an M.D. or a D.O. who has finished medical school and a three-year residency in obstetrics and gynecology. Unlike family practitioners, OB-GYNs are highly trained surgeons who specialize in treating complications related to pregnancy and childbearing. An obstetrician is the most skilled (and most expensive) maternity-care provider. If your pregnancy or birth requires extensive medical involvement, an OB-GYN may be best for you.

2. Consult a variety of sources. Maternity care is expensive in the United States. Services differ from place to place, and practices vary dramatically between providers. It's wise to look around before you "buy," especially if your community offers a wide array of birth services. Once you learn that you're pregnant, take time to learn about birth options by reading several current books and talking to as many people as possible. If pro-life issues are a concern to you, call your local crisis pregnancy center and/or pro-life groups to inquire about recommended pro-life providers. Other excellent referral sources include local childbirth and breastfeeding associations, health-care organizations and consumer support groups, state and county health agencies, and hospital staff persons.

33

3. Conduct a pre-exam interview. Before selecting a specific provider, set up an appointment to meet with her or him before making your choice. Expectant parents do this as a matter of course with pediatricians before their baby is born, so why not do this with your birth attendant as well? If necessary, the interview can take place immediately before a new-patient visit if you are fairly certain that this is the provider you will choose. Before the interview, prepare a brief list of questions to ask based on the information you've been accumulating. Jot down a few things about your medical history to discuss. During your conversation, share a little bit about yourself and talk about the kind of health care you're looking for.

Your choice of a birth attendant—the person who will provide health care throughout your pregnancy and the birth of your baby—is one of the most important decisions you make during pregnancy. By making the decision carefully *and* prayerfully, you will be more likely to be satisfied in your pursuit of a happy and healthy birthday.

Birthplace Options

by Debra Evans

Since training to become a childbirth educator in 1973, I've witnessed a virtual explosion in maternity-care options across the United States. Most hospitals now incorporate the kind of family-centered maternity care I could only dream about two decades ago.

Because current birthplace options vary widely in philosophy, types of services offered, fees charged and attitudes toward patients, it's important to learn as much as possible about maternity-care choices in your community before deciding where to have your baby. (When preexisting medical conditions rule out options that can't accommodate a higher degree of risk, flexibility is essential. For this reason, it helps to view your chosen birthplace as a preference rather than an absolute goal.)

Here are the advantages and disadvantages associated with each option to help you think through what's best for you and your baby:

Out-of-Hospital Options
Free-standing Birth Center. For Nancy and Jim Bennett, the choice was clear: Having their third baby in a birthing center offered an appealing alternative to traditional in-hospital delivery. Dissatisfied with the lack of

personal attention they had received during previous labors, Nancy and Jim also wanted to avoid routine medical interventions such as IVs and episiotomies.

"The family birthing center offers a homelike setting with little interference in the birthing process," explains Nancy. "They encourage parents to determine what they want, but a doctor or nurse-midwife is there to supervise."

The Bennetts found the birth center a good compromise between home and hospital: Nancy wanted good prenatal care and medical backup in case an emergency arose, and Jim was able to become more involved in this delivery by being the one to "catch" his daughter while the doctor watched.

Advantages:

• Birth is seen as a normal, physiological process requiring little intervention in low-risk labors.

• Considerable emphasis is placed on promoting a mother's comfort in labor: nearby kitchens supply nutritious foods and beverages; large bathtubs accommodate a variety of labor positions; regular beds with plenty of pillows are available.

• Few routine procedures are used, reducing the cost of care.

• The homelike setting reduces anxiety.

• Family decides who is present at the birth and what roles they assume in conjunction with health-care providers.

• Personnel may consist of a widely varied team, including nurse-midwives, lay midwives, OB nurses, birth assistants, childbirth educators, pediatric specialists, lactation consultants, family practitioners and on-call physicians.

• Insurance usually covers the center's charges.

• Emphasis on early return home after the birth promotes family involvement and responsibility in mother-baby care.

Disadvantages:

• Certain medical conditions may require the mother's and/or baby's transfer to a hospital.

• The center may place restrictions on what obstetrical drugs may be administered (epidural anesthesia, for example, is usually not available).

• Location of the setting may make a hospital transfer difficult.

• Medical liability varies between centers.

Home Birth. Stephanie and Chuck Ehrlinger experienced two deliveries in a hospital before deciding a home birth might be right for them.

Dick was initially skeptical. "I have good insurance that pays for everything done in a hospital," he says. "I felt the safest way to have a baby is in the hospital with expert resources available. Yet when I met with our midwife, I realized that a home birth can be at least as safe."

The Ehrlingers found a doctor who was willing to offer them medical care in case hospitalization proved necessary. The baby arrived right on schedule—exactly on his due date—with friends and family gathered in the living room.

"When Isaac was born, I nursed him immediately," Stephanie recalls. "Later, I was served breakfast in bed. It was a wonderful experience in the privacy of our own home."

Advantages:
- Birth is viewed as a non medical, family event.
- Little, if any, intervention is used.
- The family controls who is present and what they do
- The home provides a familiar setting—with familiar bacteria—significantly reducing the chance of infection for the mother and baby.
- Parents assume legal responsibility for the outcome of the birth.
- Home is the least expensive birthplace.

Disadvantages:
- In most cases, emergency medical treatment is not immediately available.
- There may be a lack of medical backup to provide ongoing care.
- There is no access to pain-relieving drugs.
- Parents must coordinate and pay for all health care and at-home support services, with little likelihood of third-party reimbursement.

In-Hospital Options

Birthing Room. Theresa and Tom Stephenson decided to have their first child in a birthing room at a hospital. Still the most widely available setting for birth, in-hospital care can often be modified according to parents' desires.

After having contractions without medication for awhile, Theresa requested pain relief and was given a small dose of analgesia. Several hours later she asked for an epidural block, an anesthetic used to numb the area between the knees and navel. Throughout the night, labor progressed smoothly, and Theresa gave birth to an eight-pound girl just seven hours after her admission.

"I was pleased with the way everything went," she said. "The doctor and nurses were great. There really isn't anything we would choose to do differently next time around."

Hospital birthing rooms are designed to be as homelike as possible, with equipment hidden or kept in the background. Some include a cradle for the baby, a rocking chair for the mom, and a recliner or fold-out bed for the dad. Most obstetrical procedures can be performed in a birthing room, with the exception of Cesarean sections.

Advantages:

• The normalcy of birth is emphasized; most obstetrical interventions used in a traditional hospital setting are available, but fewer routine procedures are used.

• Transfer to a delivery suite for birth is often unnecessary.

• Insurance covers many in-hospital expenses.

• Medical liability is assumed by physician and hospital staff.

Disadvantages:

• A birth in this setting may include routine interventions and may not substantially differ from a traditional in-hospital approach.

• In general, hospital staff controls who is present and what roles they play.

• Unfamiliar bacteria are present.

• Birthing rooms may cost the same as a traditional hospital birth.

LDRP Room. This is an increasingly popular in-hospital alternative. Early discharge from an LDRP (labor, delivery, recovery, postpartum) room saves the expense of prolonged hospitalization by keeping the mother in the same room throughout her hospital stay.

Advantages:

• LDRPs offer most of the same advantages and disadvantages as

---

Birthplace Resources

Write or call these organizations for more information on birthplace options.

• International Childbirth Education Association, P.O. Box 20048, Minneapolis, MN 55420. 612/854-8660. Promotes family-centered maternity care throughout the United States and abroad by training and certifying childbirth educators, sponsoring workshops and conventions, and publishing the International Journal of Childbirth Education.

• InterNational Association of Parents and Professionals for Safe Alternatives in Childbirth, Route 1, Box 646, Marble Hill, MO 63764. 314/238-2010. Offers information, support and educational resources regarding safe home-birth practice.

• The National Association of Childbearing Centers, 3123 Gottschall Rd., Perkiomenville, PA 18074. 215/234-8068. Provides information on the location, philosophy, and operation of free-standing birth centers.

---

birthing rooms, but often cost less because the mother and baby leave sooner.

• If the baby stays in the LDRP with the mother, chances of picking up an infection in a centralized nursery are reduced.

• Staff is shared with the nursery, enhancing continuity of mother-baby care.

• Insurance companies prefer the lower cost of LDRPs and provide excellent coverage of birth-related costs.

• Hospital personnel are legally responsible for all medical treatment provided.

Disadvantages:

• The disadvantages are primarily the same as those with birthing rooms, with the exception of reduced infection risks if a centralized nursery isn't used.

Traditional Hospital Setting. Cindy and Steve West had planned to have their baby in a birthing room, but when Cindy's water broke and labor didn't begin spontaneously, Cindy was admitted to the hospital. After two days without progress, their baby was delivered by Cesarean section in the delivery room.

"My first response," says Cindy, "was fear of the unknown. But I had a really good nurse, and she explained exactly what would happen."

Steve adds, "It was hard to make decisions because we were both really tired. Unless you spend a good deal of time becoming knowledgeable beforehand, you feel you have to go with what the medical staff thinks is best."

If you know you will undergo a Cesarean birth, or if you have encountered complications during pregnancy, becoming familiar with this setting can significantly allay anxiety. Tour the facility and ask questions.

Advantages:

• Any woman may use this setting.

• Mom moves to a delivery suite for vaginal or Cesarean birth.

• Many types of emergency equipment are available.

• Anesthesia and other obstetrical interventions are widely used.

• Staff consists of nurses, nurse clinicians, OB aides, physicians, and may include nurse-midwives.

• Medical personnel are liable for the mother's and baby's health care.

• Comprehensive insurance coverage is available.

• Recovery is medically supervised throughout the length of the hospital stay.

Disadvantages:
• A hospital setting can seem unfamiliar and cause maternal anxiety and apprehension.
• Maternity care often seems high-tech and routine.
• Transfer to delivery suite may be disorienting and uncomfortable.
• Hospital staff stipulates who accompanies the mother through the birth process.
• Foreign bacteria increase the chance of infection for the mother and baby.
• The traditional hospital setting is the most expensive type of maternity care.

For parents-to-be, the variety of birthplace choices available today makes it possible to have a safe labor and delivery that meets a family's personal needs. The type of birth style may vary considerably, but for most couples the primary factor in their choice is the desire for the birth to have a positive impact on their child's development. A healthy baby in the arms of thankful parents is everyone's main objective, regardless of the means used to achieve it.

Questions to ask so you and your baby receive the best care.
by Debra Evans
When considering an out-of-hospital option:
• Should transfer to a hospital become necessary, where is the closest emergency medical facility located, and how will I get there?
• Who will manage any complications?
• What emergency supplies, medication and equipment will be immediately available should the baby or I require it?
When considering an in-hospital option:
• Are there birthing rooms? LDRP rooms? When is the delivery room used?
• What supports are provided for women's comfort in labor (rocking chairs, padded recliners, bean bags, Jacuzzi tubs, dimmed lighting, extra pillows, squatting bars, music, showers, food and beverages, birthing chairs/beds)?
• What is your current Cesarean rate?
• Is an IV or continuous electrical fetal monitoring required by the hospital, or does my doctor or nurse-midwife decide when they should be used?
• Who stays with a woman throughout labor? Is there a limit to the

number of people allowed?

• Are labor nurses skilled in teaching and applying non-invasive pain relief and active labor techniques (back massage, breathing, thermal stimulation, water therapy, physical movement and positions)?

• How long does the baby stay with the family after birth? Is a stay in the nursery required? How often and for how long? May all of the baby's care take place at the mother's bedside, if requested?

• What are visitation policies? Are visitors allowed to hold and care for the baby? What rules govern sibling visits?

• Does the hospital employ a specially trained lactation specialist to assist mothers with breastfeeding? Are water supplements and pacifiers routinely used?

• Is this a teaching hospital? (If so, you may be examined and treated by medical students, interns, or residents unless you request otherwise.)

• Is a neonatal intensive care unit (NICU) located in this hospital? If not, where are babies who require special care sent?

The Language of Labor and Delivery
by Debra Evans

active labor: regular uterine contractions associated with increasing dilation of the cervix and descent of the baby.

afterbirth: a term used for the placenta, amniotic sac and umbilical cord.

afterpains: cramplike, postpartum contractions usually lasting up to 48 hours, resulting from efforts of the uterus to expel the afterbirth and prevent bleeding from the placental site.

amniocentesis: the removal of amniotic fluid with a syringe for diagnostic or therapeutic purposes.

amnion: a thin, transparent, tough sac which holds the baby in amniotic fluid.

amniotic fluid: a clear to slightly cloudy fluid that protects the baby from injury in the uterus, helps to maintain an even temperature, and prevents the amniotic sac from adhering to the baby's skin.

analgesia: the relief of pain without loss of consciousness.

analgesic: a drug used to produce analgesia.

anesthesia: the partial or total loss of sensation, with or without loss of consciousness.

anesthesiologist: a physician who specializes in anesthesiology.

anesthesiology: the science of administering anesthetics.

anesthetic: a drug that produces anesthesia.

anomaly: a condition that deviates from the common type or form.

antepartum: the time before the baby is born.

Apgar Score: a means of evaluating the baby's breathing, heart rate, muscle tone, reflexes, and color at one, five, and 10 minutes after birth.

anterior position: the crown of the baby's head faces the mother's abdomen as it descends into her pelvis.

back labor: the condition during labor resulting from pressure of the baby's presenting part against the back of the mother's pelvis.

bag of waters: see *amnion.*

bearing-down reflex: the involuntary pushing effort of the uterus during the second stage of labor.

birth: the process by which the baby is expelled or removed from the mother's uterus and begins life outside the mother.

birth canal: the term applied to the structure formed by the vagina and uterus when the cervix is completely dilated in the second stage of labor.

bradycardia: a slow heart rate. (In the preborn or newborn baby, a rate less than 120 beats per minute.)

Braxton-Hicks contractions: intermittent contractions of the uterus occurring throughout pregnancy that do not produce lasting changes in the cervix.

breech presentation: the presentation of the baby's buttocks instead of the head during birth.

brow presentation: the presentation of the brow toward the cervix during birth.

caput: the baby's head.

centimeters: the unit of measure used to describe cervical dilation.

cephalic presentation: the presentation of the head during birth.

cephalopelvic disproportion: the condition in which the baby's head is larger than the space of the mother's pelvis.

certified nurse-midwife: a registered nurse who is a graduate of an approved training program and who has passed a certification examination to practice midwifery.

cervix: the fixed, necklike segment of the lower uterus.

Cesarean birth/Cesarean section: the birth of a baby through an incision in the abdominal and uterine walls.

chorion: the outermost membrane surrounding the baby and the placenta.

coccyx: the tailbone.

conception: the fertilization of the egg by a sperm that initiates the growth of a human being and triggers the onset of pregnancy.

congenital: present at birth.

contraction: a unit of work performed by a muscle over a period of time. In labor, uterine muscles contract to dilate the cervix and press the baby out of the mother's body.

crowning: the time during the second stage of labor when the largest part of the baby's head appears in the vagina and does not retract between contractions.

dilation: the stretching open of the cervix brought about by uterine contractions during labor.

eclampsia: a rare condition of late pregnancy characterized by high blood pressure, severe headaches, visual interference and convulsions.

edema: the presence of an excessive amount of fluid in body tissues.

effacement: the thinning and shortening of the cervix, measured in terms of a percentage.

electrode: a small electrical conductor used to monitor the baby's heart rate directly during labor.

electronic fetal monitoring: the continuous monitoring of the baby's heart rate through a transducer positioned on the mother's abdomen, by telemetry or via an electrode inserted through the cervix and attached to the baby's scalp.

embryo: the term used to describe the baby between conception and the 12th week of development.

endometrium: the lining of the inner surface of the uterus.

enema: the insertion of fluids into the rectum to empty the lower intestine.

engagement: the entrance of the presenting part of the baby into the midpelvis.

epidural: regional anesthesia produced by injecting medication through a tiny tube into the epidural space adjacent to the spinal cord sheath.

episiotomy: the incision of the perineum at the end of the second stage of labor.

estrogen: a hormone secreted by the ovary and placenta throughout the menstrual cycle and pregnancy.

face presentation: the presentation of the baby's face toward the cervix during labor.

false labor: Intense Braxton-Hicks contractions that mimic labor.

fertilization: see *conception.*

fetal distress: a term used to describe a shortage of oxygen to the baby resulting in a disrupted heart rate.

fetus: the term applied to the baby after the 12th week of pregnancy.

first stage of labor: the time of labor during which the cervix dilates from one to 10 centimeters.

fontanels: the soft spots lying between the unjoined sections of the baby's skull.

forceps: an instrument used to hold the presenting part and extract the baby from the vagina.

fourth stage of labor: the phase of childbirth between the delivery of the placenta and the end of a six-week recovery period.

fundal massage: massage of the uterus during the fourth stage of labor to assist the uterus in contracting and controlling bleeding.

fundal palpation: checking the height and tone of the uterus by feeling it through the abdominal wall.

fundus: the rounded portion of the uterus from which contractions originate.

general anesthesia: a temporary loss of consciousness that produces insensibility to pain, induced by drugs or gas.

gestation: the period between fertilization and birth.

gravida: a pregnant woman.

hemorrhage: excessive bleeding.

hemorrhoids: swollen veins around the rectum.

hormones: chemical substances that stimulate various organs to act in specific ways.

human chorionic gonadotropin (HCG): the hormone secreted by the developing embryo measured during a pregnancy test through urine.

hypertension: high blood pressure; in pregnancy, a blood pressure over 140/90.

hyperventilation: an imbalance between carbon dioxide and oxygen in the bloodstream created by overbreathing.

implantation: embedding of the embryo in the uterine lining.

induction of labor: the artificial production of labor.

intravenous feeding (IV): the introduction of fluids, medications and other substances into the body through a thin, flexible, plastic tube inserted into a vein.

involution: the return of the uterus to its normal size after pregnancy.

labor: the series of stages during the process of childbirth through which the baby is born and the mother's uterus returns to its normal state.

lactation: breastfeeding a baby.

lie: the position of the baby in the uterus.

lightening: the descent of the uterus into the abdominal cavity that accompanies the engagement of the baby in the pelvis.

lochia: the discharge from the uterus after the baby is born that consists of blood, mucus and tissue cells.

midwife: one who practices midwifery.

midwifery: the art or practice of assisting women during pregnancy and childbirth.

miscarriage: the loss of a baby before the 28th week of pregnancy.

molding: the temporary shaping of the baby's skull to conform to the size of the birth canal during the second stage of labor.

multigravida: a woman who has been pregnant two or more times.

multipara: a woman who has given birth to one or more babies.

natal: pertaining to birth.

neonatal: the first four weeks of life.

non-stress test: a test during pregnancy to measure the baby's heart rate.

obstetrician: a physician who specializes in obstetrics.

obstetrics: the medical management of pregnancy, labor, birth and postpartum.

oxytocin: the hormone secreted by the posterior pituitary gland which stimulates uterine contractions and the milk-ejection reflex.

paracervical: a regional anesthetic injected into the cervix to numb it during labor or gynecological procedures.

pelvic floor: the set of muscles attached to the pelvis that supports the contents of the pelvic cavity.

pelvimetry: the series of X-rays used to determine the exact measurements of the pelvis.

pelvis: the bony ring that supports the spine and gives articulation to the lower limbs.

perinatal: the period from the 28th week of pregnancy to one week after the baby's birth.

perineum: the external area between the vagina and the rectum in the female.

pitocin: the synthetic form of oxytocin used to induce or stimulate labor.

placenta: the flat, oval structure attached to the uterus during pregnancy that supplies nutrients to the baby, removes waste products and secretes hormones.

placenta previa: a condition in which the placenta is over or near the cervix.

posterior presentation: the crown of the baby's head is facing toward the mother's back as it descends into her pelvis.

postnatal: after birth.

postpartum: following childbirth.

preeclampsia: a condition in which a pregnant woman has high blood pressure, edema, protein in the urine, and sudden weight gain.

presentation: the position of the baby during pregnancy and labor.

presenting part: the part of the baby lying closest to the cervix.

preterm: a baby born before the 37th week of pregnancy and weighing less than five-and-a-half pounds.

primigravida: a woman during her first pregnancy.

primipara: a woman who has had, or is giving birth to, her first baby.

progesterone: a hormone produced by the corpus luteum, then the placenta, during pregnancy.

prostaglandin gel: a transparent jelly containing prostaglandins used to induce labor by inserting the gel into the cervix to soften it.

prostaglandins: substances secreted by the body that stimulate uterine contractions.

psychoprophylaxis: a method of childbirth popularized by Dr. Ferdinand Lamaze.

pubis: the bones forming the front part of the pelvis.

pudendal: a regional anesthetic injected into the nerves that supply sensation to the genitals to numb the perineum during birth and repair of the episiotomy.

sacrum: the bone the forms that back of the pelvis at the base of the spine.

second stage of labor: the period of labor following complete cervical dilation and lasting until the baby is born.

show: the discharge of bloodstained mucus resulting from cervical dilation.

sonogram: see *ultrasound*.

spinal anesthetic: regional anesthesia that is produced by injecting medication into the spinal fluid.

station: the measurement of the presenting part in relation to the bones in the pelvis.

stillbirth: the delivery of a dead baby after 28 weeks of pregnancy.

stress test: a diagnostic test used during late pregnancy that measures the baby's heart rate under stress.

tachycardia: an abnormally fast heart rate. In a newborn, faster than 160 beats per minute.

telemetry: electronic fetal monitoring that uses radio waves.

term: a pregnancy is said to be "at term" between 38 and 42 weeks of pregnancy.

third stage of labor: the phase of labor between when the baby is born and the placenta is delivered.

tocodynometer: A pressure gauge that records uterine contractions, attached via a belt on the mother's abdomen.

toxemia: see *eclampsia* and *preeclampsia*.

tranquilizer: a drug that acts to reduce mental tension and anxiety without inducing unconsciousness.

transducer: an instrument sensitive to the echoes of high-frequency sound waves that bounce off the baby's body and translate into an image on a television screen or record the information on a recording device. See *electronic fetal monitoring* and *ultrasound*.

transition: the third phase of the first stage of labor in which the cervix dilates from seven to 10 centimeters.

trimester: period of three months; one of the three phases of the nine months of pregnancy.

ultrasound: inaudible, high-frequency sound waves used to outline the shape of the baby during pregnancy. Also called *ultrasonography*.

umbilical cord: the attachment connecting the baby to the placenta.

uterine inertia: ineffective, weak uterine contractions during labor.

uterine tetany: contractions marked by continued, severe muscle tension and interference of the baby's oxygen supply.

uterus: the thick-walled, hollow, muscular organ of the female that serves to contain and nourish a developing child.

vacuum extraction: an alternative to forceps that uses a suction cup applied to the baby's scalp to remove the baby from the vagina.

vagina: the muscle/membrane, tubelike structure which forms the passageway between the uterus and the entrance to the vagina between the external genitals. It receives the penis during intercourse and forms the canal through which the baby passes during birth.

Avoiding an Unnecessary Cesarean Birth

by William Sears

While a Cesarean section may be life-saving surgery in certain circumstances, I believe that at least half of Cesarean surgeries could be prevented. Specifically, here's what you can do:

Choose birth attendants and birthplace wisely. Determine your prospective obstetrician's birth philosophy. What is his patients' success rate of vaginal births after Cesarean? It should be at least 70 percent. What is his personal Cesarean rate? Anything over 15 percent suggests a predominantly surgical mind set.

Ask about "routines." Is continuous electronic fetal monitoring used? What percentage of the mothers need fetal monitors? And what about ambulatory labor and vertical birthing? Does the doctor insist on sitting at the end of the bed and catching the baby while you are horizontal, or can squatting or side-lying positions be used?

Bring a birth buddy. If you choose the obstetrician-hospital delivery system, studies have shown that your chances of having a surgical birth go down with a professional labor assistant.

Think upright. Research has shown that laboring upright increases uterine efficiency, shortens labor, dilates the cervix better, and allows your labor to progress better—and more comfortably.

Insistence on horizontal deliveries is one reason long labors often progress to the operating room. This doesn't mean you can't rest horizontally during labor. Many women do periodically lie on their sides while being attended to by a back-rubbing and face-caressing partner.

Take a walk. Once you're thinking vertical, get moving. Research has shown that walking helps labor progress and is good for the baby.

Use electronic fetal monitoring and interventions wisely. Numerous controlled studies of low-risk mothers show no difference in infant outcome when electronic fetal monitoring is compared with using a fetal stethoscope to monitor the baby's heartbeat. These studies found that mothers who had the use of the new technology were twice as likely to have a surgical birth.

Evaluate the epidural. In a study of 500 first-time mothers, those who received elective epidurals were more likely to require Cesareans for failure to progress. Other studies suggest that epidurals do not increase the chances of a surgical birth. But we have witnessed labors where a well-timed epidural relaxed the mother and actually improved her progress toward a vaginal birth.

Take your time. Don't feel pressured to give birth in a hurry because of others' timetables. There is no evidence that long labors are necessarily harmful to babies. The worry about long labors is based upon the belief that with each contraction the uterus delivers less oxygen to the baby; therefore, the more and longer the contractions, the less oxygen the baby gets. This has never been scientifically documented.

Use discernment about managed births. While there is a back-to-basics trend toward non-intervention, managed births are increasingly popular: A pregnant woman, screened for normalcy and certified by ultrasound to be near term, books her delivery near her due date. She enters the hospital in the morning, gets a pitocin drip to start labor and an epidural to keep from hurting. Parents and the baby go home that evening. But before you sign up for this new way of birthing, consider the probability that a disproportionate number of *mismanaged* births wind up in the operating room.

Remember your vulnerability. Plan ahead. When offered a surgical birth as an alternative to two more hours of pain, you are often in no condition to make a wise choice. Part of your prenatal preparation should be learning about the indications for Cesarean births—which ones are absolute and which are judgment calls that can go either way. Here is where having a professional labor assistant helps. Also, be sure you understand the risks and benefits of interventions and are aware of alternatives should things not go as planned.

When a Cesarean *Is* Recommended
by Debra Evans

In certain circumstances, a Cesarean is necessary to ensure the health of a baby and/or its mother. Any of the following conditions may lead a doctor to recommend surgery:

Abnormal quality of uterine contractions. When contractions are too weak to open the cervix, or are so strong they threaten the baby's oxygen supply, a Cesarean may be performed if alternative measures prove ineffective.

Coexisting maternal disease. The following conditions require special care and monitoring during pregnancy and may make a Cesarean birth necessary for the safety of both mother and baby: anemia; diabetes; genital herpes infection; high blood pressure; incompetent cervix; lung, kidney or heart disease; malnutrition; pelvic infection or PID (pelvic inflammatory disease); preeclampsia, eclampsia and toxemia; previous Cesarean birth (vertical or classical incision); Rh blood incompatibility between maternal and fetal blood; vaginal bleeding during pregnancy.

Congenital anomaly. Some present-at-birth conditions, including spina bifida and certain heart defects, warrant bypassing the vaginal route of birth to prevent additional stress on the baby.

Difficult position. When a baby presents himself with his buttocks, feet, shoulder, face, brow or chin towards the cervix, a vaginal birth may be difficult, if not impossible. In some instances, the baby may be "turned" externally to a head-first position by the mother's midwife or doctor, but if the baby engages with the pelvis in a difficult position prior to labor, a Cesarean may be required.

Fetal distress. During labor, the baby's heart rate is monitored frequently or continuously. If the heart tones become irregular and cannot be improved by medication or maternal positioning, a Cesarean will be done to prevent the stress of a vaginal birth.

Large baby, small pelvis. A discrepancy between the size of the baby's head and the size of the mother's pelvic passageway is termed cephalopelvic disproportion, or CPD. This may be diagnosed by ultrasound or X-ray pelvimetry, where the distance between the pelvic bones is measured on X-ray films.

Multiple gestation. In the case of a multiple pregnancy, the likelihood of premature labor and malpresentation, and a Cesarean, increases.

Placental difficulties. Placenta attached between the baby and the cervix is called *placenta previa*. This condition is suspected if an expectant mother experiences vaginal bleeding, especially after the first trimester of pregnancy. Placental attachment jeopardized by labor indicates a need for Cesarean birth. Another placental condition, in which the placenta begins to loosen its grip on the uterus before the baby is born and breathing on its own, is known as an *abruption of the placenta*. Occurring with varying degrees of severity, symptoms include vaginal bleeding and sharp abdominal pains. Immediate Cesarean delivery is usually advisable.

Premature labor. In order to avoid the stress of a vaginal birth on the baby, a Cesarean may be needed if labor starts prematurely.

Prolonged rupture of membranes. If the amniotic sac has been broken for longer than 24 hours, the risk of intrauterine infection goes up. Your health-care provider will determine the necessity of a Cesarean based on your vital signs, exposure to infection, and reaction to labor induction.

Umbilical cord prolapse. On rare occasions, the cord may descend ahead of the baby when some of the amniotic fluid escapes, interfering with the baby's oxygen supply. Called *cord prolapse,* this requires an immediate Cesarean to relieve pressure on the cord.

Unsuccessful induction. If the birth attendant has attempted to start labor with poor results, a Cesarean may be necessary.

Uterine dystocia or arrested labor. When the cervix doesn't dilate, even though measures such as walking, nipple massage, relaxation and medication have been used over time to stimulate contractions, a Cesarean may be advisable.

Finding Your Pediatrician

by Debra Evans

In spite of the many things competing for your attention right now, it's important to take time out before the birth of your baby to choose a pediatrician. Selecting a doctor based solely on convenience might bring you regrets in the long run.

Begin by talking to your friends and neighbors about the doctors their children see; ask your childbirth educator, lactation consultant, prenatal baby care instructor and birth attendant for referrals; look in the Yellow Pages for a complete listing of who's currently available. Find out as much as you can about their competence and ability to communicate with their clients. Their Christian commitment may be an important factor to you as well.

Think through your approach to parenting, and try to find a physician for your baby who, in addition to providing top-notch medical care, will be sensitive to your beliefs. Because so much of the advice doctors and nurse practitioners give at "well-baby" checkups is parenting rather than medical advice, choosing a doctor for your baby is different from selecting other types of health-care providers.

Make a list of the candidates you are considering and set up prenatal interviews with your first choices early in your pregnancy. If possible, attend the appointment as a couple.

During the prenatal interviews, watch for these initial cues of compassion and competence:

• Ability to listen. Does the doctor seem concerned about the same things that concern you? How does she respond to your greatest concerns about your baby's care?

• Openness. Do you feel comfortable with the practitioner? Are you encouraged to ask questions and invited to engage in a dialogue about them, or are you given textbook answers? Were time constraints managed appropriately?

• Training. Where did the practitioner receive his training? How long ago? What additional interests or certifications has he received?

• Fee schedule. What does the practitioner charge for in-hospital consultations after the birth and for office visits? Does her office bill your insurance company directly or expect you to pay when services are rendered?

• Back-up. Who is available for emergencies when the practitioner isn't? How often does he rely on a back-up person for clients' urgent medical needs?

• Perspective. How involved is the practitioner in advocating child-development and safety issues? What are her opinions on parent-infant bonding, methods of childbirth, breastfeeding and bottle feeding, colic and crying? Does the practitioner encourage you to grow into your parenting role without dominating your decision-making responsibility?

The key factor in selecting a health-care provider for your baby is your confidence in the practitioner—the type of confidence that develops over time, beginning with your first experience at the prenatal visit. If for any reason the practitioner makes you question his ability to respond to your concerns, set up a consultation with another practitioner.

"A caring pediatrician [or family physician] and intuitive parents are a winning combination that brings to your child a level of pediatric care that most parents and children want and deserve," explains William Sears, M.D., in *Christian Parenting and Child Care* (Thomas Nelson).

As parents, our part is to seek knowledge and wisdom prayerfully on behalf of our children. Finding a physician who will recognize and support us in this role is essential; recognizing and supporting our physicians in their role is an important part of this too—a winning combination that benefits us all.

Ready for Delivery:
Things to Ask, Take and Know

Fill out these checklists, and keep them in an easily accessible place for quick reference when the time comes for you to need them.

Contacting Your Physician or Midwife

I am to call _____ at _____ (number) when my membranes rupture (❑ yes ❑ no), when contractions are ____ minutes apart and last for _____ seconds. Other conditions about which I should notify my birth attendant: _____
_____

What to Pack for Labor

❑ two pairs of clean, warm socks
❑ lip gloss, Carmex, or Chapstick
❑ Bible
❑ sweet/sour lollipops or peppermint sticks for flavor
❑ corn oil or lotion for massage
❑ watch that can time seconds
❑ your own nightgown and pillows
❑ clean, seven-inch paint roller or two tennis balls in a sports sock for applying counter pressure to the lower back
❑ birthday cake (frozen ahead), candles, and sparkling cider or grape juice
❑ posters and pictures for visual stimulation
❑ tape recorder and favorite cassettes for auditory stimulation
❑ hot water bottle, ice pack, eucalyptus gel for thermal stimulation
❑ breath spray or mouthwash
❑ food for yourself and your labor partner
❑ camera, film, flash
❑ phone card or pocket change, phone-number list

What to Pack in Your Suitcase

❑ toothbrush, toothpaste, brush, comb, other toiletry items
❑ clean underwear, bras, sleepwear (designed to facilitate nursing if you've chosen to breastfeed), robe, socks, slippers
❑ birth announcements, stationery, pen, stamps
❑ reading material about parenting, baby care, breastfeeding
❑ packets of herbal teas and dried fruits to help alleviate constipation

❑ outfit and blanket in which to take your baby home, loose-fitting clothing for your return home

❑ personal tape recorder and cassettes or radio

Entering the Hospital

(❑ I am ❑ I am not) preregistered. When in labor, I'll go to _____ hospital/birth center. During business hours, I'll be admitted at _____; after _____ P.M., I'll be admitted at _____. These areas are reached from _____ (street name). Parking will be available at _____ and costs _____. After admission, I'll go to the _____ floor. The usual length of stay after a vaginal birth: _____ days. After a Cesarean birth: _____ days. Visiting hours are from _____ A.M. to _____ P.M., and the people who may visit are _____
_____.

Personalized Care

My personal preferences concerning routine hospital procedures are:

Site of care:
❑ LDRP room   ❑ birthing room
❑ labor room   ❑ delivery room

Clothing:
❑ hospital gown   ❑ own gown

Listening to the   ❑ fetoscope
baby's heart tones: ❑ amplified stethoscope
❑ intermittent EFM (electronic fetal monitoring)
❑ continuous EFM

Fluids/emergency medication:
❑ drink to thirst
❑ IV   ❑ heparin lock

Pain medication:
❑ non-invasive pain reduction
❑ analgesia   ❑ epidural

Prep:
❑ enema   ❑ natural bowel movements
❑ shave   ❑ no shave/wash only

Rupture of membranes:
❑ spontaneous   ❑ artificial

Birth assistance: ❑ episiotomy ❑ perineal massage

Medical care: ❑ staff and own physician only
❑ doctors/nurse in training

Vaginal exams: When? _____ How often? _____
By whom? _____

Postpartum room: ❑ private ❑ semiprivate

Baby care: ❑ rooming-in ❑ bedside care of baby
❑ central nursery

Feedings: ❑ on-demand ❑ scheduled
❑ night ❑ water
❑ breast only

For further information, enroll in a local childbirth education program, talk about your preferences with your birth attendant, and read additional materials about labor and birth choices available to parents today.

CHAPTER TWO

~

The First Days of Life

~

Chapter Two

Your Baby's First Exam

by William Sears

Within a day after birth, newborns get their first checkup. Ask to be present—you will learn about your baby's body and appreciate what your doctor looks for.

Head-to-toe checkup. Your doctor will form her first impression about the general health of your baby by just looking at him. Is he pre-term, post-term or done just right? Is he lying in the frog position that indicates good muscle tone? Is he alert, active, pink, healthy and breathing normally?

Next, your doctor will examine your baby's head to see if there are any abnormalities and may point out to you all the lumps on a newborn's head. Are the fontanels (the soft spots on a baby's head) normal? The doctor will measure your baby's head circumference and compare it with norms to be sure it is proportional to your baby's length and weight.

By shining a light inside your baby's eyes, your doctor can determine if your child has any cataracts or internal eye problems. Sometimes a newborn's puffy eyelids prevent a thorough exam of the eyes, so your doctor may wait a few days.

Are the nasal passages open wide enough to allow air through? Next, your doctor will check the inside of your baby's mouth. Is the front of the tongue attached to the floor of the mouth, which may prevent good latch-on during breastfeeding? (It has been customary to leave tight tongue tips alone, because most loosen with time. In recent years, how-

> *Your doctor will form her first impression of your baby just by looking at him."*
>
> Dr. William Sears

57

ever, I have been clipping the tight membranous frenulum immediately beneath the tip of the tongue if it appears tight and a baby is not latching on to his mother's breast well. This painless, one-minute office procedure makes breastfeeding easier.) Is the palate, the roof of the baby's mouth, fully formed?

By shining a light into the ear canals, your doctor can tell if they are correctly formed. The appearance of the outer ear varies greatly among babies; some are pinned against the head, some flop over, some stick out. As the cartilage in your baby's ears develops, they will assume a more attractive shape. Bruised earlobes are normal.

The doctor will run her hands around your baby's neck, checking for abnormal bumps, and over the collar bone, which commonly breaks during a difficult delivery and heals easily. Your doctor will then listen to your baby's heart for any abnormalities that may indicate structural problems. At the same time, your doctor will move the stethoscope around your baby's chest to be sure air is moving in and out of the lungs properly.

The abdomen gets the next exam. Your doctor will feel for the vital organs (liver, spleen and kidneys) beneath the thin muscles of your baby's abdomen to determine whether they are in correct position and size, and to see if there are any abnormal growths in the abdomen.

Then the doctor will check the genitalia. Is the vaginal opening normal? An egg-white type of vaginal discharge, often blood-tinged, is normal. Are both testicles descended? Are there any hernias (protrusion of the intestines) beneath the skin of the groin?

Is the anus open and located properly? Your doctor may also determine whether your baby has passed any meconium stools yet.

While in the groin area, your doctor will hold your baby's thighs and move them around the hip joints. She is checking for dislocated hips—a condition which is easy to diagnose and treat in the newborn period, but more difficult to diagnose and treat later. Your doctor will place a finger in the center of your baby's groin and check for femoral pulse. The strength of the pulsation of these large arteries assures the doctor that the vessel coming out of the heart is large enough.

Now on to the legs, which are normally bowed, and down to the feet, which normally curve in. If the front half of the foot is curved in too much in relation to the back half (called a clubfoot), it may need cast-correction. Toes are a familiar curiosity: Webbed, oversized and overlapping toes are commonly inherited traits. The doctor may also check your newborn's reflexes, but by the time she has gone through this head-to-toe exam, your doctor will already have a general impression of your baby's neurological development.

At the nurses' station, your doctor will review the birth events to see if any problem occurred which may require special attention. Your history and nurses' notes are also reviewed. The doctor also checks your baby's blood type to see if there is any potential incompatibility between your blood types that may lead to abnormal jaundice.

Depending on special birth circumstances or physical findings, your doctor may perform other examinations or tests. While in the hospital, your baby's doctor and your attending nurses will help you get used to caring for your baby.

In addition to the newborn exam, an important part of routine newborn care is what I call "the discharge-from-the-hospital talk." Make a list of all your questions and concerns before you leave the hospital. On that day, your doctor will answer these questions, discuss your concerns, and go over what to expect when you get home. Also, be sure you know how to reach your doctor and when your first office appointment should be.

The first newborn checkup also has a special meaning to your doctor. She has made a new acquaintance; you have begun a lengthy friendship. It is the first in a long series of checkups as parents, doctor and baby grow together.

Newborn Assessments: How Your Baby Scores

by William Sears

Life's little tests begin early—as soon as a baby arrives, in fact. A newborn must undergo a battery of routine tests to determine his initial health. While these tests can seem overwhelming to parents, they are necessary and helpful. Here's a description of the most common types of post-delivery evaluations:

Apgar Score. At one and five minutes after birth, your baby is given a "grade"—a quick assessment of his initial health. This score assesses skin color, heart rate, breathing, activity and muscle tone.

What does the Apgar Score really mean? Is a 10 healthier than an eight? Not necessarily. The Apgar Score was devised primarily to determine which babies need more careful observation. A baby who has a five needs more intense observation than a baby who receives a seven to 10. It is a which-baby-to-worry-about score.

Even though infants who have good skin tone, breathe rapidly, have rapid heart rates, show strong muscular movement and cry lustily are given scores of ten, most healthy newborns do not achieve perfect scores.

The Apgar Score is often an unnecessary source of anxiety for parents of low-scoring babies. There is seldom a correlation between the Apgar Score and the long-term development of babies. If your baby has good skin tone and is breathing normally, chances are he is a healthy newborn.

Vitamin K. Immediately after birth, your baby is given an injection of vitamin K to promote normal blood clotting and lessen the risk of abnormal bleeding into vital tissues. Because the injection may disrupt your bonding with your infant, ask the nurse to delay it for a few hours.

Eye ointment. To protect against germs that may have entered your baby's eyes during passage through the birth canal, an antibiotic ointment, erythromycin, is put into her eyes. This ointment will in no way harm your baby's eyes, though it may temporarily blur her vision. Because it is important for your baby to establish eye contact—one of the high points of bonding—you may safely ask the nurse to delay administering this ointment.

Blood tests. After birth, a sample of your baby's umbilical cord blood is taken to determine blood type and Rh factor. A small amount of blood is taken from your baby's heel to screen for a number of illnesses including:

• Hypothyroidism, which is caused by an inadequate thyroid gland and occurs in one out of every 5,000 infants. If undetected and untreated, hypothyroidism may cause mental retardation. Early treatment is most effective.

• Phenylketonuria (PKU), which is an extremely rare disease occurring in approximately one out of 15,000 infants. If left untreated, it can result in brain damage; if detected early and treated properly, the child may develop normally.

• Galectosemia—the rarest condition, occurring only in one out of every 60,000 infants. Galectosemia is caused by an enzyme deficiency that allows harmful substances to build up in a baby's blood, damaging vital tissues and resulting in death if not treated. Like PKU, this disease is treatable by a special diet.

Bilirubin Tests. Most newborns develop some degree of jaundice—yellow coloring of the skin and eyeballs. Jaundice is caused by the buildup in the blood of a yellow pigment (bilirubin), and the deposit of this excess bilirubin in the skin.

Your doctor will monitor the degree of jaundice by blood samples that reveal bilirubin levels. If these levels are low, there is nothing to worry about. If these levels are too high and rapidly rising, your doctor may begin treatment by giving your baby more fluids to wash out the excess bilirubin and placing your baby under phototherapy lamps that dissolve the excess yellow pigment.

A more severe, "abnormal" kind of jaundice is usually caused by an incompatibility between a mother's and her baby's blood types—a mother may have type O, while her baby may have type A or B. Or a mother may be Rh-negative, her baby Rh-positive. In these cases, some of a mother's blood products circulate through her baby's bloodstream, and a war of sorts develops between the opposing forces. As a result, many red blood cells are damaged, bilirubin is released, and jaundice occurs.

If your baby develops jaundice, be sure your doctor explains the type you're dealing with. There is more unnecessary anxiety and misinformation about newborn jaundice than any other concern in the newborn period. Most cases of jaundice disappear naturally after a couple of weeks. Even the abnormal kind of jaundice rarely harms a full-term, healthy baby.

Understanding the Apgar Test

The Apgar Score, designed by anesthesiologist Virginia Apgar in 1952, represents your newborn's initial capacity to adjust to extrauterine life. Its five measurements are based on a three-point scale (from 0 to 2) which are added to obtain the final total. These scores are:

	0	1	2
Heart rate	Absent	Less than 100/min.	More than 100/min.
Color	Blue or pale	Body pink, extremities blue	Pink all over
Breathing	Absent	Slow, irregular, weak cry	Good cry
Muscle tone	Limp	Some flexion of extremities	Active motion
Reflex irritability	No response	Grimace with some motion	Strong cry, withdrawal of foot

Babies who receive low Apgar ratings immediately after birth but are given higher scores later demonstrate that they have responsive nervous and cardiovascular systems. Totals of 8-9-9, given at three-minute intervals, are considered to indicate optimal adjustment, whereas scores of 4-6-8 show that the baby's responses, though stressed initially, are gradually adjusting. When scores remain consistently below six, a baby needs special care to help stabilize his responses.

Circumcision: Yes or No?

by William Sears

Until recent years, circumcision was considered a routine procedure for newborn males, but parents are beginning to ask if circumcision is really necessary.

The biblical basis for circumcision is found in Genesis 17:10-14. This passage makes it clear that, according to Mosaic Law, God commanded all males to be circumcised.

However, in the New Testament, many verses state that circumcision is not necessary: "Circumcision is nothing and uncircumcision is nothing" (1 Cor. 7:19; see also Gal. 5:6; 6:15 and Rom. 2:29).

The ancient covenant of circumcising males was probably designed as a method of preventive hygiene. If the living conditions that prompted the custom of circumcision no longer exist, should circumcision still be performed?

The American Academy of Pediatrics has taken the stand that routine circumcision is unnecessary. The following questions and answers are intended to help you make an informed decision regarding the procedure:

How is circumcision performed? The baby is placed on a restraining board, his hands and feet secured by straps. The tight adhesions between the foreskin and the penis are separated with a metal instrument. The foreskin is held in place by metal clamps while a cut is made into the foreskin to about one-third of its length. A metal bell is placed over the head of the penis, and the foreskin is pulled up over the bell and cut circumferentially. About one-third of the foreskin is removed.

Is circumcision safe? Does it hurt? Circumcision is usually a safe surgical procedure, and there are rarely any complications. However, as with any surgical procedure, there are occasional problems such as bleeding, infection, or injury to the penis. And yes, it does hurt! We are sometimes erroneously taught that a newborn baby does not feel pain during circumcision. But studies have shown this is not true.

Can a baby have anesthesia to lessen the pain? Yes. A local anesthesia can and should be used. Painless circumcision should be a birthright. Ask your doctor about this safe and effective procedure.

Does circumcision make hygiene easier? The glands in the foreskin secrete a fluid called smegma. These secretions may accumulate beneath the foreskin and cause the penis to become irritated and infected. Removing the foreskin removes the secretions and makes care of the penis easier.

What happens if the foreskin is left intact? At birth it is impossible to make a judgment about how tight the foreskin will remain, since almost all boys have tight foreskins in the first few months. In about 50 percent of boys, the foreskin loosens from the head of the penis and retracts completely by 1 year of age. By age 3, 90 percent of uncircumcised boys have fully retractable foreskins. Once the foreskin retracts easily, it becomes a normal part of male hygiene to pull back the foreskin and cleanse beneath it during a bath.

If the foreskin does not retract naturally, will he need a circumcision later on? Circumcision is rarely necessary for medical reasons, but occasionally the foreskin does not retract, becoming tight and infected, obstructing the flow of urine. This condition, called phimosis, requires circumcision. However, if circumcision for phimosis is necessary later in childhood or adulthood, an anesthesia is given, and the boy is involved in the decision process.

If he isn't circumcised, will he feel different from his friends? Parents cannot predict how their son will feel if he is circumcised *or* intact. Children generally have a wider acceptance of individual differences than adults do. It is difficult to predict whether the majority of boys will be circumcised or intact in the future, but the number of circumcised boys has been steadily declining in recent years.

We have a son who is already circumcised. Should brothers in the same family be the same? Many parents feel that sameness is important among the males in a family since little boys do, in fact, compare their penises.

Do circumcised boys experience any particular problems? The foreskin acts as a protective covering of the sensitive head of the penis. Removal of the protective foreskin allows the head of the penis to come in contact with ammonia in diapers. Sometimes this irritation causes circumcised babies to develop painful sores on the tip of the penis that may obstruct the flow of urine.

When should circumcision be performed? Genesis 17:12 states, "Every male among you who is 8 days old must be circumcised." The probable reason for this was that the newborn baby's blood clots faster by the eighth day. Today, it is medically unnecessary to wait until the eighth day, because almost all babies routinely receive an injection of Vitamin K shortly after birth to enhance clotting.

Premature Birth and NICUs: Early Arrival

by Patricia Rushford

Michelle had gone into labor in her 25th week and delivered her baby 16 hours later. Weighing in at only three pounds, six ounces, Mary Elizabeth Whiting was smaller than her name. The NICU (neonatal intensive care unit) staff worked to stabilize her, then tucked her into an incubator and took her away.

In spite of reassurances from her doctor, feelings of grief, guilt, emptiness and helplessness consumed Michelle. Had she done something wrong? Would her baby live?

Mary Elizabeth is just one of about 350,000 babies (around 10 percent) born prematurely in the United States each year—babies born before the 37th week of completed pregnancy. Premature infants, because they leave the womb too early, present parents and medical staff with many challenges. Since their organs are not sufficiently developed, premature babies are often placed on life support systems in an intensive care environment with high-tech equipment and specially trained medical personnel. The trauma of a premature birth is especially hard on parents. Below are suggestions that might help parents cope with the stresses:

Spiritual distress. Parents' spirits are often crushed. They are often angry with God for allowing so much suffering to come to their child. God does care and, if you ask, he will soothe your pain. God can handle your anger and understand your grief.

Marital stress. Some couples, perhaps because they are able to communicate their feelings and give one another support, grow stronger through the severe strain of dealing with a premature birth. Others are not so fortunate. Talk with one another. Avoid placing blame. Express your feelings of anger, guilt and fear. Ask for and accept help from other family members.

Financial stress. Medical care is expensive. Some preemies who develop complications will require long hospital stays, while others with severe handicaps may need lifelong care. Try not to be anxious over finances. When the ordeal is over or has leveled off, you'll be able to view your financial picture more objectively. Check your resources. You may be able to qualify for assistance, grants, or programs that alleviate undue financial stress. In the meantime, be thankful that even though it's expensive, your child is getting the medical care he needs.

Emotional stress. Nearly every day brings another crisis. The impact of caring for a preemie and not knowing from one minute to the next whether your baby is going to live or die can take a terrible toll on parents. You can ease your emotional stress in several ways:

• Be informed. Stress often occurs when we face unknown fears. The best way to alleviate this kind of stress is to make the unfamiliar familiar. Ask questions. Read. Get to know all you can about premature babies.

• Participate as much as possible in your baby's care. You may not be able to work all the high-tech equipment, start an IV, or read the monitors, but you can hold and cuddle your child often. Breastfeed or pump your milk if you can afford to give your baby the benefit of your milk. Medical experts agree that talking, touching, stroking and cuddling have a profound effect on a child's development.

• Spend as much time as you can with your baby, but be flexible. Try to work with the medical staff in coordinating feedings, bath times and weighings. Because the NICU is a busy place, medical staff may ask you to leave the unit for brief periods of time so they can perform necessary tests and procedures.

• While you do all you can to care for your baby, you'll need to care for yourself as well. Get enough rest. Eat regular and nourishing meals. Don't blame yourselves. Often parents add to their already stressful lives by ruminating about the past. If only I'd stayed off my feet. If only I'd called the doctor sooner. If only I'd asked for help with the other children. If only I'd helped my wife more with the housework.

• Ask for help. Realize your limitations. Don't be shy about letting people know you need someone to cuddle and love your baby when you can't, or help with meals and childcare. Be part of a parents-of-preemies support group. Take pictures to share with your family and friends so your baby can become an important part of their lives as well.

Sadly, not all premature infants survive, and some who do have serious handicaps. But now more than ever before, premature babies as small as 16 ounces not only survive but go on to live healthy, normal lives.

Practical Helps for Critical Moments

While the crisis is happening:

• Pray for your baby, for one another, and for those caring for you. Enlist the prayer support of friends, family and fellow church members to bathe each of you in prayer.

• Stay calm. Ask God to strengthen you so you can understand your feelings of anger, disappointment or loss. Don't be ashamed of how you feel. Instead, acknowledge the reality of your emotions and express them appropriately.

• Get accurate information. Ask questions often to remain involved in what's going on. In this way, you will better understand how you can help, what can be done, and what the true outlook is.

• Keep your options open. The more critical the situation, the greater the psychological stress. As a result, try to get all the facts before making any ethically complex decisions. Ask your pastor or priest to pray with you if you feel overwhelmed by your circumstances.

After the crisis:

• Know that you aren't alone—it just feels that way sometimes. Others have experienced a similar crisis; many are willing to offer you support and information. Resist isolating yourself and denying the benefits of allowing others to reach out to you in love.

• Avoid making comparisons. Your baby or birth may not fit your picture of what is ideal. Though it's natural to compare, remember that each situation is unique. Try not to compare your experience to what you consider to be the norm. Instead, be attentive to how the Lord is ministering to you specifically in your situation right now.

• Realize that any loss brings grief. Grieving is a process marked by a variety of emotions, including numbness, irritability, restlessness, anger, sorrow, fantasy, loneliness and frustration. It's a process that normally runs its course over time, eventually leading to a restoration of physical and emotional well-being.

• Seek pastoral or professional help as needed. Never hesitate to ask for help. There are times when even the strongest among us needs ministering to. Locate someone who will offer help and advice that is compatible with your beliefs, and make a sincere effort to follow the recommendations you're given.

• Make peace with God. You may never know why things happened as they did. Move toward accepting that God heard your prayers, knew your desires and expectations, and is working all things together for your good. Be honest about your feelings, presenting them to God and allowing him to help you face your emotions one day at a time.

What We Know (and Don't Know) about Babies and Pain

by Clara Shaw Schuster

Premature and newborn infants often give delayed or weak reactions to pain. Their inability to tell us whether or not they hurt has led some health-care providers to assume that infants feel little or no pain. Consequently, newborns frequently do not receive any pain medicine for circumcision or other painful procedures.

However, the vigorous withdrawals and anguished cries of some babies in response to a simple heel stick lead other medical personnel and psychologists to believe that infants feel pain acutely. Concern is growing about the side effects of pain stress and the potentially long-lasting impact of circumcision or other painful procedures—even those needed to save the life of a high-risk infant.

Whether infants can understand or respond to pain, it is increasingly evident that they are fully able to *feel* it. The density of nerve endings in infants is similar to or greater than those found in adult skin. By the 30th week after conception, the baby is capable of feeling pain with the same intensity as an adult. In fact, recent research indicates that stress responses to pain are three to five times greater in the infant than in the adult. Heart rate, blood pressure and pressure on the brain are all elevated when painful procedures are performed on infants without pain medicine. Use of medication eliminates or reduces these physical effects of pain and stress.

During the first 24 hours after the procedure, newborns who have been circumcised without pain medicine don't respond as well as other infants to people and objects. For the next two days, they show greater irritability and difficulty maintaining attention when their parents talk to them. This psychological effect can harm parent-child interaction.

In light of this evidence, doctors can no longer act as if infants are indifferent to pain. Although many doctors provide appropriate pain relief for young babies, many still do not use pain medication even for circumcisions.

You may need to play an active role in your child's care from his first day of life by requesting that pain medicine be provided when necessary. Young, nonverbal infants need to receive the same humane attention and pain relief as do children and adults in similar painful and stressful situations.

Going Home with Baby

by Debra Evans

After nine months of waiting and the standard interminable labor and delivery, the time has finally arrived. You're ready to take your new baby home.

Preparations have been in the making for weeks. There's a frozen casserole thawing in the refrigerator; an ample supply of disposable diapers and handsewn breast pads line the bottom shelf of the bathroom linen closet; the phone-machine message is ready to go.

Imagining yourselves curling up on the couch after tucking the baby in bed, sparkling cider in hand, you and your spouse look forward to basking in the settled-in warmth associated with being back on your own turf. In other words, life as usual—with a few minor adjustments.

The fantasy quickly disappears as soon as you walk in the front door. Rather than peacefully sleeping, your baby starts crying loudly. Well-intentioned friends arrive, asking for a peek.

Then Aunt Martha phones from Wyoming. As you graciously try to excuse yourself from the conversation, your milk suddenly lets down and soaks your clothes. Meanwhile, your husband tries to clean up the remainder of the baby's surprise bowel movement that somehow managed to escape the diaper. Two hours later, with your baby asleep at last, you both collapse, exhausted, on the couch.

Sound like a disaster? It doesn't have to happen this way. First, realize that with a new baby your life is going to change substantially. Then, take the following steps to ease this major transition:

• Say no to visitors. For at least the first week, restrict visitors. Say you're tired and you need to rest because your baby's schedule is highly unpredictable. Ask friends and family to call before stopping by. Children under the age of 5 should be discouraged from visiting for a week or two—they're more likely to pass communicable illnesses to you or your baby, and their energy levels tend to be demanding. Limit visits that can't be avoided to a maximum of 10 minutes.

• Go to bed as soon as you get home. By getting into comfortable pajamas and climbing into bed, you'll be more likely to get the rest you need—and to send a strong message to others that you're unavailable.

• Surround yourselves with plenty of good music and food. You can stock up on these ahead of time, as well as on paper plates and cups. The less preparation and clean-up time required, the better.

• Accept offers of help. For the first week home, new moms shouldn't do any laundry, cooking or cleaning. If people say they want to help, *take them up on it*. Be specific about what you want done.

• Snuggle with your baby. Make your bedroom a sanctuary where you can get to know your newborn, away from household activities and outside demands. You may even want to keep the baby in a cradle or bassinet next to you while you snooze during the day. A rocking chair in the privacy of your room encourages lullaby singing and uninterrupted cuddling.

Marveling at the wonder of your newborn, putting the rest of the world on hold for a few days, and taking time out as a family will make these days to be remembered for the rest of your lives.

Now You're Mom and Dad

Chapter Three ————————————————————

Mothering the New Mother

by Debra Evans

The days and weeks immediately following a baby's birth bring many changes to a woman's life. This is period of transition, a time of assuming new roles and responsibilities. It also is a time of learning to accommodate to new schedules and routines.

In the prenatal classes that I teach at a local hospital, I offer couples these words to help this transition go more smoothly: For at least one to two weeks after the baby is born, new mothers are not to do any of the following activities: laundry, shopping, cooking, cleaning, assuming primary care of the older children, and attending church.

Invariably, this statement is greeted with big grins by the women and looks of surprise by the men. I then explain how husbands, mothers, mothers-in-law, sisters, friends, neighbors and one's church congregation can be enlisted for performing these tasks.

But wait a minute—do *real* women need all this help? Many of us have heard about women elsewhere in the world who give birth and then immediately resume working. This is a myth. In traditional cultures, women are pampered and cared for (normally by female relatives) while they take time out to recover and establish their milk supply.

Sadly, our culture is dismally inadequate when it comes to supporting women who give birth. We have somehow forgotten that new mothers need *mothering.* Here are some practical ways we can help the new mom:

Food and rest are top priority. New moms (even if they have eight

———— ∽ ————

New mothers are not to do any of the following: laundry, shopping, cooking, cleaning . . . .

Debra Evans

———— ∽ ————

73

children) appreciate time alone with their new baby and time to rest at regular intervals throughout the day and night. Frequent snacks should be provided as needed, and a pitcher of juice or water kept available at all times. During breastfeeding, a woman requires 300 to 500 extra calories daily, and an extra one to two quarts of fluids. Often, friends at church offer to prepare meals; take them up on it!

The "babymoon" is not a time for extensive socializing. Don't feel reluctant to limit phone calls and visitors; you didn't hesitate when you were first married. Like a honeymoon, the transition period after a baby's birth is a time of bonding, intimacy, and learning new ways to communicate. Consider setting "visiting hours" for a period of 60 to 90 minutes every evening. Some families refrain from accepting visitors during the first week to give the mother and baby a chance to rest.

Encourage relaxation. A new mother benefits from back rubs, long showers, fresh flowers and a peaceful atmosphere within the home. A new robe, softly scented body lotion, or a brightly colored cotton sweat suit lets her know that she is valued and deserves special attention. If she is tired, bathe and change the baby while she rests, or lie down together—just the three of you—to take a nap.

Minimize isolation. Eventually, friends and family retreat, dad returns to work, and mom and baby are home alone for the first time. *New mothers need others.* Make sure your alone times are interspersed with brief walks with your baby, attending new-mother groups, accepting visits from friends, and calling your husband. (If he can come home at lunch time, that's even better.) In our culture, women at home are often isolated from their extended family and must develop their own support system to provide companionship.

The transition from pregnancy to postpartum is a time of discovery and personal growth—a time made easier by the caring involvement of others.

Helps for Common Postpartum Concerns

Problem	Help
Fatigue	Eat good food; plan a two-week break from outside activities; sleep—especially when your baby sleeps; simplify housework; limit visitors; minimize stair climbing; accept offers of help
Chills after birth	Warm blanket; heating pad; hot water bottle

Hot flashes	Cool cloth on forehead; lightweight clothing
Backache	Massage; heating pad for 10 minutes every hour as needed; pelvic tilts; slow breathing
Mood swings	Talk about your feelings with someone supportive; try to rest and take a break several times each day; have a good cry to release tension; remember, it's temporary—things will get better
Afterpains	Use pain-relief techniques used during labor; take pain medication as needed
Change in color of lochia (back to red)	Slow down—you're probably doing too much too soon; temporarily refrain from laundry and other housework
Sore, itchy perineum	Apply anesthetic ointment or spray; take sitz baths and pain medication; use Tucks
Abdominal wall flabbiness	Gradually resume doing curl-ups, pelvic tilts; realize muscle wall recovery takes time; sign up for postpartum fitness classes
Constipation	Increase fruit, liquid and fiber intake; take stool softeners if needed
Hemorrhoids	Avoid constipation (see above); use Tucks or anesthetic ointment
Breast fullness, sore or leaky nipples	Wear a supportive bra; apply ice packs; if you aren't nursing, don't express milk—wear a binder instead (your body will gradually reabsorb the milk); if nursing, breastfeed baby—or express milk—frequently; position baby properly on your breast

Postpartum Symptoms You Should Notify Your Doctor about *Now*
 • Temperature above 101°F
 • Bad-smelling vaginal discharge
 • Faintness, dizziness
 • Increased frequency and burning upon urination
 • Heavy gush of blood from vagina after flow has tapered off or changed color

- Hallucinations, fears of harming the baby, suicidal feelings
- Chills
- Severe headache
- Passage of clots with heavy bleeding
- Vaginal bleeding that soaks more than one pad per hour over a couple of hours
- Reddened area of the breast that feels sore and hot, especially if you have flu-like symptoms or a fever
- Any other symptom your doctor asks you to immediately report

Postpartum Depression: Chase the Blues Away
by Debra Evans

New mothers commonly experience an unexpected onslaught of emotions they don't understand or can't cope with. While the most common symptom is crying, moms dealing with the "baby blues" may also have trouble sleeping, or they may have feelings of agitation and emotional exhaustion. Four out of five new mothers encounter these to some degree, with most feeling a wave of sadness in the first days after childbirth. How can you overcome these unwelcome feelings?

- Give yourself permission to grieve. Normal grief is a process which runs its course and eventually leads to emotional restoration. Knowing it's OK to grieve is an important first step in the healing process.
- Sleep often. Interrupted sleep, light sleep and inadequate amounts of sleep can all contribute to depression. As a result, getting the sleep you need should be your primary self-care strategy. If you can sleep while your baby sleeps—either in your room or in a nursery—you may not need additional help. But if you're worn out from vigilant watchfulness, or if you have other young children to care for, you'll need someone you can rely on to take over while you snooze. If no one is available to assist you, consider hiring a reliable teenage baby-sitter to help after school. On evenings and weekends, ask your husband to cut back on outside activities temporarily to support you at home.
- Eat smart. Eating small, nourishing snacks throughout the day will boost your energy. Avoid caffeine, nicotine (including secondary smoke), alcohol, MSG and sugary foods. Instead, drink fruit juice, herbal teas with a little honey and lemon, or Postum. Buy easy-to-fix nutritious foods: plenty of fruits and vegetables, whole grains such as bran muffins and oatmeal, yogurt and other low-fat dairy products, and frozen meals that include all essential food groups.

• Talk about how you feel. Find someone who can understand what you're going through. Contact Depression After Delivery, a national support group with over 70 local branches: P.O. Box 1282, Morrisville, PA 19067. 215/295-3994. A skilled, sensitive counselor may be able to help you reduce emotional stress while caring for your baby. If you don't feel any better after two weeks of therapy, ask to be evaluated for additional treatment with antidepressant medication. Depending on which drug is prescribed, breastfeeding is still possible.

It takes time, but the symptoms of postpartum depression will subside, and babies are wonderfully adaptable if their basic needs are met. Until then, take care of yourself. Choose not to neglect your well-being no matter how pressing others' needs may be. Your baby deserves to have a mom whose needs are met.

Moms' Support Groups

by Debra Evans

I remember very clearly my first time at a mothers' support group. Five months pregnant, dressed in a long, handmade maternity dress, I sat quietly, listening to each mom introduce herself. I was a novice, a rookie—not even a bona-fide mom yet. But I openly acknowledged my first-timer status to the others, asking plenty of questions when my turn came.

We all shared something in common: We needed support from women who had traveled the road before us. Childrearing, breastfeeding and mothering aren't easy for anybody, and the journey is eased by the companionship and assistance of friends.

Recent studies confirm that women who lack an adequate support system run a significantly higher risk of developing depression after giving birth. As a solution, experts recommend that women fill the gap by joining or forming a mothers' support group—preferably one that is compatible with their individual style of mothering.

Babies and toddlers are some of the most demanding people on earth. They're not automatically easy to understand or care for. The only way to learn how to be a mom is by being one, and, at least initially, that's a pretty overwhelming method of education.

Mothers' groups make the learning more bearable as well as more fun. But in order to be a help rather than a hindrance, any group you are considering forming or joining should follow these basic rules:

Rule #1: Don't compare, share. The best support groups allow each member to openly express her unique foibles and frustrations. The group leader (if the group has one) acts as a gentle facilitator and wise source of information instead of The Perfect Mom. Don't set a strict agenda and discourage any departure from it. Group members shouldn't feel forced to compare themselves to one another.

Rule #2: Feel free to ask anything. Sure, you may sound stupid. Who doesn't at first? But that's exactly why you need a support group! You're a beginner, and you might as well admit it. You'll learn more, laugh more, and love being a mom more by dropping pretenses and opening up.

Rule #3: No apologies necessary. In order to build you up, your support group shouldn't tear you down—or cause you to tear *yourself* down. You are who you are, and that goes for everyone in your group. If in your group you feel inadequate, tearful, or full of second thoughts, you're in the wrong place. The *last* thing you need are a bunch of Job's comforters trying to "help" you by piously putting you down. When it comes to being a mom, none of us is perfect.

As women, we have much to gain from sharing our most valuable resources: the Lord *and* ourselves. As mothers, we know and understand things that professionals can't possibly know or understand unless they've been through it, personally, as mothers—day in and day out.

By supporting one another through times of failure and frustration as well as success, we make learning how to be a mother easier, and also discover how to take better care of ourselves and our families.

Notes for New Dads

by Patricia Rushford

"Isn't she the most beautiful baby in the world?" Joy, love, pride, and wonder fill Ken as he holds his daughter for the first time. He longs to protect her, care for her, nurture her. He wants to do more than to provide a paycheck. He wants to be part of her life.

But Ken has no idea how.

Most dads want to be involved in caring for their infants, and many, like Ken, waver in uncertainty. Their nurturing instincts have never been encouraged. If you find yourself in a position like Ken, these 10 steps can help point the way to being the kind of father you really want to be:

1. Share the pregnancy. Intimacy and bonding begin before your baby is born. Learn all you can about pregnancy and childbirth. Go with your wife to at least some (if not all) of her prenatal exams, and attend childbirth classes together so you can empathize with your wife and assist in the delivery.

2. Share intimate moments. Place your hand on your wife's abdomen and feel the baby move. Listen to the heartbeat. Talk to your baby so the sound of your voice becomes as familiar to the baby as your wife's. Talk openly about your excitement, joy, concerns and fears. Pray together for a healthy, happy child, a smooth delivery and a loving partnership.

3. Prepare for parenthood. Take a parenting class with your wife. Learn about baby development. Ask questions. Hang around other children to get some hands-on experience. Education can prevent feelings of insecurity and inadequacy.

4. Attend the baby shower. Traditionally, friends and relatives shower the mom and baby with gifts, making pregnancy and childbirth "a woman's thing." Why not suggest a baby shower where both sexes are welcome?

5. Take some time off work when the baby arrives. The Family and Medical Leave Act requires most employers to grant moms *and* dads at least 12 weeks of unpaid leave for the birth or adoption of a child. Take what time you can. Use your paid vacation time also. Your wife and baby need you.

6. Care for your newborn. With the exception of child-bearing and breastfeeding, dads can do anything for their babies that moms can. Feed and burp your baby. Rock her to sleep. Change her diapers. Schedule time together to talk, goo, coo, laugh and play.

7. Be persistent. You may be criticized for your active role in childcare. "After all," someone may say, "men are meant to work, not take time off to play mommy."

Even wives who long for their husband's involvement may resist it. Some moms may become overprotective, bossy and critical in an attempt to maintain control as the primary care giver. Again, talk about it, share your feelings, and work together toward the goals you both want.

8. Allow time for your nurturing instincts to develop. If you've never had a good role model, you may need to look to your wife or mother as a parenting teacher for a time. According to a study done by Kyle Pruett, M.D., a psychiatrist with Yale University's Child Study

Center, after about six months of hands-on fathering, the dads observed became increasingly confident in their roles. "They were so tuned in to their children, they felt they could trust their own instincts."

9. Be aware of others' unconscious attempts to undermine your efforts to co-parent. It's easy to back off when you feel ridiculed for your fathering. Instead, stand firm in your commitment and reap the rewards of being "the best dad a kid ever had."

10. Help other dads. As you become a nurturing, caring dad, consider sharing the joys of fatherhood with other men. Teach a Sunday school class, or lead a Bible study where dads and would-be dads can learn what fatherhood is really about.

Build Your Own Dads' Team
by Paul Lewis

Step One. Contact three to five men who face fathering responsibilities similar to yours.

Step Two. Introduce the idea to each of them. Say: "I notice you work at building a good relationship with your kids. I want that to be a strength of mine as well. A support network is an idea I'd like to experiment with for a few weeks with some other dads. Would you be interested?"

• Limit the time commitment: "This is an experiment. We'll meet weekly six times and then decide whether to continue."

• Express a clear focus: "Each time we'll discuss one or two fathering challenges we all face. We'll look for biblical and practical solutions. We're fellow learners—any ideas will be welcome."

Step Three. Meet for one hour in a place where there's enough privacy to pray. Spend about five minutes socializing, 40 discussing fathering, and 15 praying for wisdom and for your kids. Close with next week's objective. Important fundamentals:

• Punctuality.
• All comments are confidential.
• Everyone participates.
• The group becomes closed to new members after the second meeting. (Other dads can join when the group re-forms for another six sessions.)

Starter Discussion Topics:
• This week, what barrier to being a better dad do you face?
• How would you describe your fathering philosophy and goals?

- What do you feel each of your children need most from you right now as a dad? What developmental stage is each in?
- What strengths and weaknesses do you and your wife have as a parenting team?
- Talk about the strongest *fathering* figure in your life (i.e., fathering role model). How are you alike and different from him?
- Talk about the personality differences between your children. How do you adjust to these?
- In what ways do you hope your children become (or don't become) like you?
- How could your relationship with your own father be strengthened or rebuilt?

Babycare Basics

Chapter Four ————————————————

Well-Baby Checkups:
The Parent-Doctor Team

by William Sears

There are two facts of parenting: Babies get sick, and parents worry. How frequently and severely your baby gets ill will depend primarily upon her susceptibility to illness, not on your parenting. But by working closely with your doctor, you will lessen your baby's chances of getting sick and speed recovery when she does become ill.

Learning to "read" your well baby helps you more intuitively recognize and help your sick baby at the first sign of illness. A sensitive response to your baby's cries, and hours of holding and nursing increase your recognition: "She's acting differently; her cries are different; I know she hurts somewhere." It's not as important to know *what's* wrong as it is to know *something's* wrong.

A close parent-infant attachment will make it easier for you to care for your sick child. Many times your doctor will say, "I don't know what's wrong with your baby, so let's wait a day or two and see what changes occur." For example, I usually suspect that a baby who has a fever of unknown origin has a harmless virus that will pass in a few days. I ask her parents to call me if the symptoms change and release the sick baby to Dr. Mom and Dr. Dad, trusting that they will report back if their baby's condition worsens.

What are the credentials of these home doctors? If they are so sensitive to their baby that they almost hurt when their baby hurts, the sick baby

> *A sensitive response to your baby's cries, and hours of holding and nursing increase your recognition.*
>
> Dr. William Sears,
> on learning to "read" your baby

85

is in good hands—and their doctor-parent partnership will function well.

Getting the Most Out of a Visit to Your Doctor

• If possible, both parents should attend. Many doctors now offer helpful extended hours.

• Make a list of the questions and problems you wish to discuss.

• If you have an especially worrisome or complicated concern (for example, a behavioral problem), request an "extended visit" when making an appointment. Respect the fact that your doctor allots the usual amount of time for each scheduled checkup in order to be on time for other patients. Avoid surprises, such as springing a question as your doctor is walking out of the room: "By the way, we're considering a divorce next week. How will this affect our baby?"

Making Checkups Friendly

• Trying to examine a screaming child wears down you, your baby and the doctor and makes a precise exam next to impossible. You mirror the state of the world to your baby. If you are apprehensive, your baby is likely to share your anxiety. Try to be calm and relaxed.

• Avoid worry-producing statements like, "The doctor won't hurt you," or, "The shot will only hurt a little." Your child may only hear the word *hurt*. She'll automatically connect "hurt" with "doctor"—an association that will mushroom into an all-out scene even before you sign in.

• Make a good first impression. Greet your doctor cheerfully. Carry on a "We're glad to be here" conversation before the exam begins. According to a child's logic, if the doctor is OK to you, he's OK to me. Do not reinforce a child's clingy behavior by clinging back. Hold your child comfortably—it will help relax her.

• Finally, if this is not already your doctor's custom, request that your baby remain on your lap at least during the initial part of the exam. I have found that examining babies on parents' laps yields a more thorough exam and is less tiresome for everybody.

Phone Communication Tips

• Respect your doctor's time with his or her own family by limiting after-hours calls to especially worrisome situations when you fear your baby will get worse before your doctor's office reopens.

• Have your pharmacy's phone number ready.

• Be prepared to communicate accurately all the details of your child's illness—your doctor must offer a medical opinion based only on your description. If you feel your doctor doesn't appreciate the seriousness of your concerns, repeat them. The most direct approach is best: "Doctor,

my child seems very sick. I'm worried, and I would like him examined."
Be sure you understand your doctor's phone advice—write it down.
Don't hesitate to call back if your child gets worse.

The BREAD List

By using this simple "BREAD" list, you'll find it easier to remember the essential components of responsible parent-doctor teamwork. If you can't answer (or answer no to) one or more of the questions below after visiting your doctor, consider taking a more active role in guiding your child's treatment or changing to a physician who invites you to play a more active role in making decisions concerning your baby's health care.

Benefits	What will my child gain from having this treatment or procedure?
Risks	What are the possible discomforts, adverse reactions, common complications and major risks (no matter how rare) associated with the treatment or procedure?
Explanations	Was the information I needed to make an informed choice for my child presented in terms I could understand? Did my child's doctor encourage discussion? Were all my questions answered to my satisfaction?
Alternatives	Were alternative treatments explained to me with enough information about each to allow me to decide between possible courses of treatment, including non-treatment?
Decisions	Was I generally supported in the decision-making process by my child's physician without feeling pressured to decide in favor of a certain treatment?

Well-Baby Checkup Schedule
by William Sears

Another way to work in tandem with your doctor to the benefit of your baby is to follow your doctor's schedule for well-baby exams. Here's the schedule I recommend, which is similar to the one advised by the American Academy of Pediatrics:

• for the first six months: monthly for first-born babies; every other month for subsequent babies
• at 9, 12, 15, 18 and 24 months

- yearly thereafter

During these exams, expect to discuss:
- growth and development at each stage
- good nutrition
- preventative medicine and accident prevention

and to have:
- immunizations
- an exam to detect abnormal development
- height, weight and head measurements
- periodic lab tests, including hemoglobin and urinalyses
- hearing and vision evaluation
- questions answered about parenting
- help with specific medical problems

During these checkups, your doctor will grow in her knowledge of your well child—a useful reference point for both you and your doctor to have when your child is sick.

Interpreting Your Baby's Cries

by Bonnidell Clouse

All infants cry. Even a "good" baby must let his parent know when he is hungry or cold or in need of being held. Crying is the signal that alerts the care giver to come, to find out what is wrong, and to provide the necessary attention. Without letting an adult know that help is needed, some infants would not survive, nor would they learn the joy of interacting with another human being.

Crying during the first month is reflexive—like breathing or sucking or hiccuping. Picking up your infant and feeding him is a typical parental response and usually does the job.

By 3 months of age, a baby learns that crying brings the attention he wants. He also associates the meeting of his needs with the one who supplies those needs. He may cry when his mother leaves the room and stop when his mother returns. At this age, your baby not only needs his physical needs met, but his social/interactive needs too. A smiling face and chit-chat will probably help stop the crying—at least for the moment.

At 6 months, your baby will cry when his freedom is restricted. Being confined to a playpen or car seat may bring strong objections. And as he becomes adept at creeping, standing and walking, he will protest even more when restrained.

Excessive crying is most apt to take place during the first three months. Sometimes referred to as the three-month colic (because the worst is over by then), your child may suffer from gastrointestinal distress. His abdomen will become distended, and he will stiffen and pull up his legs in pain. Placing him on his tummy over your knees and rubbing his back may help. Some parents experiment with walking the floor, rocking their child, burping him, and offering him the bottle or breast.

But sometimes, no amount of cuddling, swinging or back rubbing will stop the crying. What then? Crying is the major non medical problem reported by parents of infants. Even knowing this, it takes a patient and well-adjusted adult to weather the first few months with a non-soothable infant. Keep in mind the following:

You know your baby better than anyone else. Advice may help, but only you can decide the best course of action.

Respond to crying promptly. Your baby will have less reason to cry if you don't delay meeting his physical and psychological needs.

Fatigue is one of the most common reasons for crying in infancy. When you have done all you can to make your baby comfortable, yet the crying continues, consider putting him to bed, closing the door, and letting him cry himself to sleep.

Take a break. It doesn't take two parents to listen to one infant cry. If you have an excessive crier, take turns taking care of him. "You go to the library tonight and I'll go to the library tomorrow night," worked well in our household.

Enjoy your infant. No infant cries *all* the time. Enjoy him when he's not crying. As the weeks go by, he will do less crying and more smiling. Both of you will live through the experience.

Tried and Tested Soothing Techniques

Burp, walk, rock. Rock your baby in a cradle, on your lap, or in a rocking chair. Burp her early and frequently during feedings, keeping her in an upright position with gentle motion for half an hour afterwards. Try creative positions to encourage burping—such as the "football-hold" (baby held horizontally in front of you, with your hand supporting her abdomen) or "tailor-sitting" (baby held sitting in a cross-legged position, facing away from you) as you walk and sway.

Pack and pat. "Wear" your baby in a front-pack carrier or side sling as you gently stroke her back; apply a little oil on her tummy and firmly massage your baby's abdomen in a continuous, circular, clockwise pattern (up her right side, across, and down the left); take her for a drive in her car seat; tuck her in a cradle with a fluffy lambskin to caress her skin softly as she rocks.

Try "white noise." Some babies calm down quickly when listening to the vacuum cleaner, blow dryer (on cool setting), washing machine, or a tape recording of rain, ocean waves, or a waterfall. For a variation on this theme, place your baby on top of your washing machine—strapped securely in her car seat—and do a load of laundry, staying by her side throughout the cycle.

Song and dance routines. Holding your baby close, support her head securely as you stand on a mattress and sway to some music; glide across the floor to the steady beat of a marching band (some babies are strangely calmed by John Phillips Sousa's "Stars and Stripes Forever"); rhythmically bounce your baby while you whistle to the latest Disney soundtrack.

Establishing Parent-Friendly Sleep Habits

by Grace Ketterman

At birth, most babies sleep from 18 to 20 hours a day, waking only to eat and have diapers changed. But not every newborn follows such a pattern—just ask the parents of a baby with colic!

As babies grow and learn to focus in on the sounds and sights around them, they sleep less and interact more with their environment and the people in it. They learn to cry, not just from hunger or discomfort, but for companionship. They get bored! So, long after the time is past when they need to awaken at night for feedings, the baby who loves entertainment will regularly call on you to provide it. Some of that is good: It helps babies grow up being able to take care of themselves. But it's best to try to prevent nighttime wakefulness. Here are some suggestions.

• Try to arrange a quiet place for your baby's crib. It needs to be close enough for you to hear the cries of genuine needs, but distant enough that your sounds, such as snoring or a mattress that squeaks when you move, do not disturb the sleeping infant.

• Provide a source of low-level, constant sound near your baby to block out other noises that could awaken him. Once your child is asleep, the sounds can fade away.

• Let your infant fuss or even cry a little while. Some experts believe allowing a baby to put out his effort before parents respond will help him develop an assertive, independent personality. Sometimes babies put themselves back to sleep after a little fussing, and this helps teach them to sleep through the night.

• When you give your baby nighttime feedings, do it quickly, efficiently, and get him back to bed. It may be tempting to cuddle or play with this new creation when all is quiet. But you may be setting the stage for a habit of waking up just to play.

There are many opinions regarding how to handle a baby's wakefulness. Some believe a crying baby of any age needs parental attention. They recommend taking your baby into bed with you. Others would keep babies remote from parents, even to the point of risking a child's sense of abandonment. They recommend you never allow your child in bed with you.

Find your own comfort zone. If your infant is in pain or is afraid, he needs the comfort and safety of being close to you. But if he is learning to manipulate you, it can't be good for anyone.

Why Kids Awaken

by Patricia Rushford

Children awaken at night for a variety of reasons:

• Habit. As an infant, Joshua needed his nighttime feedings. Now it's an expected part of his routine. As long as his parents comply, why change?

• Hunger. Normal, healthy babies (1 to 2 years) don't need nighttime feedings. Most children can safely sleep through the night by 12 pounds or three months.

• Fear. Nightmares, separation anxiety, stress or significant changes may contribute to nighttime fears. If these are a significant problem, you may want to discuss the matter with your pediatrician or counselor.

• Too much sleep. Sarah still put Mandy (15 months) down for a nap twice a day. Mandy woke up at three in the morning, expecting her family to rise with her. Sarah solved the problem by cutting one nap.

• Sleeping with parents. Whether children should sleep with their parents is the subject of much debate. Some find the family bed works well for them, but co-sleeping is not for everyone. Bringing a child into her parents' bed on occasion provides a sense of comfort and security, such as when a child is frightened or ill. But habitual co-sleeping patterns (when a baby can't sleep any other way) can decrease levels of self-confidence and increase and/or create sleep problems. Parents may become irritable, frustrated and resentful at having their sleep interrupted.

Occasionally, a child's disruptive sleep patterns may indicate a sleep disorder. If you have any questions or suspect abnormal sleep problems, you may want to talk with your child's doctor and research the matter more thoroughly.

Happy Napping

by William Sears

In the first year, your baby will need at least a one-hour nap in the morning and a one- to two-hour nap in the afternoon. Between ages 1 and 2, most babies drop the morning nap but still require a one- to two-hour afternoon nap. Most children require at least a one-hour afternoon nap until around age 4. If your young napper is reluctant, try these approaches:

• Nap with her. You probably look forward to her nap time so you can finally get something done. Resist this temptation. Naps are as important for you as your child. Even if your baby doesn't want to nap, she may need a little down time.

• Be consistent, napping at the time when you are most tired.

• Prepare your baby for a nap. Take her into a dark, quiet room, turn on some soft music, nestle together in a rocking chair, or lie down on a bed. Set aside a special quiet time every day during which you read a story together or give her a massage to condition her into a nap.

• If you're caught in a juggling act, trying to get your baby to nap while chasing down a busy toddler, try making a nap nook. Use a large box with a cut-out door, a card table with a blanket over the sides, or the space under the grand piano. Lure your older child into his special place reserved just for napping. Then you can lie down with your baby.

• If your baby still resists a nap, try a car ride or a baby carrier. The monotonous movement of a car will often lull the resistant napper to sleep. Also, put your baby in a baby carrier, preferably a sling-type carrier, and wear your baby around the house awhile until she falls asleep. Slip out of the sling while you place your baby down on her bed, using the sling as a cover. Then join her. Chances are good you could use a break yourself.

Oh, Colic!

by Grace Ketterman

Colic is often designated by its expected duration: six-week colic, six-month colic—or longer. A friend told me one of her children slept only a few minutes at a time for over a year.

The symptoms of colic are well known: The most annoying is crying—loud and long. Generally, babies with colic draw up their knees and then kick their feet; they clench their fists and wave their arms. You think they are in agony and must need emergency medical care. That is usually not the case, and for most infants, there is no apparent cause for such crying. Walking the floor, rocking and crooning may relieve the crying for brief moments. So may helping your baby burp, expel gas or have a bowel movement. But these methods do not significantly relieve the long-term problem.

Pediatricians know little more now about what causes colic than they did decades ago. Some breastfed babies with colic have allergies to dairy products or other foods in the mother's diet, whereas bottle-fed babies can react adversely to various formulas. If breastfeeding, contact your local lactation consultant for advice on how to adjust your diet to reduce your baby's discomfort. If bottle-feeding, switch to a soy-based or meat-based formula with the supervision of your nutritionist or health-care provider.

Get your doctor to confirm there is nothing seriously wrong with your child. Pay plenty of attention to your baby; cuddle and carry him. Save enough money to hire someone to give you a night's relief now and then. Or ask a friend or relative to provide a respite. If you can look forward to a quiet half-day once a week, you'll maintain your poise more easily.

Although health-care providers try to use as little medication as possible, prescriptions can help extreme cases. Many new mothers are reluctant to administer medication for excessive crying, but it may be what's needed to break the vicious cycle of tension. If so, try medicine for at least one week to relieve the colic and to give you and your baby some rest. Then gradually stop using the medication.

In the midst of the daily challenges of caring for a colicky baby, here are some points to remember:

Believe in yourself. As a parent, you have within you all the resources to raise your child. If you remember that, you will not be as anxious during difficult times.

Believe in your child. The Creator has implanted in every child a will to survive. In some children, that survival instinct is stronger than in others. But it is there, and you can count on it to pull your child through this difficult time.

Develop a positive attitude. Knowing that colic is only temporary can help parents survive the weeks or months of its duration. By doing what you can to enhance your baby's comfort—and knowing you're not to blame for your baby's crying—all of you will make it through this trying time a bit more easily.

Recommended reading: *Crying Babies, Sleepless Nights,* by Sandy Jones (Warner); *Crying Baby,* by Sheila Kitzinger (Viking Penguin).

Tips for Treating a Colicky Baby

- Burp your baby early and frequently during feedings.
- If using a bottle, enlarge nipple holes or buy nipples with smaller openings. (To test size, turn the bottle over. Formula should drip out freely, but not exit in a steady stream.)
- If you have a strong "let-down" while nursing, remove your nipple from your baby's mouth and allow the initial burst of milk to spray onto a cloth diaper or cotton towel.
- Always feed and burp your baby in an upright position.
- To help relieve gas, press your baby's knees gently toward her chest, legs folded; hold briefly, then release. Repeat several times.
- Feed your baby in a quiet, dimly lit room.
- Try abdominal massage: Warm a little oil in your hands, then rub continuously in a slow, circular motion on your baby's tummy, following the direction of his colon, up the right side, then across and down the left.
- Clear your baby's nasal passages—mouth breathing may cause her to swallow more air.
- Avoid exposure to sudden startles and noises.
- If nursing, assess your diet for possible offenders and eliminate them, one at a time, from your diet for several days. (Dairy products, iron supplements and citrus foods are common irritants.)
- Discuss the benefits and risks of intestinal relaxant medications with your doctor.
- Hold your baby in a relaxed and secure fashion.
- Carry your baby in a cloth sling or infant carrier.
- Ask someone to care for your baby while you take a break away

from the house. A 15-minute walk can quickly restore your sense of calm, and your baby will benefit from your being more relaxed.

- Consider chiropractic care: Many chiropractors cite success in relieving infant colic by performing spinal adjustments.
- Securely swaddle your baby in a blanket, and rock her frequently.
- Seek help from new-parent or moms' support groups.

Diaper Rash and Treatment

by William Sears

Take a close look at your newborn's blemish-free bottom. The complexion may never be so clear for the next year. As soon as you begin diapering, a rash is bound to come.

Diapers were invented to protect the surroundings from your baby's excrement—and skin rebels at losing its freedom to enjoy fresh air and sunshine. Start with ultra-sensitive skin, add the chemicals of urine and stools, obstruct the area with a big "bandage" and rub it all together. Presto! Diaper rash.

Excessive moisture on sensitive skin is the main cause of diaper rash. This moisture removes the skin's natural oils, and wet skin is more easily damaged by friction. Once the skin has been irritated by excessive moisture, it no longer provides a good natural barrier. Bacteria and fungi attack the weakened skin.

How to relieve diaper rash and comfort your baby:
- Quick changes. Change wet or soiled diapers quickly. Although breastfed babies have a stool right after feeding, they are often in a deep sleep that allows changing without waking.
- Frequent changes. Studies show that infants who are changed at least eight times a day have less diaper rash.
- Rinse and wipe well. Rinse your baby's bottom during each change, especially if the diaper is "soaked" or you smell ammonia. Experiment with what gets along well with your baby's bottom. Sensitive skin does well with plain water; some bottoms need a mild soap. Some react to chemical wipes; others accept them without a rash.
- A gentle pat. Blot your baby's bottom with a soft towel or a clean cotton diaper. Avoid excessive rubbing. One of our babies had such sensitive skin that even blotting reddened her skin. We used a hair dryer

(coolest and lowest setting, held 12 inches away) to dry her bottom.

• Air condition your baby's bottom. Allow the diaper area to breathe. If you use disposable diapers, apply them loosely, and avoid tight-fitting plastic pants that retain moisture. Some mothers even poke holes in disposable diapers to allow air to circulate more freely. Experiment with both cloth and disposable diapers to see which ones cause the least diaper rash. If you wash your own diapers, remove soap residues and irritants by adding one-and-a-half cups of vinegar to the rinse cycle. You can request this of diaper services too.

• Bottoms up. While your baby sleeps, expose his bottom to the air and occasionally to a 10-minute ray of sunlight near a *closed* window. Place him on a cloth diaper with a rubber pad underneath.

• Remove friction. Fold the plastic liner of disposable diapers outward so that only the soft area touches the skin. Apply a lubricant such as A and D ointment or zinc oxide cream to reduce chafing. Creams and ointments aren't needed for most rashless bottoms. They may prevent your baby's skin from "breathing" naturally. However, at the first sign of an irritated bottom, apply barrier cream *generously*.

When conditions change at one end, expect changes at the other. Teething, medicines, or a change in diet or formula affect the chemistry of stools and urine. Different rashes may follow. As soon as the "mouth end" conditions change, apply barrier creams before rashes begin, especially if your baby is prone to diaper rash. Adding acidophilus or lactobacillus bifidus to baby's antibiotic regimen may lessen antibiotic-produced diarrhea. If a rash doesn't improve, contact your doctor.

Which rash is which:

Allergy ring. A red ring around your baby's anus indicates a dietary irritant as the culprit, similar to a rash around the mouth when beginning a new food. Wheat and citrus fruits and juices are the main irritants. Discontinue a new food to see if the red ring goes away. If you are breastfeeding, you may need to drop the food from your own diet.

Contact dermatitis. This is a red, scald-type rash over the area of the skin touched by diapers. It is caused by chemical irritants in the diaper, detergent, or urine and stools. It also can be caused by chemical changes in stools during diarrheal illnesses or antibiotic treatment. To treat it, soak your baby's bottom in a baking-soda solution of one tablespoon soda to two quarts of water.

Intertrigo. This rash occurs where skin folds rub together and is caused by heat and moisture retention in the creases. If urine touches the irritated areas, it may burn the skin, causing your baby to cry.

Seborrheic dermatitis. This is one of the most sore-looking diaper rashes. Its sharply demarcated margins look like a big red patch placed over the groin, genitalia and lower abdomen. This rash is more raised, rough, thick and greasy than any of the others. Besides the above preventative measures, this type of rash is usually treated with a prescription cortisone cream. *Do not use cortisone cream on the diaper area longer than prescribed by your doctor,* as overuse may damage the skin.

Yeast rash (also called candida). This is a reddish-pink, raised, patchy rash primarily over the genitalia, with satellite spots sprinkled around the rash's main area. If a diaper rash persists despite the preventative measures, suspect yeast rash and try an over-the-counter or prescription anti-fungal cream. Yeast infection may occur on top of other diaper rashes if they persist more than a few days. Some persistent yeast rashes require a prescription oral anti-fungal medication.

Impetigo. This rash, caused by a bacteria (usually streptococci or staphylococci), appears as coin-sized blisters that ooze a honey-colored crust. These are spotted around the diaper area. This type of rash needs a prescription antibiotic cream and sometimes oral antibiotics.

Is it Serious? Questions to Ask about Diaper Rash

Are there any broken or intact blisters? If so, a bacterial infection that requires antibiotic therapy may be present. Be sure to notify your baby's doctor now to get proper treatment.

Are there bright, strawberry red patches on the skin? The diaper rash may be complicated by a monial (yeast) infection—contact your doctor by phone for specific advice concerning home treatment and which cream to use.

Is the rash more severe in skin creases between fat folds? Then steroid cream may need to be prescribed. Call your doctor's office.

Has there been any improvement in the rash since starting treatment? Any rash that lasts longer than three to four days without improvement should be seen by a doctor. Regardless of what's causing the rash, however, it's safe to begin the home therapy as described in this chapter right away.

Facts about Hernias

by Grace Ketterman

Judy was fearful when she discovered a lump in her newborn son's groin. His scrotum looked strangely large too. Fortunately, the actual truth was not nearly as dreadful as Judy's fears had been. Her son was born with an *inguinal hernia.* He also had a *hydrocele,* a fluid-filled sac in the scrotum. Neither, the nurse assured her, was cause for alarm.

A hernia is the weakness of lower abdominal muscles in the area commonly called the groin. As a baby grows in his mother's womb, a canal or tract develops through which the boy's testicle and spermatic cord move from his abdomen into his scrotum. When a baby's abdominal muscles are weak, a segment of his intestines may protrude when he cries or strains. The bulge this creates—a hernia—can be seen and felt.

Here are a few facts about infant hernias:

• Hernias occur in five percent of baby boys and one percent of baby girls.

• Hernias are often present at birth. A baby might also be born with a physical weakness that will result in a hernia later.

• They are more common in boys than in girls, due to the process of development of the sexual anatomy.

• Hernias may be accompanied by a condition known as an *undescended testicle.* (A baby boy's testes stay in the lower abdomen instead of moving into the scrotum.)

• Hernias, undescended testicles and hydroceles are easily corrected by simple surgical procedures.

The surgical procedure to repair an infant hernia is typically routine, and most babies tolerate it well. Surgical correction is necessary to prevent a section of the intestine from getting caught in the narrow tract that has developed, such that it can't return to its proper place in the abdomen. A caught intestine can result in a *strangulated hernia,* in which swelling and interference with blood circulation to that part of the intestine are likely to occur. If this condition is severe and lasts long enough, emergency surgery is necessary to prevent permanent damage to vital tissues.

Good Sense about Vaccines

by William Sears

Immunizations have received a lot of bad press lately. Unfortunately, this has done more to confuse than to educate the public. Like most parents, you may feel caught in a dilemma: If your child is immunized, he may experience a bad reaction; if he's not, he may get the disease itself.

Today's parents do not remember the pre-vaccine era, when infectious diseases posed serious threats to the health of children. I can still remember as a young child seeing or reading about other children spending years in iron lungs for treatment of polio. As a young intern in pediatrics, I heard on the whooping cough ward the coughing and choking of infants who had not been immunized. I remember the encephalitis caused by measles, and the birth defects in babies of mothers who had German measles during pregnancy. These diseases are not common anymore, perhaps because of vaccines.

Immunizations stimulate your child's immune defenses to produce antibodies against the germ that causes a particular illness. A vaccine is made from a part of the germ itself, or from a germ changed so that it does not cause disease but nevertheless stimulates the body to react as if the germ were the real thing. If the real germ enters the body, the antibodies produced by the vaccine will be able to fight it.

Questions to Ask Prior to Immunizing Your Child
by Debra Evans
1. How effective is this immunization?
2. What adverse reactions may result from this vaccine?
3. Who might experience an adverse reaction to it?
4. Does my baby have any conditions to contraindicate immunization at this time?
5. For how long does this vaccine guarantee immunity?
6. Is the vaccine free of contaminating agents?

Evaluating vaccines. Every vaccine (and, in fact, any substance that is put into a child's body, be it a medicine or a food) has both risks and potential benefits. When evaluating a vaccine, we try to determine its risk/benefit ratio. If the risks of a reaction to a vaccine are worse than the risks from the disease that the vaccine is designed to prevent, then the vaccine has a high risk/benefit ratio and is not a safe vaccine.

The smallpox vaccine initially had a low risk/benefit ratio. However, worldwide vaccination was so effective that, nowadays, smallpox has been nearly eradicated. The risks associated with the vaccine outweigh the now extremely small risk of contracting the disease, so routine smallpox vaccination has been discontinued.

There are currently eight vaccines in common use: diphtheria, pertussis (whooping cough), tetanus, measles, mumps, rubella (German measles), polio, and the newer Hib vaccine (for the bacteria Hemophilus influenza type B, a common cause of respiratory infections and meningitis in young children). Diphtheria, pertussis and tetanus are usually given together in a DPT shot; measles, mumps and rubella are combined in the MMR. The polio vaccine is given orally. All of these vaccines have a low risk/benefit ratio.

Pertussis vaccine concern. The pertussis vaccine has been a cause of increasing concern. Of all the vaccines, it is the least effective in preventing the disease it is designed to combat, and it presents the greatest risk of serious reactions. The media, along with concerned parents and health-care professionals, have called attention to the fact that the whooping cough vaccine is not a very good vaccine. This has stimulated researchers and manufacturers to work on a safer and more effective vaccine, which will probably be available within a few years. Countries that have temporarily stopped the routine use of the pertussis vaccine have encountered whooping cough epidemics shortly thereafter, resulting in the resumption of routine vaccinations for whooping cough.

Unfortunately, the concerns about the whooping cough vaccine have created a lot of fear about vaccines in general. As a result, some parents withhold all immunizations from their child. This is unfortunate.

In my opinion, unless special medical circumstances are present, children should be immunized according to the dosage and schedule recommended by the Committee on Infectious Diseases of the American Academy of Pediatrics:

at 2 mos:	DPT, oral polio
4 mos:	DPT, oral polio
6 mos:	DPT, oral polio (optional)
1 yr.	Tuberculin test
15 mos:	Measles, mumps, rubella (MMR)
18 mos. to 2 yrs:	Hib, DPT
4 to 5 yrs:	DPT

The immunization schedule should be followed as closely as possible. The initial series of three DPT vaccines may be given as closely as one month apart. Interrupting the recommended schedule does not interfere with the development of immunity; it is not necessary to start the series again, regardless of the time elapsed. While it is not necessary to delay your child's immunizations if he has a cold, immunizations should not be given while your child is generally sick or is running a fever. Other special health considerations may also prompt your doctor to alter the schedule and dosage of your child's immunizations.

For More Information

by Debra Evans

In addition to talking to your baby's doctor about vaccinations, you may also want to become familiar with a variety of other viewpoints. As a parent it is your right—and your responsibility—to make the best choice possible for your baby.

What You Need to Know, American Academy of Pediatrics. Presents general information about routine childhood immunizations; distribution of this booklet to parents has been required since 1992. Some parents feel coverage of severe adverse reactions and death rates is too vague and advise additional reading about vaccine-related risks. Available free from your physician's office or public health clinic.

Health Information for International Travel, U.S. Government Printing Office. Gives information on a wide variety of vaccines, including risks and benefits. May be obtained for $5 from the Superintendent of Documents, U.S. Government Printing Office, Washington, DC 20402, or call 202/783-3238 to order by credit card.

Vaccines: Are They Really Effective? by Neil Z. Miller. Explores current controversies and asks key questions related to adverse vaccine reactions, mandatory immunizations, and adequacy of new-product testing. $7.95 plus postage and handling. National Vaccine Information Center, 512 W. Maple Ave. Suite 106, Vienna, VA 22180. 703/938-DPT3.

Feeding
Your Baby

Chapter Five ————————————————————

Breastfeeding Concerns

by Debra Evans

Breastfeeding is a natural process, but is also a *learned* ability. In the past, women learned to breastfeed by example. Today, breastfeeding knowledge is acquired primarily through self-education and skilled support. While few women encounter long-term breastfeeding difficulties, even minor concerns can seem major at the time. Prenatal preparation, getting help when needed, and ongoing support can ease the way.

As a nursing couple, you and your baby interact frequently to foster healthy breastfeeding. After lactation begins, your body will require the regular removal of milk as a signal for your breasts to produce additional food for your baby. Excessive fullness, or *engorgement,* prevents this process. Breastfeed your baby soon after birth and frequently during the first few weeks to help alleviate this problem. I suggest you nurse your baby at *least* every two to three hours during the day and every three to four hours at night. Wake your baby for feedings if she is sleepy, making sure her mouth is open wide for proper placement on the breast. If your breasts are overfull, apply warm compresses to encourage milk to flow before each feeding, and express a little milk by hand or breast pump to enable your baby to latch on easier. After feeding, apply cold compresses to your breasts to relieve any tenderness or swelling.

Normally, breastfeeding doesn't hurt. If nipple soreness persists beyond the first few days, it's probably because your baby isn't positioned properly. While nursing, your baby should be in a flexed, comma-like

> *Prenatal preparation, getting help when needed, and ongoing support can ease the way.*
>
> Debra Evans,
> *on beginning to breastfeed*

position with her entire body facing yours, "chest to breast." Holding your baby close at breast level, cup your breast throughout the feeding with your free hand, all four fingers beneath and your thumb on top. Using your nipple, tickle your baby's lips until she opens her mouth *very* wide, then quickly place as much of the breast as possible inside. The key here is *open wide*. If the baby's mouth isn't open enough, she'll latch on too low to press milk out adequately, which will result in nipple damage. Alternating positions one out of every three feedings during the first two weeks also helps. After feedings, allow the milk to dry on your nipple and the dark skin around it, air drying for at least five minutes before covering your breast. If your bra is wet, change into a fresh one. I also recommend you avoid breast pads at first—they trap moisture against the skin and prevent toughening. When bathing, wash your breasts only with water to prevent skin dryness.

Nursing a Sleepy Baby

Undress your baby. Help keep your baby more alert and interactive by feeding him "skin-to-skin" instead of swaddled in blankets and covered with clothing.

Manually express milk. Express a little milk—either by hand or with a breast pump—before your baby latches on. This softens your breasts and enables your baby to take more of your nipple and areola into his mouth. If necessary, rhythmically compress your areola while nursing to encourage milk flow until your let-down reflex takes over.

Tickle, tap, nibble. Wake him up if he starts to doze off or lose interest by stroking his back, tickling his feet, talking, and stretching his free arm in and out.

Bubble and switch. If he's still stubbornly sleeping, sit him up, allow any air bubbles in his stomach to rise, and then burp him. Often, the gentle jostling and thumping of bubbling will wake your baby up so you can resume the feeding. Repeat this technique as needed.

Relax. Your baby will outgrow this tendency. Small babies, jaundiced babies, and contented babies are more likely to be sleepers than high-need babies, babies who love to suck, and easily-startled babies.

If you notice a painful, lumpy area in one of your breasts, you may have a blocked milk duct. Breastfeed frequently, starting on the affected side, and apply warm, moist cloths to the area. Position your baby's chin towards the blocked duct, even if it means laying him upside down on the bed next to you. Gently massage the affected breast every few hours, starting at your chest with each stroke, repeatedly moving down over the lump toward the nipple. Be sure to rest, drink plenty of fluids, and *keep nursing*. If a red, lumpy, painful area on the breast is accompanied by fever, chills, and/or other flu-like symptoms, treat it as a blocked duct and call your doctor today. You may have a mastitis, a type of breast inflammation common among nursing mothers. If so, continue to breastfeed often and take a pain reliever with the antibiotic prescribed by your doctor.

Be encouraged: *None* of the problems I've just mentioned are an indication for you to stop nursing; *all* can be quickly resolved with proper treatment. Few breastfeeding difficulties—including slow weight gain, nursing a premature baby, newborn jaundice or a low milk supply—totally preclude breastfeeding. If you don't want to wean your baby right now, but are encountering a difficulty I haven't discussed, consult an up-to-date breastfeeding manual or call La Leche League (800/LA-LECHE) for further information.

Dispelling Nursing Myths

When you make the decision to breastfeed, you may find yourself becoming the target of all sorts of comments and advice. Much of what you hear will be based on false information or what was believed to be true about nursing many years ago.

Ignore any breastfeeding advice if it is: based on belief rather than fact; a recycled idea left over from someone else's unsuccessful or unpleasant nursing experience; taken from any books published prior to the 70s; intended to prove that the person who's stating her opinion is right (in order to prove you wrong); or offered to ease the other person's concern, rather than to genuinely support *you* with accurate information.

The most helpful source of breastfeeding knowledge, beyond current books, classes, support groups and videos, is a friend or relative who enjoyed nursing her baby for at least six to eight months. Your health-care provider is likely to be supportive if he or she values breastfeeding as a special relationship that involves both you and the baby, rather than simply a means of providing your baby with nutrients.

If you're faced with comments that reflect myths or misunderstandings about breastfeeding, keep in mind Proverbs 15:23: "How good is a timely word!" You'll soon find that your "timely words" about nursing can quickly clear the air—and calm your mind.

Night Nursing and Ear Infections

Middle ear infections result from the spread of infection through the eustachian tube—the passageway connecting the middle ear to the throat. Because the entrance to the eustachian tube lies close to the tonsils and adenoids, it's a fertile environment for the growth of bacteria and viruses when fluid collects inside the ear.

If your baby nurses at night in a lying-down position and frequently develops ear infections, try nursing him while sitting up or lying down at a 45-degree angle. In addition, avoid nursing your baby on the same side throughout the night. Although this may be less comfortable, it may solve the problem of a stubborn ear infection that doesn't completely clear up following antibiotic therapy.

Making these simple changes will accomplish two important things: First, when your baby has a cold or nasal congestion, gravity promotes fluid drainage through the eustachian tube into the throat; second, periodically switching sides when you nurse decreases skin warmth near the ear and allows the susceptible area to cool down, thereby discouraging bacterial growth.

Expressing and Storing Breast Milk

• Express your milk by hand or with a breast pump. Electric breast pumps are the most simple and efficient. If your baby is hospitalized or your lactation consultant recommends pumping, rent a commercial pump. Many women rent electric pumps when returning to work to save time and effort. Other methods of expression—hand expression, manual breast pumps and battery-operated pumps—require practice and patience to learn, but are considerably less expensive.

• The best time of day to obtain milk is when your milk supply is highest—usually in the morning. Don't be discouraged if you only get one-half ounce at first. It normally takes a little time for your let-down reflex to become conditioned to alternate methods of expression.

• To establish a let-down response to manual or breast pump expression, relax and avoid expressing for the first few times if you're under pressure to obtain milk. Practice in a soothing setting (in the tub or while showering), realizing that you may not get much at first. This may seem awkward, but soon it will be much easier.

• Store collected milk by expressing it directly into a container that has been washed in the dishwasher or sterilized for five minutes in boiling water. Cover the container tightly and refrigerate the milk immediately.

• If you won't be using expressed milk within 48 hours, freeze it after chilling. A plastic cube tray works great for this purpose—no matter how much milk you obtain, you can fill at least *one* cubicle! Tightly cover the tray with plastic wrap, then aluminum foil; after several cubes are frozen, transfer them to a plastic freezer container with a fitted lid for longer storage.

• You can store your milk up to 48 hours in your refrigerator, two weeks in a refrigerator freezer, or two months in a free-standing freezer.

• Never thaw frozen breast milk at room temperature, in boiling water, or in a microwave: Defrost it in the refrigerator or by shaking the bottle under lukewarm running water.

• Once the milk is thawed, it should be used within 24 hours. Once you've warmed it, discard any remaining milk.

When You Can No Longer Breastfeed

Once lactation has been established, a number of conditions or circumstances may interrupt breastfeeding. Unfortunately, there is no quick or easy answer for immediately stopping the flow of milk or the feelings connected to nursing. These tips, however, may help ease your physical and emotional discomfort:

1. Relieve excessive breast fullness, or engorgement, by nursing or pumping—just enough to relieve the fullness—about every two hours. This can also be done during a warm shower or bath by applying warm washcloths to your breasts and then gently pressing milk out. An added advantage of bathing and showering: Warm water soaks will help to relieve stress. Tension caused by infant loss, hospitalization, postpartum depression, returning to a stressful job, and other circumstances related to sudden weaning will also decrease your milk supply.

2. Every third day, decrease the number of nursings/pumpings and increase the time between them. This signals your body to make milk more slowly and reduces the possibility of breast infection or plugged ducts. Over a period of time, your milk will eventually change in color and consistency from a whitish-blue to a thinner, clearer fluid. After one week, the constant feeling of fullness should subside; after two, you will probably feel a marked decrease in fullness, discomfort, leaking and tenderness. It will take about three weeks before your breast size and comfort level return to a pre-lactation state.

3. Some people believe that binding the breasts is helpful; if you decide to try this, consult with La Leche League or a knowledgeable health-care provider first. (Binding, if applied incorrectly, can cause infection.) Instead of binding, try wearing a well-fitting, supportive bra.

4. If you develop plugged ducts: Treat plugged ducts with warm heat and gentle massage. If you develop a fever, see any large, painful lumps, or notice a red streak or red area on either breast, call your doctor or lactation consultant for advice.

5. Cutting back on fluids may help, but don't stop drinking liquids altogether, especially if signs of breast infection are present. For your own health, you need a sufficient amount of fluids. Drinking just enough to satisfy your thirst will meet this need.

6. Although you may be facing a painful situation or difficult time right now, you may, in the future, find comfort in knowing that you did your best. Even a day or two of breastfeeding—during which time your baby received a blend of nutrients and antibodies that weren't available anywhere else—was beneficial for your baby.

Bottle-feeding Update

by Debra Evans

Are you confused by the overwhelming choices of bottles, nipples and formulas on the market today? In spite of this, bottle-feeding can be quite simple once you understand what goes into it.

Here's a list of do's and don'ts designed to help simplify this process. Direct any additional questions and concerns you may have to your baby's doctor:

Do buy the variety, color, type of nipple and brand of bottle, whether disposable or refillable, that you like best. If your baby has difficulty with the nipple shape you select, feel free to try other brands until you find one she likes.

Don't bother with sterilizing. Today's infant formulas are pre-sterilized. Never leave unopened formula at room temperature for more than two hours, and don't freeze formula. Refrigerate opened, pre-mixed formula or concentrated liquid formula; if you don't use the remainder within 48 hours, toss it out. Any formula left in the bottle after feeding should be thrown away, because it has been mixed with bacteria and saliva from your baby's mouth. Carefully wash all equipment with a mild dish detergent and a bottle brush, followed by a thorough rinsing to remove soap film. Air dry and reassemble bottles before storing.

Do become familiar with available infant formulas, and make a list of questions to ask your baby's doctor. Most full-term babies use milk-based formula made from non-fat milk and a milk protein called de-mineralized whey. Vegetable oils replace the butterfat naturally found in cow's milk to provide essential nutrients. Babies who experience difficulties with this type of formula are often switched to a soy-based formula.

In some cases, your doctor may recommend a protein hydrolysate formula if your baby is unable to digest or tolerate other formulas.

Do watch the flow of formula as your baby sucks. Air bubbles rising in a steady stream up the side of the bottle as your baby's mouth moves rhythmically indicates all is in order. Gulping means the formula is flowing too fast. Check the nipple opening. It may be cracked or too large for your baby. If your baby is actively sucking without getting much milk, the flow is too slow. Perhaps the nipple is clogged or the cap screwed too tight. If your baby sucks in a quivering motion, the nipple may be collapsed. Removing the nipple will break the vacuum.

Don't heat bottles in the microwave. The composition and nutritional value of the formula may be altered, and even if the bottle feels cool to your touch, "hot spots" can form in the milk. It isn't necessary to heat formula, but because babies like consistency, offer formula at about the same temperature at each feeding.

Do hold your baby whenever she needs to be fed. Allowing for normal variations in your baby's appetite, feed your baby until she seems satisfied. Bottle propping causes dental decay when your baby falls asleep nursing on her bottle. Besides, the snuggling time associated with feedings will be a bonding boon for both of you.

How Much? How Often?

The following general guidelines are based on the amount of formula an average-size baby drinks each day. A larger or more active baby will require more formula; a smaller baby, less. The total daily amount of formula should not exceed 32 ounces. Be sure to ask your baby's doctor for additional advice concerning your baby's specific needs.

	0-2 wks	2-8 wks	2-3 mos	3-6 mos
ounces per feeding	2 to 3	3 to 5	4 to 6	5 to 7
feedings per day	6 to 8	5 to 6	4 to 5	4 to 5
average daily total	22 oz.	28 oz.	30 oz.	32 oz.

The Trials of Teething

by Debra Evans

Teething. Ask any parents what they remember about their kids' teething experiences. You're likely to hear stories about saliva-soaked shirts and blankets, crying toddlers who can't stay asleep, and the anxious pursuit of pain-relief on rough days. These are all part of a normal phase of child development, but one that can still cause worry. Familiarity with the teething process can ease your concerns.

"It's important to understand that teeth erupting is as natural as hair growing," explains Marianne Neifert, M.D., assistant professor of pediatrics at the University of Colorado. "Although teething can produce excessive drooling and chewing, mild discomfort and fussiness, the process usually requires little special treatment."

By the time most babies reach their first birthday, they will have cut six incisors—four on top and two on the bottom. Six more teeth normally appear by the age of 24 months, including the remaining two bottom incisors and the first four molars.

Around the second birthday, two pointed teeth called canines erupt between the upper incisors and molars, followed by the four second molars by age 2½. Your baby will erupt a total of 14 teeth in the second and third years of life.

Most children begin teething actions several months before the first tooth appears. Watch for these common signs:

• Drooling. Plan on a lot of saliva before teeth appear, possibly accompanied by diaper rash and loose stools. Ask your baby's doctor how to distinguish between true diarrhea and teething-induced bowel irritation.

• Fussiness and irritability. While teething doesn't normally cause much difficulty, it still hurts. Your patience, understanding and pain-relief efforts can ease your baby's discomfort and lessen your own frustration.

• Decreased appetite. Gum discomfort may make it temporarily uncomfortable for your baby to suck or chew, reducing her desire for food. Try preparing favorite snacks and foods, providing plenty of low-sugar, low-acid liquids (such as highly diluted apple juice) in a sipper cup, and not forcing your baby to eat.

If your baby is nursing, she may refuse the breast due to discomfort and go on a "nursing strike." This doesn't necessarily mean your baby is ready to wean. Consult a lactation consultant, the La Leche League, or an up-to-date resource for advice on how to manage this problem.

• Wakefulness. When your baby's sleeping patterns suddenly become disrupted without accompanying signs of illness, suspect teething and initiate appropriate comfort measures. However, a high fever, vomiting, coughing, a body rash or a runny nose and watery eyes may indicate something more serious.

- Chewing, "gumming" and finger-sucking. Your baby will automatically attempt to relieve discomfort through these typical teething-related behaviors. Older babies and toddlers employ expanded options as their ability to apply other forms of relief changes.

Try these safe, soothing techniques:

- Massage your baby's gums firmly with the padded part of a well-washed finger. The pressure feels good and you'll be providing extra cuddling—one of the most powerful measures—at the same time.
- Make a variety of chilled teethers available: a frozen banana or raw carrot; ice chips in a washcloth; commercial devices made of rubber (cold plastic can chip and splinter) such as a teething ring, pacifier or smooth toy. Don't let your baby teethe on a bottle, however—it causes cavities.
- Consult your baby's physician about the use of liquid acetaminophen (Tylenol or Tempera) when teething pain is severe. Since babies' teeth erupt off and on for months at a time, some doctors recommend reserving medication for bedtime only.
- Topical, over-the-counter oral anesthetics may temporarily numb affected gums, but should be used sparingly. Your baby may develop sensitivity to specific ingredients contained in these products. Don't use pain-relief remedies that contain alcohol (rubbing alcohol) or a narcotic (paregoric or cough syrup containing codeine).

Introducing Solid Foods

by Clara Shaw Schuster

Parents sometimes introduce solid foods to their baby's diet as early as 2 weeks of age. However, too early an introduction of solids is a waste of money and may be harmful to your child. While an infant may tolerate solids, the food can interfere with adequate milk intake, increase the risk of allergies, and lead to obesity. A young baby's digestive system does not produce the enzymes and chemicals essential for breaking down simple solid food products until 5 to 6 months of age. By then, most infants can coordinate tongue movements sufficiently to bring solid food from the front to the back of the mouth for swallowing.

Parents who start solids too early often complain that their baby doesn't like the food. In fact, the spitting up they experience is caused by natural tongue-thrust movements used in sucking the nipple. Some parents compensate for this lack of skill by adding solids to the formula or using an infant feeder or sucking cup to feed the baby. Two dangers emerge from this practice. One is overfeeding. The other is inadequate stimulation and use of the tongue and mouth muscles, which can lead to speech difficulties as the child matures.

The American Academy of Pediatrics Committee on Nutrition recommends waiting until 6 months of age before introducing foods other than cereal. Since infants may be allergic to various foods, new foods should be introduced one at a time, starting with only one tablespoon a day for five to seven days. When no sensitivities (rash, vomiting, diarrhea) are observed, then another food can be introduced.

A recommended order for introducing solids with the foods that are least likely to cause allergies is:

1. Cereal—rice
2. Vegetables—yellow, peas
3. Fruit—apples, bananas, pears
4. Meat—lamb, chicken, turkey
5. Egg—yolk only

Many parents start solids or introduce mashed and textured foods at about 7 or 8 months, when their child joins them at the dinner table. By this time, a baby has begun chewing and is able to move his tongue sideways to push food into the gum line. Favorite foods for babies of this age include teething biscuits, oven-dried toast, and cheese sticks. Since the child may bite off a piece that can be breathed into the windpipe, avoid carrots, apples, hot dogs, celery and potato chips. Small, hard foods—such as popcorn, peanuts, berries and raw peas—are especially dangerous. The most critical point in providing finger or textured food: remain nearby in case your child chokes.

Try to avoid sweet and sugary foods (such as cookies and soft drinks) as well, because they will decrease your child's desire for more nutritious foods, such as meats and vegetables. This is why vegetables should be introduced before fruits; it encourages children to accept a wider variety of nutritious foods.

Mealtime is not only a time for physical refueling, but for emotional refueling also. It needs to be a rich social time between you and your baby, with plenty of eye contact and talking. Children play with the textures of their food, feel hunger and fullness, see colors and shapes. As you talk about your baby's sensations, you enhance language, social and physical development. The relaxed, happy baby is able to digest and absorb food more easily. When you recognize and respect your child's cues for hunger and fullness, you help to cement the bond with your child.

Iron-Boosters

• Iron is a life-supporting element essential for oxygen absorption; in addition, it's also necessary for many of the body's biochemical reactions.

• The result of getting too little iron is a common nutritionally-caused condition called anemia, which results in muscle weakness, fatigue and listlessness.

• There are two types of dietary iron: heme iron, present in animal foods, and non-heme iron, provided by vegetables. Heme iron is the type that's easiest for the body to absorb.

• To increase the amount of iron you get from vegetables, include some meat along with them. Potatoes, potato skins and spinach are especially good sources of non-heme iron.

• To boost the amount of iron absorbed from iron-rich foods, a food that's high in vitamin C should be eaten at the same time, such as papaya, sweet red or green peppers, cantaloupe, broccoli, or an orange. Also, avoid serving caffeinated drinks with meals. They decrease iron absorption.

Safe Foods for Small Children
by Becky Ladewig

Foods like raw apples and hot dogs are leading culprits of choking in small children. By preparing foods differently, you can serve them safely.

Raw apples need to be cored and have their skin removed. Slice apples into thin wedge shapes that are easy for children to hold.

Grapes need to be cut in half with seeds removed, otherwise toddlers may try to swallow the grapes whole. Seedless grapes are the safest.

Meat with bones (such as chicken or pork) needs to be cut away from the bone and served in bite-sized pieces. Toddler gums are usually too tender to thoroughly chew large pieces of meat. Chicken bones tend to splinter.

Hot dogs can swell when lodged in a child's throat. Rather than cutting a hot dog into circular shapes, slice it lengthwise into four equal sticks.

Popcorn should not be given to children under 3. Children over 3 should have their own popcorn to eat slowly.

Playing Up Food Play

by Laurie Winslow Sargent

Feeding babies—and babies feeding themselves—is messy business. Unfortunately, this sometimes prevents parents from allowing their infants to experience self-feeding. Infants learn about food flavors and textures, hand-eye coordination and independence by feeding themselves. Specific attitudes can encourage this process:

Be sensitive to your child's physical readiness to begin eating solids. Carol Harrison, R.N., advises waiting until your infant has developed enough muscle control and reflexes (for swallowing) before making solids routine. If your infant continually rejects baby cereal with his tongue, he probably isn't ready.

Most pediatricians recommend beginning solids at 4 to 6 months of age. Introduce new foods one at a time so that if allergic reactions occur, you can pinpoint the cause.

Be sensitive to your child's readiness for self-feeding. Harrison continues, "If you feed infants past the point when they are ready to learn, they may get the message that they aren't competent to do it themselves."

Encourage your baby to feed himself by letting him hold his own spoon. Help guide it to his mouth. As for liquids, some 8-month-olds can successfully handle a covered sipper cup with large handles.

When your infant tries to pick up objects, he is showing some readiness to learn self-feeding. Letting your baby use a spoon or pick finger foods off a tray will encourage autonomy and coordination.

If you continue to feed your baby only puréed foods when he is ready for others, he may reject unfamiliar textures later or show boredom with eating. Offer finger foods in varied colors and shapes. Contrast tiny pieces of cooked carrot with fistfuls of sticky rice. Rinsed vegetables and meats from canned soups make terrific instant finger foods.

Don't fret about perfect nutrition. For his first year, your infant should get most of his nutrition from breast milk or formula. This takes pressure off you to provide a perfectly balanced diet of solids. Of course, foods offered should be nutritious: low in sugar and salt. Iron-fortified baby cereal should meet any need for iron supplementation. But for now, emphasize the enjoyment of the eating process.

Try not to fret about the mess. Instead, observe and enjoy the learning taking place. Having to wash out the goop massaged into your daughter's hair after every meal can be discouraging. Minimize the mess by offering small portions. Make a game out of wiping hands once in a while.

But don't be in too big a hurry to wipe off a tray finger-painted with cereal, or squashed banana oozing between plump little fingers. The "don't play with your food" rule doesn't apply to infants—table manners come later.

Don't forget the social aspect of eating. If you feed your infant before the rest of the family, interact with him. He might get the giggles feeding *you* bites off his tray as you smack your lips and exaggerate your enjoyment. During family meals, place his infant seat or baby swing nearby. Include him in conversations and in thanking God for your food.

Before you know it, your baby will be clutching sticky hands together, bowing his own little head, and wielding a spoon with amazing proficiency.

How a Baby Learns to Eat

Age in Months	Feeding Skills
birth to 3	swallows by sucking
4 to 5	sits with support; gains control of neck and head; learns to swallow with tongue
6 to 7	drinks from a cup with assistance; begins to chew; plays with a spoon; grabs finger food and puts it in mouth; sits without support
8 to 9	masters chewing; picks up finger food with thumb and finger
10 to 11	feeds self finger food
12 to 14	uses a spoon; drinks from a cup without help

How and When to Wean

by William Sears

Some people believe that waiting to wean a child will create unhealthy dependence, cause parents to lose authority, and generally contribute to a "spoiled" child. However, experience and research, along with my own professional experience, contradict this.

Recent studies have compared groups of babies identified as securely attached to their mothers with groups of infants described as insecurely attached. The studies show that the securely attached babies (those who were not weaned before their time) actually grew up to be more independent toddlers, separated more easily from their mothers, moved into new relationships with more security and stability, and were easier to discipline.

Over the past 10 years, we have studied our own patients who were not weaned early. We noticed the following qualities in these children: They were easier to discipline; they showed less anger; their transition from one developmental stage to another was smoother and less anxious.

What happens to a child who is weaned too early? Children who have been prematurely weaned exhibit what we call "diseases of premature weaning": anger, aggression, tantrum-like behavior, anxious attachment to care givers; and in general, shallower and less-intimate relationships.

The American Heritage Dictionary says weaning is "to withhold mother's milk and substitute other nourishment." From this it seems that there are two phases in weaning: detachment and substitution. Just as your baby is detached from the *nutritional* nourishment of your milk and solid food is substituted for it, other forms of emotional nourishment also should be substituted for the *emotional* detachment from your breast. Here are some tips:

Try to breastfeed your infant for nutritional reasons for at least one year. One year is an arbitrary figure, but it seems to be most in keeping with current medical teaching. Most mammals breastfeed their young until they triple their birth weight, which in human infants is around 1 year old. Weaning begins naturally between ages 1 and 2, because a child has the physical abilities to separate from his mother (for example, he has learned to walk). Also, a child has an interest and the necessary fine motor skills to take in alternative forms of nourishment, the ability to maneuver food with his hands, and the verbal ability to express his desires.

An important developmental ability that helps a toddler wean from mother also kicks in at this age—the development of "person permanence," or memory. During the first 9 to 12 months, a baby does not yet have sufficient memory skills to imagine that his mother exists when he cannot see her. But between 1 and 2, an infant can develop a mental picture of his mother even when she is in another room; in essence, he "carries" his mother with him as he explores his environment. This cognitive ability facilitates weaning.

Weaning should take place from person to person, not from person to thing. As your baby weans from you, another person should substitute other forms of nourishment; ideally, this person should be your husband.

Wean gradually. Avoiding weaning by desertion (such as a getaway holiday). Detachment from your breast *and* detachment from you entirely may be combined stress that is too much for your baby to handle. The time-honored weaning method of "don't offer, don't refuse," seems to work best for most mothers and babies.

Between 1 and 3, as babies naturally wean into other relationships, they periodically return to mother as their "home base" for nutritional and emotional refueling. Be prepared for an increase in nursing frequency as toddlers return to their secure home base during periods of high need or stress. While this sometimes will be perceived as a nuisance or an overdependency, it is a normal and healthy state of development. A baby returns to nursing in order to be filled with a relationship he knows, and from which he develops a feeling of security that reminds him it's OK to proceed into less-known relationships.

Develop creative alternatives to breastfeeding. After your infant has been nursing a year, this relationship is so beautifully fixed in his developing mind that he may give absolutely no indication of slowing down his nursing frequency. Many mothers have told me, "He waits for me to sit down and then pounces." This happens because a child's developing memory is like a big record into which grooves are cut. The nursing groove is probably one of the deepest your child will ever cut; therefore, he returns to this frequently until other grooves are cut in his memory "record."

As you develop more playful interactions as alternatives to breastfeeding, your child will gradually learn to be content with these alternatives with *you* as a substitute for breastfeeding. The age at which children willingly accept alternatives varies. Expect nap-time nursing and night nursing to be the last aspect of the breastfeeding relationship to wean.

Questions to Ask about Weaning
by Debra Evans
If you're currently considering weaning your baby, or will be facing this decision in the near future, here are a few questions to think about:

Are you taking both your and your baby's needs into account before deciding when to wean? As with other aspects of mothering, your baby's needs are normally more immediate and intense than your own. What will weaning mean to your baby? Is weaning her necessary at this time, or might it be possible to wait another month or two? Are there stressors in your life or your baby's, such as illness or family tensions, that would make weaning traumatic right now? Do the benefits of breastfeeding still outweigh the costs?

Where is the pressure to wean coming from? Does weaning make sense or not? Much of the pressure to wean comes from others. Family, friends and fellow employees all tend to add their three cents' worth when it comes to weaning. Instead of listening to outside advice, listen to your heart and look to your baby. Use as a sounding board (versus a you-should-do-it-this-way information source) someone who has been an encouragement to you regarding breastfeeding.

CHAPTER SIX

Bonding with Baby

Parent-Infant Bonding

by Clara Shaw Schuster

The word "bonding" frequently is used inappropriately by persons who only partially understand the phenomenon. A mother and baby spending 30 minutes together in the delivery room does not necessarily mean they are forever attached by some invisible super glue.

Some people are convinced that the quality of a parent-child relationship and a child's future personality are intrinsically related to the magic of these moments. It is true that early research studies indicate that mothers who spend extra time with their infants in the delivery room and during the first 72 hours of life tend to have healthier relationships with their child during the early years of life. Some research found a lower incidence of child abuse and increased maternal sensitivity to a young child's needs.

Other studies indicate that children of early-contact mothers seem to possess more confidence and less anxiety than their peers by the time they're 1 year old. By age 2, they talk more and show more curiosity through exploratory behaviors. By age 5, they score higher on IQ tests, especially on the verbal skill sections. Thus, it appears that the advocates of early contact for the sake of bonding may be right. With studies like this, it is obvious why parents and professionals, looking for a "good-parent recipe," advocate early contact between parent and child.

There are, however, some inherent problems in accepting this thesis uncritically. What about the parents who completely miss out on their

Some people are convinced that the quality of a parent-child relationship is intrinsically related to the magic of these moments.

Clara Shaw Schuster,
on mother-infant contact in
the delivery room

123

child's first few hours (or even days and weeks) of life because of complications of childbirth, prematurity, illness or adoption? Are these parents doomed to raise the child without that essential element of the parent-child relationship coined "bonding" by T. Berry Brazelton?

———————— ∼ ————————

Ways to Nurture the Bonding Process
by Allen Johnson

1. Trust that God will bring you and your child together in a bonding attachment when that can realistically occur.

2. Don't be too anxious about bonding. Rather, focus your thoughts on your love for your child.

3. Play with your child at every opportunity. Quiet, affectionate play forms the beginning of strong bonds.

4. Speak and sing to your child words of love and affection. Repeat them often. Bible verses and Christian lullabies will bring a sense of well-being and peace to both of you.

———————— ∼ ————————

Some clinicians report that, regardless of the amount of contact, one out of three mothers does *not* love her infant at first sight, and some mothers may take up to five months to completely fall in love with their infants. Yet these parents can go on to have a healthy relationship with their children.

What, then, is bonding? *It is the complete emotional commitment of one person to the welfare of another.* As a concept, it incorporates more than the parent-newborn relationship. It occurs between friends, between husband and wife, between parents and children of all ages. Bonding is a sense of belonging to the other person, a sense of loving that other person as highly or even more keenly than one loves himself. Bonding includes a sensitivity to the subtle cues of the other's needs. It serves as an impetus to communicate with, to make life interesting for, and to seek ways to maximize the potentials of the other.

With the utmost dependency of your newborn on your care, it is essential that you experience this sense of absolute dedication to the needs of your new family member. Since your baby's repertoire of skills is so limited, your focused, adult attention is essential for her both physical and emotional survival. Food and diaper changes are not enough. Infants who do not have an emotionally sensitive, interactive parent frequently experience failure-to-thrive syndrome. Some babies literally die from lack of an adequately caring adult.

During the first few hours after birth, most babies experience a wide-awake, alert state. This is an optimal time for you and your child to become acquainted, since your baby will look you directly in the eyes (which gives many parents the feeling that their babies recognize and accept them). Love and bonding may be facilitated by your baby's alertness, but they are not limited to this behavior.

Neither is this the only or the last time your baby will be so bright-eyed and responsive. In cases when parents are unable to have immediate contact, it may take a little longer to discover the child's alert periods, but they will come. Love and bonding are within the power of any parent for any child at any age.

Why Babies Need Cuddling

by Clara Shaw Schuster

Newborns look so fragile that some adults fear they might hurt the tiny newcomers. Other parents are concerned that their baby may become ill from over-handling. But touch is essential for a child's physical and emotional growth. Cuddling will not spoil them.

History lessons. For centuries, infants in orphanages wasted away and died before their first birthdays. King Frederick II of Sicily set up an experiment in the 13th century to determine what languages babies spoke naturally. He created a nursery where the babies' physical needs were met, but the staff was forbidden to talk or play with them. His experiment failed, because all the babies died.

During World War II, psychologists compared orphanage babies who were well cared for, but who received no affection, with poor babies receiving good mothering at home. They discovered that loving touch was more important than outstanding physical care. When nurses were encouraged to hold, caress and cuddle institutionalized babies, the death rate declined dramatically.

The meaning of touch. The first way babies get to know the world and people is through the concrete reality of touch. Although your child has vision and hearing at birth, her limited focusing skills and lack of experience prevents her from understanding what she sees and hears. Touch provides meaning. Your child is essentially isolated from the world if not touched or allowed to touch.

Many babies with failure-to-thrive syndrome have a history of inadequate touch. The increased activity a child uses to cope with boredom and with having to meet her own emotional needs depletes the calories available for growth. But these babies begin to gain weight when their parents provide more caressing and physical attention.

Gentle, soothing touch helps your baby relax. Since the growth hormone is released during sleep, a relaxed baby grows more effectively.

125

Premature babies who are rocked, cuddled and touched gain weight more quickly.

Tactile stimulation is also essential for your child's healthy emotional development. A child learns to love by being loved. Touching helps your child become aware of others and of her environment. Warmly caressing and touching your infant will help her be less fearful and irritable, and more resilient, cooperative and friendly.

Ideas for touching. What are some ways to stimulate your baby through touch? Bath time, diaper changes and mealtime offer opportunities for massage, skin blowing, finger rubbing and gentle roughhousing. Avoid carrying your infant around in an infant seat, which deprives her of the warmth and softness of your arms. Use a soft baby carrier to multiply her opportunities for close contact.

Babies from 6 to 12 months begin to pull away and crawl, but they continue to need touching. This lap-baby time is critical for cementing the bond between you and your infant. It's also a good time to allow your baby to explore your face and to teach social games such as "peekaboo," "pat-a-cake" and "this little piggy."

Throughout infancy and beyond, children need joyful play and physical contact to affirm their presence and to help them become loving, sensitive little people.

Keeping in Touch

By loving and accepting your child, you demonstrate in a tangible way what the Lord has done for you. By affirming your baby through touch, warmth, words, eye contact and milk, you also convey God's goodness and loving care. These gifts from you teach your baby important lessons about trust—an essential element of all healthy relationships at any stage of life.

In saying, "I'm thankful you're here," and "I'll take care of you," you tell yourself as well as your baby that you accept her and will meet her needs as best you can. Notice how your baby's body moves to the sound and changing rhythms of your speech. By varying its tone and pitch, you'll quickly discover how responsive your baby is to your voice and smile.

Our Creator designed babies to be lovable! Although they can also be exasperating, babies thrive on the tender, loving care expressed through rocking, cuddling, singing, bathing, stroking, and keeping them near. These expressions of parent-baby togetherness foster attachment, enhancing your ability to care for your baby.

Opening your heart to completely love this new person in your life involves risk-taking, personal growth and abiding trust in the sovereignty of God. Your love for your child is already causing your faith to grow and deepen as you trust the Lord in new ways. Touch works two ways—it's important to you *and* your baby as a tangible means of strengthening the bond you share.

Rocking Babies

by Patricia Rushford

"If we're going to have a baby, we need a rocking chair," I told my husband prior to the birth of our first child.

"Why?" he asked.

"Because our mothers rocked us, and their mothers rocked them. Because babies need rocking, and that's what rocking chairs are for."

That was 28 years ago. We've had a rocking chair ever since. Why do I so strongly recommend rocking infants? I offer common-sense answers from observation and experience:

Why rock? To provide comfort and security. The gentle movement reminds babies of their prenatal environment. There, the swaying, the sound of their mom's heartbeat and the warmth of her womb all added up to a secure place for fetal development. This same secure feeling can be simulated by snugly wrapping your baby in a soft blanket, cradling him against your chest and rocking.

Rocking relieves stress—in both a baby and parent. I've rocked my babies and my grandchildren to calm myself as well as the child. In our fast-paced society, there's nothing better for a baby and his parents than to spend many quiet moments rocking—especially when you work full time outside the home. Take time every day to relax and rock with your baby.

What if we don't have or can't afford a rocker? In my family, the benefits of rocking far outweighed the expense of the rocker. A better question might be: Can we afford not to have one? But if you truly can't buy one, there are some alternatives:

• Babies don't always need to be held to benefit from the rocking experience. Cradles, hammocks and baby swings are designed to offer comfort when arms are unavailable.

• In recent years, baby packs, which allow a parent to secure a baby to the chest or back, have gained popularity. These snuggle packs also simulate the womb experience and enhance parent-child bonding.

Will my baby be emotionally hurt if I don't rock him? Not necessarily. In fact, some babies may not like being rocked. All children do, however, need to be nurtured, cuddled and loved. Our responsibility as parents is to comfort and provide security so our children can develop a sense of trust. We must be in tune to our infants' needs and do whatever is necessary to meet them. This way, we provide a healthy environment in which our babies can grow and develop physically, emotionally and spiritually.

Will rocking spoil babies? Never. Babies whose needs are met, who are cared for and comforted appropriately, learn to trust, which is foundational to their emotional growth. Once children learn how to reason and manipulate, we can concern ourselves with discipline. Until then, enjoy.

Benefits of Rocking

Rocking your baby provides a number of physiological benefits, including:

- increased cardiac output, which aids baby's circulation
- increased respiration, which discourages lung congestion
- stimulation of the digestive tract, which relieves gas buildup and constipation
- enhanced brain activity, which reduces anxiety and brings about stress reduction

Wearing Your Baby

by William Sears

Ever wonder how mothers in biblical days transported their babies? It is unlikely they used carriages, prams or strollers. Most likely they wrapped their babies around themselves in a sling made out of their shawls, as if the baby were part of their apparel. New research is proving what experienced mothers have long known—that something good happens when they carry their babies this way.

My personal preference for baby-wearing began several years ago while I was doing research in preparation for one of my books. I noticed that the more babies were carried, the less they cried. Mothers with fussy babies would calmly say, "As long as I carry him, he's content!" Based upon these observations, we designed a sling-type carrier and advised parents to begin carrying their babies as much as possible, right after birth. We noticed the following effects:

Carrying organizes the baby. A newborn comes disorganized, and one of the most important functions of a new parent is to organize her baby. The unborn baby has a sensitive vestibular system. This system is constantly stimulated, because the fetus is in almost continuous motion. This is why motion, not stillness, is the normal state for most babies. A baby is born to expect movement similar to what he experienced in the womb. Carrying reminds a baby of the womb, which is why he seems more content.

Carried infants cry less. Carrying creates an environment which lessens a baby's need to cry.

Carrying helps babies thrive. All babies grow, but not all babies thrive. Thriving means growing to baby's fullest potential. I believe that carried babies thrive better because of the energy-sparing effect of re-duced crying. If a baby wastes less energy in crying, he has more energy left over to thrive. One of the most popular myths is that it's good for a baby to cry. Crying serves absolutely no benefit to the baby, and in fact, prolonged crying may have harmful physiological effects.

Carried babies learn better. Carried babies show enhanced visual alertness and seem more tuned in to their environment. Here's the reason: A baby who is carried more cries less and spends more time in the state of quiet alertness. This is the behavioral state in which a baby interacts most with his environment. Carried babies become more aware of their parents' faces, walking rhythms, voices and scents. They are intimately involved in their parents' world. A baby worn while Mom washes dishes, for example, hears, smells, sees and experiences what his mother is doing. Despite the recent publicity about infant stimulation and super-baby classes, it seems that the simple art of baby-wearing is one of the most natural modes of infant stimulation.

Baby-wearing fits in well with today's busy lifestyles. Mothers in other cultures have fabricated various sling-type carriers because it is necessary to carry their babies with them when they go to work or are on the go. Mothers in Western cultures are also on the go—they just "go" differently. For example, my wife Martha, mother of our eight children, is a lactation consultant and teaches breastfeeding classes. One day, just before one of her seminars, our then 6-month-old, Matthew, developed an ill-timed fussy period. Not wishing to cancel her class, but even more, not wanting to leave Matthew in a high-need period, she "wore him" in a sling while delivering a one-hour lecture to 150 pediatricians. After "they" (mother and happy baby) finished this talk on parenting styles, a doctor came up to Martha and exclaimed, "What you did made more of an impression than what you said!"

All in all, baby carriers are nurturing devices which make rediscovering the lost art of wearing your baby easier for parents—and a good time for baby.

Help for Separation Anxiety

by Debra Evans

Separation anxiety, or "stranger anxiety," is a healthy sign of parent-infant attachment. "As infants grow and develop, their attachment to their parents becomes more complex, more laden with feelings and meanings for all involved," writes Dr. Nancy Balaban in *Learning to Say Goodbye*. "It's as if the baby were saying to the stranger, 'I really know the person whom I love the best—and it's not you.'"

When even momentary separations become traumatic, considering stranger anxiety a compliment is often the last thing on a parent's mind. Yet it helps to know that it's normal for your infant to want to be close to you. Your child will eventually outgrow her intense dislike of goodbyes.

Dr. John Bowlby, who did groundbreaking work in the 60s on the experience of separation in infants, believes that a baby's state of *helplessness* is present "at its maximum at birth and diminishes more or less steadily until maturity is reached." On the other hand, he points out that *attachment* "is not strongly in evidence until after an infant is past six months." Bowlby then explains attachment as a condition to be cherished, and dependency as a condition to be avoided.

So how does a parent foster attachment while easing babyhood dependence? Unfortunately, no cookbook answers exist for that one! Since each child is unique, each will experience separation anxiety differently. But parents have found some general techniques that help lessen the burden while awaiting further growth and development.

• If your baby is not used to you being away, schedule brief separations initially—about 30 to 45 minutes. Rather than both you and your spouse going out, perhaps one of you or another familiar relative could stay with your baby the first few times. Plan activities that allow you a break but don't require extended time away from your baby.

• When you leave, tell your baby why you are going and when you will be home. Your baby will learn that goodbyes are only temporary and that he can rely on you to return. Avoid long, drawn-out exits. Instead, be confident in your need for a brief break and the benefit your baby will receive in learning that you are dependable.

• Until your baby outgrows this phase, accept her need to express displeasure at your departures, and take her with you whenever you can. Keeping a sense of perspective helps tremendously. A strong, healthy attachment now may mean less emotional dependence later.

Well-known pediatrician and author T. Berry Brazelton expresses it this way: "The goal of attachment is detachment." Investing time and energy in your baby now will pay off. Until then, know that what you're doing matters to this little person, who loves you more than anyone else in the world.

When Mom Works

by Kay Kuzma

These days, mothers who need or choose to continue working after they have a baby have many options. Realistically, you'll have to make certain sacrifices that will affect your family life. If you're in this situation, consider these options:

Try to find childcare close to where you work, which will make it possible to continue breastfeeding during the day.

Part-time work may be a possibility. Some moms work an evening shift so their husbands can take care of the children. (For most families, this option is better than denying the children a relationship with their dad because he has to work a double shift in order make ends meet.) Single moms sometimes split shifts and trade childcare responsibilities.

Consider working from your home. More and more mothers are choosing to work at home. In fact, some are probably working harder and longer hours at home than they would ever consider working outside the home.

Determine from the outset to pace your career as it best fits your family needs. Jeannette was a popular junior high teacher who accepted a job as an educational director for a local church so she could work out of her home during the week. Her husband took care of their baby on the weekends. Connie quit her office job to sell Tupperware and Avon products so she could have flexible hours and take her baby along. Lisa took a year off from managing a restaurant in order to write a cookbook she had always wanted to write.

Remember, a mother isn't the only person who can meet her baby's needs. Maybe your husband has a more flexible job. Many fathers are as nurturing as their wives and enjoy caring for the baby while their wives work.

Just because you work outside your home doesn't mean that your newborn will be denied a parental bonding experience or will suffer from unsterile conditions at a daycare center. If you spend significant time together, talking, looking at each other and touching, you and your baby will bond. (And good infant-care programs are often more concerned with the spreading of germs than mothers usually are!)

Regardless of your working arrangements, your newborn must grow up believing that she is your number-one priority. Here's how a working parent (Dad included!) can communicate that message:

Tuck love into little pockets of time. It may not be easy to find a free hour to spend with your baby. But seizing free minutes as they come is equally valuable. Play peekaboo, sing your baby a song, do a finger play, tell a story, take her on a five-minute tour through the house to look at family pictures, exercise her arms and legs, or clap hands together.

Plan special times to be together. As your baby grows, make sure you don't miss mealtime and bedtime appointments.

Enjoy your baby. Laugh, smile, and show enthusiasm when you're together. Babies love to be around positive people.

Make it a habit to surprise your baby with something special. Babies love surprises, like going to the park, petting a gentle dog, looking at a new book, or playing a game of crawl tag on the carpet.

You *can* be a good mother and work too. You do have options. Choose what is best for you *and* for that precious little one entrusted to your care!

Childcare Choices

by Susan Gilliland

A real home away from home—that's what all working parents would choose for their children. But how do you find good childcare? Some parents advertise in newspapers or local churches. Others rely on referrals from friends and co-workers. The key, however, is not how many places you look into for childcare, but how thoroughly you check each option and compare it with your standards.

Here's how to start your search.

Learn the specific needs of your child. "I didn't know that 20 2-year-olds were too many for one teacher at Jenni's daycare center," says Kathryn, who admits she was too involved in her own divorce problems to learn what was proper for her daughter's care. Kathryn recommends, as a starting point, that you find out your state's minimum standards for the care of little ones your child's age.

As a general rule, experts recommend that children under 3 be cared for in a home setting or in small, separate groups in a larger center. These little ones need lots of adult attention, not peer interaction. In contrast, older preschoolers enjoy socializing and can thrive in larger group care.

Besides being a toddler, preschooler or older child, however, your child is also an *individual*—fast or slow, solitary or sociable, shy or bold, compliant or difficult. A good caregiver needs to take into account the characteristics of each child. It's up to you to find a situation where your child's special needs will be understood and met.

Know the style of care you want and what's being offered. Ask directors about their centers' basic approach. Some places emphasize discipline, order and formal instruction. Others emphasize individual activity and informal play. Though some balance of freedom and structure is best, you have to decide what emphasis suits you.

A caregiver working out of her home should also be able to tell you her ideas about childcare. If a caregiver can't answer your questions well, it may mean she hasn't taken time to plan what she's doing.

Observe each care setting personally. When Kathryn heard second-hand about a Christian family who did daycare, she assumed it was a good home and inquired only about costs before placing Jenni there. After a while she began to notice that the house was filthy and the adults cool toward her daughter.

It's best to evaluate a daycare home or center with your own eyes and ears, rather than relying on others. One expert claims you can learn a lot even in a half-hour visit (as long as you don't visit during nap time). You can note whether the setting is clean, safe and pleasant, the space adequate, and the play materials plentiful and varied.

More important, you can observe the people. Note whether the children seem generally happy and busy in activities. Check how closely the caregivers watch and interact with the children.

Look for people with good training and good attitudes. Besides watching the caregivers, talk to them. Find out about their training and experience. As a rule, the best care givers are those educated in child development, whether or not they've had children of their own.

"Ask them how long they've had their jobs," Kathryn recommends. The number of years of experience can indicate the person's commitment to—and contentment with—the work and the center.

The care giver's attitude toward children may be the most important of all. Jean frequently heard her sitter say, "These kids are driving me crazy!" And at the end of a day, Geoffrey's first sitter would tell Becky about all the housecleaning she'd accomplished. *What about Geoffrey?* Becky would wonder. In contrast, Mrs. Harper frequently told Becky that the children were her top priority during the day. In this personality probe, it's important to pray and listen to your gut feelings. Don't ignore a sense of uneasiness about a place.

Maintain your high standards. The *Parent's Guide to Daycare* notes that "enrolling your child in daycare is not like parking your car in a garage—you need to stay in touch and be involved." For Kathryn, staying in touch means stopping to see her daughter at lunch time occasionally, instead of just rushing in at five o'clock. It means asking the care giver, "How was Jenni's day?" and waiting for more than a one-word answer. It means being willing to confront issues and discuss problems.

Finding good childcare requires a lot of effort, but it's worth it. "My stomach still turns when I think of how vulnerable my children are, and how many rotten things can happen in the world," says Jean. "The comfort of having quality childcare is worth the energy you spend finding it."

Avoiding Daycare Dangers
by Susan Gilliland

Though only a tiny portion of child abuse occurs in daycare settings, it does happen, even in Christian centers. Here are some helps for avoiding abuse in childcare situations.

• Try to assess if the care giver and others in the setting seem emotionally stable. Get to know the person a little, and don't ignore your "gut feelings." In chatting about family, work and activities, you may notice less-than-healthy attitudes: low self-confidence, dissatisfaction with life, or a lack of trust and close relationships with others. A person whose comments hint at unresolved problems with an extremely negative family background may be a walking time bomb.

• Evaluate the care giver's attitudes toward children. One single mother told me of a care giver who took more and more children into her home until she had an after-school total of 25. Recognizing a potential for neglect, she moved her son elsewhere.

Persons who physically abuse children may be looking for something to control. They might pride themselves on harsh discipline, and use phrases such as, "I'll show *him* who's boss!" They often expect too much of children and can swing from affection to anger when faced with normal crying, toilet-training problems, thumb sucking or messy eating.

Many of those who sexually abuse children also expect too much. They seek from children the physical and emotional fulfillment they have not found in adult relationships.

• Notice how the person copes with stress. A crying, defiant, messy or energetic child (that is, a *normal* child) can put stress on any care giver. How well does the person cope? "Most child abusers are normal people like you and me who act occasionally totally out of control," says one expert.

• Be alert to unusual happenings. If a teen or adult takes particular interest in your child and wants to take him alone to special outings, respond cautiously. Though the situation may be fine, it may also spell potential sexual abuse. If your child has some distress, illness, or injury that a care giver does not notice, it may mean he or she is being neglected. If the explanation for an injury seems far-fetched, the care giver may be hiding something.

• Communicate with your child. No parent, however vigilant, can protect a child from all harm. But we can speak to our children about how to respond in potentially abusive situations, just as we teach them about fires, traffic and stray dogs. Know your child. A young one who does not yet talk may signal a problem to you by a sudden change in behavior—as will an older child if she feels afraid to speak. An open, caring, listening relationship with your child will make it more likely that he will trust and communicate with you, rather than carry around a terrible secret.

• Ask God to guide you in protecting your child.

Daycare Quality Checklist
by Marjorie Lee Chandler

1. Is the facility licensed? (It's estimated that half of all daycare is unlicensed and 90 percent of family-home providers are not licensed.)

2. Does the program help children learn your family's values?

3. Do all caregivers provide a warm, nurturing atmosphere? Do they take listening to children seriously?

4. Is the atmosphere challenging yet non-threatening? Do children experience success more often than failure?

5. Is the center clean, attractive and stimulating? Are all play areas safe?

6. Does the program encourage self-help so that children learn to cope with real life? Does the teaching approach open up the world for children or dictate orders and advice?

7. Do staff members discipline with a positive approach? Is all communication directed at building the child's self-esteem?

8. Are meals/snacks nutritious? Are good eating habits encouraged?

9. Are parents involved in policy making and program planning?

10. Does the center have an "open-door policy" so parents may drop in at any time?

Finding a Babysitter

by Debra Evans

Who might be qualified and available to care for your baby? Think about the following criteria:

Experience. Preferably, the person you ask to sit with your baby has spent lots of time changing diapers, soothing teething toddlers, warming bottles, and rocking fragile newborns. A young woman at your church or a member of the high school youth group with younger siblings might fit the bill.

Maturity. This isn't necessarily an age issue. It has to do with responsibility, staying calm under stress, and the ability to focus appropriately on meeting the needs of others. Be open to babysitters of a wide variety of ages. Personal preferences come in handy, as does inviting a potential babysitter over to meet you and your baby. Watch how she handles the baby, and listen to her responses to your questions.

Expectations. What will your expectations of your babysitter be? How much responsibility are you willing to assume in letting your sitter know what your expectations are? What are her expectations of you? What does she expect to be paid? Good sitters don't come cheap these days. (Ask other moms in your town about the going rates.) Your babysitter will be worth *every penny* you pay her if she fulfills your expectations, so be generous.

Make sure your expectations are realistic and your sitter understands what you want her to do (and not do—phone calls, visitors, refrigerator rights). Give clear, concise directions. Write everything down in advance.

If you aren't sure where to look for a babysitter, check out these sources: your neighborhood, extended family, church youth group and singles ministries, local babysitting classes and associated referral services, university "job wanted" lists, nursing schools, and word-of-mouth networks. It may take a little work to find a sitter who is right for you, but the effort will be worth it.

If you aren't happy with your babysitter, consider talking kindly with her about your concerns before trying someone new. She may be more than willing to adapt and conform to your expectations. If she isn't, don't hire her again.

Be forewarned: The best babysitters usually are booked weeks in advance. This is an indication that they are well-liked by parents. Finding the best sitter can be extremely discouraging for last-minute planners.

CHAPTER SEVEN

~

Uniquely
Created

~

Chapter Seven ————————————————————————

Your Baby's Character

by Kay Kuzma

Watching your baby's character emerge and develop during the first year of life is like watching a living miracle. This year marks the laying of the foundation:

Month 1—adjustment. A child's feelings about himself and others start developing at birth. If his basic needs are met during these first months in a loving respectful way, he will learn to treat others in the same way. If not, he will begin to feel that he's not valuable, and he will have a difficult time learning to trust.

Months 2 and 3—crying and erratic sleeping. Take courage; there is light at the end of the tunnel. After three months, a baby's crying usually decreases markedly, and his sleeping becomes more regular. At this age, babies need happy, loving parents who have developed a support system that prevents either parent from feeling the pressure of continuous infant care. Most parents do a better job of character building if they take an occasional break and can nurture their own relationship.

Months 4 and 5—reaching out. By 4 or 5 months of age your baby will no longer be a passive "sponge" soaking up his environment. Now you'll observe an active, responsive little human being who laughs, babbles and reaches out to people or things that catch his attention.

At this stage, you need to begin molding your baby's behavior gently but firmly. For example, when he is wiggling and you are trying to change him, he doesn't need a swat; he needs someone who will distract

> *Most parents do a better job of (baby's) character building if they take an occasional break and nurture their own relationship.*
>
> Dr. Kay Kuzma

him from moving. He needs a parent who will say consistently, "Be still," and will gently hold his little legs and body. This tells him that the parent is the loving authority of the family who should be obeyed.

Months 6 through 8—moving out. This is the age when a baby perfects his rolling-over skill and immediately progresses to sitting up, crawling and creeping. At this age, children need parents who exhibit both common sense and wisdom. Since babies need to move, provide a safe environment for them that includes child-proof door fasteners and electrical outlet covers. And since babies need limits, lovingly teach some. For example, "If you touch Mommy's vase of flowers, she must put them up out of your reach." Because babies learn through sensory stimulation, movement and play, provide heavy doses of each.

Months 8 through 12—recognizing the familiar. By the time a baby is 8 months of age (and often as early as 5), he begins to recognize the familiar things in his environment: "My blanket, my mommy, my daddy, my bed." This achievement is the result of consistency in his life. This consistency needs to be continued, because by recognizing the familiar, he also recognizes the unfamiliar—such as strangers—and is frightened by it. Coaxing and pleading only force the child to retreat further into the familiar. Don't force the unfamiliar upon him. Wait until the unfamiliar becomes familiar, and then encourage him to reach out.

During your child's first year, it is most important that he come to understand that, "I'm an OK person and I can trust Mommy and Daddy to meet my needs in a loving way—even though my behavior isn't always good." This will gives your child the confidence and security he needs to begin stepping out and testing the limits—which is what the second year is all about!

Your Baby's Temperament Type

by Bonnidell Clouse

"I thought environment was everything, until I had my second child," my friend told me. "I don't see how two children with the same parents can be so different."

We all know that children are different, and, like my friend, we tend to attribute these differences to the environment—to the way children are reared. If a child is friendly, cooperative and eager to learn, we say his parents know how to raise him right. If a child is perpetually unhappy, given to temper tantrums, and refuses to cooperate, we assume that faulty parenting is the reason.

Not until we have children of our own and *know* that our method of child-rearing is not that different from one child to the next do we realize environment is not the sole reason why a child is the way he or she is.

There are characteristics present at birth that predispose a child to be active or passive, pleasant or fussy, shy or bold. These inborn qualities have been studied by child psychologists and are referred to as temperamental traits. They tend to cluster together into one of four temperament types: easy, slow-to-warm-up, difficult, or variable.

The "easy" baby is the "good" baby. He is regular in eating and sleeping habits, generally cheerful, and readily adapts to new foods, schedules, and people. This is the baby pictured in advertisements for baby products—beautiful, smiling, the picture of health. And this is the baby everyone expects to have. Approximately 40 percent of infants fall into this category.

The "slow-to-warm-up" infant will react negatively to anything that is new. If she has not experienced an event before, her immediate response to it will be withdrawal. If it is not what she is used to, she wants no part of it. But new things are constantly happening to babies: the first time they go outside, or stay with a relative, or are introduced to fruit juice or cereal. As they get older, there are changes in how often they eat, what kind of clothes they wear, and where they sleep. Fortunately, familiarity with any situation reduces the initial negative reaction, and with repeated exposures, "slow-to-warm-up" children can adjust. About 15 percent of infants are in this category.

The "difficult" baby also reacts negatively to new experiences, but he has other problems as well. High in activity level, irregular in eating and sleeping habits, intense in reactions, and downright cranky and miserable, he is appropriately dubbed by baby literature "the mother killer." Approximately one baby in 10 is "difficult" in the true sense of the word.

It's hard to know when "variable" babies will be "easy," "slow-to-warm-up," or "difficult." Their temperament varies depending on the circumstances. Thirty-five percent of all infants are "variable."

Neither the sex of a child nor the order of birth appears to be related to any of the four temperament types. Nor does the disposition of an infant correlate with the disposition of his parents. Long-term studies show that initial temperament tends to persist into childhood and even into adulthood. But this does not mean that environment is not important. By the age of 10, the way a child is handled in the home is as important as his original disposition.

Here are some suggestions for parents:

If you have an easy baby, be thankful. For you, child rearing will be a pleasure, and you will be more successful in your efforts to bring the child to an understanding of the Lord. Providing love and setting appropriate limits as your child grows older will produce optimal results.

If your baby balks at everything new, be patient. Gentle persuasion and continuous exposure will bring your "slow-to-warm-up" child around to appreciating the variety of life's experiences.

If your baby is "difficult," don't blame yourself. It does not mean you are not a good parent. But don't blame your child either. Just remind yourself, "This is the child God has given me. I will try to be a good parent."

Respect your infant as a person created by God, regardless of his innate temperament. God has always used people with different dispositions to further his cause. He will continue to do so.

The "High-Need" Baby

by William and Martha Sears

Babies don't come with directions, but if they did, Hayden's would have been written in a foreign language. Hayden, our fourth baby, was one of those children who expect every ounce of energy from both of us. She wanted to be held, nursed and comforted constantly.

Because she was content only when held, we were always playing "pass the baby." Hayden was in our arms by day and in our bed at night. She craved skin-to-skin contact and often fell asleep on my chest after her mother had given out.

Like all babies, Hayden had a special language of needy cries, and we had ears and hearts that listened and responded. She snuggled against our bodies in a baby carrier, rather than being wheeled in a stroller. She could not be left in a church nursery, as our other babies had. We took her with us into the church service, but during particularly high-need periods, we took turns; one would be in church while the other walked Hayden around the church grounds. Our friends prayed for us and supported our realization that we had a baby with a special temperament.

The need-level concept. Birth and adaptation to life outside the womb reveal the temperament of a baby, since for the first time she must do something to have her needs met. A baby's needs must be met if she is to thrive. So infants come wired with the temperament to communicate those needs.

A baby's early language is a language of need. An infant with a high level of needs comes programmed with an intense way of communicating these needs. For example, babies who need a lot of holding in order to thrive will protest if they are put down.

Those infants labeled as easy babies are content in a variety of care-giving circumstances. They don't cry much because their needs are easily met. They are somewhat consistent and predictable and adapt easily to a variety of schedules and parenting styles.

Other babies, labeled as difficult babies, may be supersensitive to changes in their environment. These babies have intense needs and voice equally intense protests when those needs are not met. Their mothers may say things like "I just can't put her down," or "She wants to nurse all the time." Rather than *difficult,* we prefer to call these infants *high-need babies.*

A baby's demands are an important survival technique. If a baby was endowed with high needs, yet lacked the ability to communicate these needs, her survival would be threatened. This baby would not develop to her full potential.

In some cases, a baby's fussing may indicate a medical problem. If a fussy baby wakes every two to three hours or less, or wakes in pain, a visit to the doctor is in order. The most obvious physical causes of night waking are ear problems, kidney infections, teething, and food or environmental allergies.

What happens if a baby's needs aren't met because her demands have gone unheard? The need never completely goes away. The resulting inner stress may eventually produce anger, aggression, withdrawal or rejection. This baby does not feel right and therefore does not act right. A baby who does not act right is less of a joy to the parent, so they drift apart. The parent becomes less adept at care giving, and the baby becomes less motivated to signal her needs.

One important point for new parents to understand is this: *Your baby fusses primarily because of her own temperament and not because of your parenting abilities.* Babies make demands because they *have to* in order to have their needs met. However, your responsiveness plays a part in determining whether or not the baby's temperament is channeled into desirable or undesirable personality traits.

Christian parents seem particularly susceptible to not responding to their baby—out of fear of being manipulated or losing their authority. Grandparents or friends may lead vulnerable new parents to feel that they are being poor disciplinarians if they give consistent nurturing responses to their baby. This quickly becomes a no-win situation. The parents lose the chance to develop their God-given, intuitive nurturing skills. And their baby loses the opportunity to develop better communication skills and refine some rough edges around her temperament.

Some well-known authors believe that high-need children, if not disciplined, are at high risk for behavioral problems later on. It is important not to prejudge the type of person the high-need child will become. By providing a nurturing, care-giving environment, we help lessen the undesirable behavior traits in these children and decrease the risk of later behavioral problems.

Survival tips for parents of high-need babies. Because high-need babies require a higher level of parenting, it is important to identify them early. You can usually spot a high-need baby when she is still a newborn, if she looks up at you as if to say: "Hi, Mom and Dad. You've been blessed with an above-average baby, and I need above-average parenting."

After 10-plus years of studying high-need babies, and through our own experience with Hayden, we have learned the following parenting lessons:

Nurture your spirit. If you keep your relationship with God alive, you have a greater chance of remaining in harmony with your high-need child. As you pray, remember these how-to-cope verses from the Bible:

• "Trust in the Lord with all your heart and lean not on your own understanding" (Prov. 3:5).

• "But those who hope in the Lord will renew their strength. They will soar on wings like eagles; they will run and not grow weary, they will walk and not be faint" (Isa. 40:31).

• "Give thanks in all circumstances, for this God's will for you in Christ Jesus" (I Thess. 5:18).

• "Do not be anxious about anything, but in everything, by prayer and petition, with thanksgiving, present your requests to God" (Phil. 4:6).

• "Cast all your anxiety on him because he cares for you" (I Pet. 5:7).

Don't feel guilty. A fussy baby can shake the confidence of a new mother or father and destroy many of the rewarding aspects of parenting. Remember, the "goodness" of your baby is not a measure of your effectiveness as a parent. The less confident you become, the less you will be able to comfort your baby and the more inconsolable your baby will become.

Don't compare babies. A mother of a high-need baby once said to us: "Why can't I handle my baby? Other mothers seem to be more in control of their babies. They can leave them and get other things done. I can't."

We advised her not to compare her baby with other babies or herself with other mothers. Some parents tend to exaggerate the "goodness" of their babies. Comparing babies adds nothing to your relationship with your child. Instead, it contributes to your own frustration and burnout.

Both parents should participate. One of the most common statements we hear from mothers who have successfully coped with their high-need babies is, "I could not have survived without the support of my husband." High-need babies require shared parenting. These babies are continuously "in arms" babies, but mothers' arms occasionally wear out.

High-need babies can be a severe strain on a marriage if shared parenting does not occur. Fathers, keep in mind that mothers are not noted for asking for help or for recognizing that they are giving out. Be tuned in and sensitive enough to know when to say: "I'll take over. You need some time for yourself."

Find a support group. Surround yourself with positive friends and others who have coped with a high-need baby. There is great consolation in knowing that your baby is not the only one in the world who fusses.

Seek advice from those who have experienced what you are going through. In our practice, we keep a list of such parents and often refer new parents of a fussy baby to someone on our list. After meeting with parents who truly *do* have a high-need baby, new parents sometimes report, "We don't have a fussy baby after all!"

Practice "gentling" techniques. Many babies seem most relaxed when things are still and quiet. Most high-need babies, on the other hand, are calmed by motion, sound and physical contact—a back-to-the-womb type of environment. In fact, one mother of a high-need baby coped by regarding hers as an 18-month pregnancy—nine months inside and nine months outside!

The art of gentling a fussy baby consists of determining what motion, sound and physical contact your baby likes and needs, and how much you can give of yourself without exhausting your parental resources.

Relax. A fussy baby can shatter the nerves of even the most shatter-proof mother. Being held in tense arms may be very upsetting to a baby who is already sensitive to tension. Here are a few relaxation tips to help

you and your baby enjoy each other:
- Take a warm bath together.
- Lie down and nurse your baby.
- Get outdoor exercise, even if you have to force yourself.

Set priorities. Most parents of high-need babies become exhausted not so much because of their baby's demands, but because they have tried to continue all of the activities and obligations they had before their baby arrived. You can't be all things to all people. If you have been blessed with a high-need baby, many of your previous commitments may have to be temporarily shelved. But only temporarily—your baby is small for a very short time.

Leaving the high-need baby. Because of the oneness that develops between a high-need baby and her mother, the pair may seem inseparable for the first year or two. Babies do not want to separate from their mothers, nor the mothers from their babies. It's important for a new mother of a high-need baby not to feel isolated or feel that she must stay home all the time. Home to a tiny baby is wherever her mother is.

Christian mothers commonly have ambivalent feelings about leaving their new baby in the church nursery while attending service. Part of her wants to rejoin the fellowship and the church service. Another part of her feels uncomfortable leaving her baby. It is vital that you take good spiritual care of yourself so that you can take better maternal care of your baby. For this reason it is important that new mothers not feel excluded from their Christian fellowship simply because they've had a baby, especially a high-need baby.

Churches are beginning to recognize this dilemma by making mothers feel welcome to keep their babies with them during the service. At the same time, they offer them the option of a nursery with nurturing care givers. If you choose that option, be sure to leave instructions with the nursery care giver that you wish to be called if your baby needs comforting. To worship or to mother should not be an either/or choice. A Christian fellowship can provide a setting that encourages the mother to do both.

Somehow we managed to survive that first year with our high-need baby, Hayden. And in the midst of it, something beautiful happened to us. Subtly and gradually, we changed. After a year of feeling that we had done nothing but give, we realized we had received much in return. Hayden taught us how to nurture.

Whatever the temperament of your baby, keep in mind that the greater the investment, the greater the return. By following the style of parenting that God has designed for you and your baby, you are likely to see a rich payoff in years to come.

Developmental Delays

by Laurie Winslow Sargent

Our son took his first steps at 13 months. The other babies from our childbirth class all walked at 10 months! Like many mothers, I wondered, *What's normal?*

Often, worry about a baby's development is needless. Walking at 13 months is well within normal limits. But sometimes, concern is justified. As a general rule, children should possess the following skills by age 2:

Gross motor skills. Your baby stands, stoops and squats. He walks forward, backward and can run without falling. He walks upstairs, jumps off one step (perhaps holding your hand), and jumps in place, landing on both feet. She can also throw and kick a ball.

Fine motor skills. Your baby can build a tower with four or five blocks. She can separate pop beads. With a crayon, she scribbles and imitates a vertical stroke. She can remove and insert pegs in a board. She can turn book pages and unwrap wrapped objects.

If your child's motor skills are significantly delayed, you *may* see delays in speech, understanding, self-help skills (feeding and dressing) and interaction with other people. Especially in babies, these skills are inter-related. You may ask yourself the following questions:

My child seems a bit slow. Should I have her evaluated by an expert?

Yes. You may want to ask your pediatrician to give your child a developmental assessment. Express your concerns and observations. Your child may be referred to a developmental pediatrician or clinic for further testing.

Call your local educational service district to ask about early intervention programs. Developmental preschools for children ages 3 to 6 are widespread, with programs for children under 3 emerging in many areas.

If my child is delayed, what can be done?

In an Ilwaco, Washington birth-to-3 program, babies receive therapy twice a week in conjunction with in-home and group treatment (which always includes the parents). An occupational therapist and a home teacher make up the primary treatment team. A speech therapist, resource coordinator and family therapist are often involved (as are physical therapists in similar programs).

After a child's skills are assessed, a family treatment plan is designed to help your child attain specific goals. Perhaps she has poor "righting reactions"—meaning she does not extend her arms to catch herself when she falls forward. Treatment might include laying the child on a physio ball, encouraging extension, and allowing her to feel her weight fall on her hands. In addition to special equipment, positioning techniques are sometimes used.

Therapists also use common items or food in therapeutic activities. Group activities are designed to teach multiple skills simultaneously. For instance, while bathing and dressing dolls, children identify body parts and nurture their "babies." They practice fine motor skills and follow directions. During snack time, many learn to use spoons instead of their hands and must verbally say, "More juice!" instead of pointing and grunting.

Parents watch the interaction between their children and the therapists. Sometimes parents realize they have been too quick to do things for their children.

I feel alone when I see other parents' babies developing right on schedule. Where can I get support?

In therapy groups, parents encourage each other. Parent support groups and information can be found through parent-training and information centers. For the name and phone number of your state's parent advocacy group, call the Federation for Children with Special Needs at 617/482-2915.

Seek out prayer support in your own church body. Remember that God knows your concerns, knows your child's great potential, and loves him as much as you do.

Parenting a Child Who Has Physical Disabilities

by Joni Eareckson Tada

A few words always come to mind when I hear of parents raising a child who has a serious disability. Overburdened. Isolated. Abandoned.

And I know how these "overburdened and isolated" parents of disabled children spend much of their time making excuses to family and friends, fighting the system, writing letters of complaint, making endless calls to the school district, and accepting and rejecting advice from well-meaning friends and from "experts" from the Department of Social Services.

But in case you feel that parents of disabled children are having a pity party, consider one special friend of mine.

"I don't feel our baby's birth is a genetic accident, as Down's syndrome is so often called," the young mother said, referring to her son's birth five months earlier. "We feel the Lord had it planned," she said calmly.

During the months of waiting, Keeta had no reason to suspect that this pregnancy was any different than her first one. With their 2-year-old daughter, Meg, Keeta and Joe eagerly anticipated the arrival of the baby. A baby boy would be Joe the Fourth, but they would call him Jess.

That's his name and he has Down's syndrome. As I listened to Keeta talk about her baby, I was jolted by the quiet, strong conviction that this little boy, still so unknown, had great worth. His mother didn't tell me what a beautiful child he was. She didn't brag about his easygoing contentment or his sweet smile. Instead she talked about his Creator.

Somehow all the debate about quality of life, self-worth, and purposefulness was inconsequential. God had made Jess. God had knit Jess together in his mother's womb. He knew Jess' body and it was made in the secret place (Psalm 139). Jess' disability didn't take God by surprise. He was just made special.

Keeta brought substance to that light-hearted slogan, "God doesn't make junk." To her, Exodus 4:11 was more than a mere recitation: "Who gave man his mouth? Who makes him deaf or mute? Who gives him sight or makes him blind? Is it not I, the Lord?"

She voiced those words out of a solid-rock foundation that was six months in the making. Those had been hard months, Keeta said. They had been rooted in disappointment. She and Joe had expected one thing and gotten something else. Together they had grieved the loss of a normal child.

But together they had determined to save their own marriage and family, knowing that four out of five couples with disabled children end up in divorce court. Now they were rejoicing in the special child God had given them.

They had soon learned that Jess required extra time. For several hours each week, he and Keeta went to infant-stimulation classes for children with special needs. The quality of time spent in classes tightened the family bond. During those structured hours, Jess became more and more able to respond to the love around him. That feeling of acceptance was crucial—and will become increasingly so as Jess moves out of his family circle in years to come.

Keeta and Joe realize that through them Jess can grow into the young man God intends him to be. In my experience, two of the most critical ingredients in this godly parenting commitment are discipline and inspiration.

Discipline your child. I am aware that no two children respond in the same way to discipline. This fact may be exaggerated if your child has a disability. But it is crucial that every child knows what behavior is expected of him. Be realistic with your standards, taking into consideration the special needs of your child. Can he really meet the standards you've set? Clearly communicate your expectations. Paul's warning not to exasperate our children (Eph. 6:4) is well applied here. Every child needs to know how to please his parents. You need to set guidelines—and then clearly articulate them to your child.

Once there is an understanding of the goals which have been established, the onus is yours to be pleased with your child's obedience. Your special-needs child wants to rest in the fact that he has done well, that he has made you happy.

Of course, your child is not always going to want to please you. During those moments and days of intentional deceit and willful disobedience, your love will be tested . . . and tested:

• Do you love your child enough to discipline him quickly, breaking down that wall of disobedience that has come between you?

• Do you love your child enough to hold him accountable to his understood standards of conduct?

• Is your love mature enough to respond as an adult in quiet firmness rather than with a loud emotional outburst?

• Is your love strong enough to allow your child to learn from his mistakes?

It's easy to make excuses for your special-needs child, delaying discipline. But God says, "Do not withhold discipline from a child" (Prov. 23:13).

Strive for a consistency in your household between the discipline of your special-needs child and his brothers and sisters, realizing that some children require more correction than others. Some require only a look from their mother or father to correct their ways. (They want to please.)

Others need repeated spankings or other age-and-situation-appropriate punishment. (They have to be reminded of how much they want to please!)

Siblings, second only to you as parents, will also touch the life of your special-needs child. If they observe inequities in treatment between themselves and a sister or brother, barriers will be built between that relationship. Joseph was not the first—or the last—child to experience vindictive jealousy because of his parent's favoritism (Gen. 37:4, 11).

Inspire your child. The church I attend has a Sunday school class for mentally retarded children and young people. A mother of one class member called my friend Greg Barshaw, the church elder for special ministries.

"I don't understand it," she said on the phone. "My son is learning things that I know he can't understand. Yet his learning is far beyond his natural capabilities." The mother was shocked, but it was no surprise to Greg. This was just one more example of the truth of I Corinthians 2: 12, 13: "We have not received the spirit of the world but the Spirit who is from God, that we may understand what God has freely given us. This is what we speak, not in words taught us by human wisdom but in words taught by the Spirit."

What better teacher than God's own Spirit? Time after time Greg has seen God, through His Holy Spirit, teaching developmentally disabled persons truths far beyond their natural capabilities to comprehend. We must not set limits to what our impaired child can achieve or understand. Perhaps it's not even our responsibility to determine boundaries.

However, it is our privilege to inspire. Your child knows his limitations. Help him to see that along with those limitations, the Lord has given him gifts that compensate for his disability.

I received a letter from the mother of 4-year-old Shon. He has cerebral palsy and was the winner of an art contest we had in our Joni and Friends Kids' Club. She wrote, "I'm writing you, Joni, to confess that God used your art contest to teach me a lesson—namely, I should never try to protect Shon from disappointment, for in doing so, I may rob him of some rich blessings. You see, I had not wanted him to enter the contest because I didn't want to deal with his disappointment. I'm ashamed to confess that I never believed he could win."

That's good wisdom from Shon's mother. Yes, there are times your child needs to be protected. But there are also times to allow him to take a chance, even risking disappointment. Prepare him for such a possibility and then be there for him—in the event of failure or success.

Sometimes even the words you use can contribute to his success or failure. He lives in a world where not everyone is as disability-aware as you and your family have become. Without building defensiveness, you can give him a language for explaining his disability. It's only as you help him understand how he is different that he will be able to tell others about it.

You can also inspire your child by helping him discover role models. Everybody needs heroes—your disabled child is no exception. Help him find godly men and women in the church, or even national figures, who are disabled or nondisabled. They have had their share of failures and successes, too.

God comforts us with these words from Jeremiah 29:11, " 'I know the plans I have for you,' declares the Lord, 'plans to prosper you and not to harm you, plans to give you hope and a future.' "

It was true for those Israelites in captivity, it's true for me, and it's true for you and your disabled child. God has hope and a future for each of us—even the most severely disabled child. Help your child see that hopeful future that will bring glory to God. Dream his dreams with him, planning realistic steps to bring him to his goals. Stretch his limitations, encouraging him to do—and be—more. And do everything in your power to help him achieve his dreams.

As Keeta and Joe have learned, it wasn't a mistake that God made them the parents of a child with Down's syndrome. Just as God hasn't given me the grace today to anticipate living another 20 years in a wheelchair, he doesn't promise to answer tomorrow's questions about caring for your child. But one thing we can all count on: God's grace is sufficient for today—as it will be for each day you lovingly parent your special child.

Emotional Needs of Kids with Disabilities

by Allen Johnson

I recall praying each night as a child that I would wake up the next day without my disabilities. But many disabilities—or "challenges," as I prefer to call them—last a lifetime. If you explain this to your child as soon as his disability is diagnosed, and continue to discuss various challenges as they arise, this will help him to cope.

Constantly reiterate that first and foremost, your child is a *person*—like every other child. His disabilities are characteristics he possesses, but they do not make up his total personhood. *He is more than a grocery list of chronic illnesses and disabilities.* Rather, he is a child made by a loving God, a child who happens to have unique challenges.

I remember asking both my parents and God, "Why me?" Anyone with a chronic condition naturally wonders why he got it and his brother didn't. Tell your child honestly that only God knows why he developed the condition. But assure him that it was not due to anything either you or he did wrong. Actually, "Why me?" is not really what the child is asking. More accurately, the meaning is, "Now that this has happened to me, how can I, with my parents' help, not only accept it, but grow from the experience?"

Although you will face many pitfalls in parenting your challenged child, the growing up process can be a time of character-building. Your entire family will learn several important lessons:

• Having a disability does not make your child a *different kind* of child. He is a child who has a unique set of challenges, some of them perhaps needing to be "fixed," just like his friends may have crooked teeth that may need to be straightened.

• The condition is not something his friends need to fear they might "catch." Most of the time his condition was caused by an accident, or by abnormal development prior to birth.

• Some people may act differently toward him because of what I refer to as *disaphobia*. Disaphobia can be defined as that social anxiety, prejudice and ignorance that nondisabled persons feel toward the challenged individual. In turn, this phobic reaction is felt by the challenged person in his interaction with the nondisabled majority.

• Children and adults who truly are friends will remain friends; a disability will not alter such a relationship.

• Encourage your child to make friends with other children who have difficulties, such as an obese child or the class "nerd." I recall a challenged child whom I saw in therapy who started his own Nerd Club and invited all his friends to join. It became one of the largest and most popular clubs in the school.

• Siblings have both positive and negative feelings about their challenged brother or sister. But in addition, there are specific feelings about the disability that a nondisabled sibling needs help to work through. Often these are negative feelings about the disability. Encourage your nondisabled child to accept the disability as natural and OK, and to discuss the matter openly with you. When not attended to, these negative feelings can cause lasting emotional difficulties for the entire family.

Parenting a child with special needs takes special knowledge. Getting involved in a parents' support group can help you to learn how best to cope. In addition, parent-guidance counseling with a knowledgeable Christian family therapist may be necessary, not only to deal with your child's social, emotional and spiritual needs, but yours and those of his siblings as well.

Early Self-Esteem Builders
by Allen Johnson

In counseling parents of children with disabilities, I find that one of their primary concerns is how to help their youngster achieve a more positive self-esteem. Self-concept begins within the first few hours of life. It is promoted by the immediate bonding that occurs naturally between parents and child. When a child is born with a disability, formation of a positive self-concept is made more difficult.

The initial response of parents to the birth of a different-than-expected infant is traumatic. Depression sets in not only for parents, but for other family members as well. Consequently, negative responses of family and friends may be communicated to the infant through care and nurturing, or lack of it. That can harm the bonding process and the child's evolving self-concept.

Ambivalence is natural, but try to resist it. Stroking and caressing your impaired infant from the first hours of her life are crucial if she is to develop a strong nucleus of positive feelings. Although you may provide adequate physical attention, your child may not be receiving the emotional care she needs due to your naturally ambivalent feelings toward the disability.

When your baby comes home from the hospital, you may be so overwhelmed by the regimen of care required that your depression may continue or even increase. Moms are often so exhausted by the daily routine of therapy and administering of medicine that the little hugs and kisses that are every infant's birthright simply don't happen.

Promote a positive self-concept. But there are some things you can do to promote your child's positive self-concept. Since every child's self-concept is based on her perception of her body from birth onward, try to discover positive aspects of your infant's body and focus on those. Since your baby's body is the focus of so much negative attention, you may miss seeing all of her positive qualities, such as her pretty brown eyes, cute smile or sweet disposition.

Focusing on areas of your youngster's body and temperament that are adorable and unaffected by the disabling condition helps her learn to focus on these positive qualities as well. In this way, her self-concept can be nurtured and you can begin to look beyond the disability to the child within the disabled body.

Access Rights Groups
by Joni Eareckson Tada
"Access"—the right or means to enter, approach or use.

Parents of disabled children are "accessing" every day, whether it's fighting for an appropriate education for their child, securing necessary rehabilitation for their child, or securing necessary rehabilitative and social services. But parents aren't alone. A variety of agencies can help parents meet the unique needs of their disabled youngsters.

One of the most important tools, which guarantees free and appropriate public education for disabled children, is PL 94-142, the **Education for All Handicapped Children Act.** Your school district will tell you how it is implemented in your area.

Another important resource is the **Federation for Children with Special Needs** (95 Berkeley St., Suite 104, Boston, MA 02116. 617/482-2915). This agency works with many Parent Training Centers across the country to help parents access educational services for their children.

The **National Rehabilitation Information Center** (NARIC, 8455 Colesville Road, Suite 935, Silver Spring, MD 29010-3319. 800/346-2742) is particularly useful to those parents seeking rehabilitation services—whether it's locating the best hospitals which serve children, or finding an innovative rehabilitation program.

At the state and local levels, parents will want to contact such agencies as **United Cerebral Palsy** (UCP, 1522 K Street NW, Suite 1112, Washington, DC 20005. 800/USA-5UCP), **The Association for Retarded Citizens/US** (500 E. Border St., Suite 300, Arlington, TX 76010. 817/261-6003), and the **National Easter Seal Society** (230 W. Monroe St., Suite 1800, Chicago, IL 60606. 312/726-6200). These associations have listings of support groups where parents can learn from others who, by trial and error, have successfully found help for their child. These agencies also provide services such as UCP's "Respitality," a partnership between UCP and a hotel chain which provides discounted weekends for parents who need a rest from the routine.

Finally, if you're having difficulty accessing services for your child, you should contact your **State Protection and Advocacy System** (PAS). (The National Association of PAS is located at 900 Second St. NE, Suite 211, Washington, DC 20002. 202/408-9514.) Each state has a PAS as authorized by the Developmental Disabilities Act. Your PAS can provide a variety of legal services to children and adults who are disabled early in life. Most PAS agencies will be aware of the education problems which exist in your state and will also be able to provide you with other local resources.

Disabilities Resources

American Cleft Palate Foundation, 1218 Grandview Ave., Pittsburgh, PA 15211. 800/24-CLEFT.

American Foundation for the Blind, Inc., 15 W. 16th St., New York, NY 10011. 212/620-2000.

Epilepsy Foundation of America, 4351 Garden City Drive, Landover, MD 20785. 301/459-3700.

National Association for the Visually Handicapped, 22 W. 21st St., New York, NY 10010. 212/889-3141.

National Association of the Deaf, 814 Thayer Ave., Silver Spring, MD 20910-4500. 301/587-1788 or 800/942-ASDC.

National Down's Syndrome Society, 666 Broadway, New York, NY 10012. 212/460-9330 or 800/221-4602.

Spina Bifida Association of America, 4590 MacArthur Blvd. NW, Suite 250, Washington, DC 20007. 800/621-3141.

Recommended Reading: *Growing Up Proud: A Parent's Guide to the Psychological Care of Children With Disabilities* (Warner Books) by James and Sally Lindemann; *Mixed Blessings* (Abingdon Press) by William and Barbara Christopher; *Out of the Ordinary: A Digest on Disability* (ARCS, Inc.) by Robert Loring.

Birthmarks That Disfigure

by Patricia Rushford

About one in 300 babies is born with a disfiguring birthmark. While they are rarely life threatening, some birthmarks can significantly impact a child's emotional and social development.

A birthmark, also called nevus, or hemangioma, is a congenital discoloration that appears on the skin at birth or later in life. The term usually refers to a benign skin tumor which is caused by an abnormal growth of blood vessels within the skin. (Because of the greater-than-normal blood supply, injury to a birthmark can cause heavy bleeding. Gentle, firm pressure applied to the wound will usually stop the bleeding. Consult your doctor about lesions that persistently cause concern.)

Some birthmarks will disappear over time, but others are permanent. They can appear anywhere on the body, but are most often found on the head, neck and face.

Birthmarks generally fall into three categories:

Strawberry birthmark: These usually appear as small raised areas, bright red in color. They tend to disappear in about three to four years.

Purple nevus (also called a port-wine stain): These birthmarks are usually flat, dark and large. While they may be small and imperceptible at birth, a purple nevus can grow over time, eventually covering a large skin area. They also can become darker and thicker and may develop a pebbly texture and appearance.

Brown nevus: These birthmarks usually are flat, dark brown, and may be covered with hair. The purple and brown birthmarks can be extremely disfiguring. Fortunately, severe disfigurements are rare, but when they do occur, the emotional trauma can be confusing—even overwhelming.

Parents of children who have a disfiguring birthmark often struggle with the following emotions:

• Guilt—This occurs in response to what parents perceive as negative feelings of anger, rejection and repulsion. Parents also blame themselves for the defect, even though they're not to blame.

• Anger—Their anger is directed toward God for allowing the disfigurement and at themselves for what they consider unacceptable attitudes and feelings.

• Grief—This emotion is experienced because of the loss of "normalcy." Parents need to know it's OK to grieve over the loss of what *might have been* so they can grow to accept what *is*.

Some parents become overprotective of their affected children, while others overexpose the problem in an attempt to compensate for it. But what is needed is balance, acknowledgment, acceptance and honesty—the honesty to say, "There is a problem, but we love you and we'll work this out together." Whether as a parent, family member or friend of a child with a disfiguring birthmark, focus on inner beauty and special strengths, and provide encouragement to help the child to develop a healthy self-esteem.

Fortunately, we live in an era of high-tech cosmetology, lasers, and specialized surgical skills. Consequently, many disfiguring birthmarks can be covered or removed. Recent research in using tunable dye lasers to remove port-wine stains in children has led to remarkable advances in treating children as young as 3 months of age. Previous attempts to erase these birthmarks often resulted in permanent, disfiguring scars.

Removing birthmarks is a highly specialized field, and great care and investigation is needed before selecting any type of treatment. But remember: While birthmarks can have an impact on a child's development, so do a parent's love, acceptance and understanding.

CHAPTER EIGHT

∾

Passages

∾

Chapter Eight

Attachments and What They Mean

by Grace Ketterman

Have you ever wondered just how long it will be before your 2-year-old gives up her binky? Or that tattered old blanket? Perhaps your attempts to lose either one have caused you and your child so much frustration that it doesn't seem worth the effort. But you worry about ignoring the "problem" for too long.

It's normal for children to cling to a variety of objects in their early years. Fortunately, these objects eventually become unnecessary. What role should you play in "weaning" your child from his teddy bear, thumb or pacifier? Understanding how these attachments form will begin to answer this question.

Forming attachments. For the first nine months of life, a child is secure, nestled in his mother's womb. New babies are quickly washed and swaddled in warm, soft blankets and cuddled in their mothers' arms. I believe that attachment to comforting objects dates to these first moments outside the womb.

Nursing is another comforting experience for a newborn. The softness of his mother's skin, the scent of warm milk and the new sensation of a full tummy bring him pleasure and security. Nursing leads to sucking. A baby discovers that his thumb feels comforting when the breast or a bottle is unavailable. Sometimes exhausted parents insert a pacifier into their baby's mouth, relieved when it stops his crying.

Touch is a third source of attachment. For example, as a baby nurses,

> *It's normal for children to cling to a variety of objects in their early years. Fortunately, these objects eventually become unnecessary.*
>
> Dr. Grace Ketterman

163

he often touches his mother's skin, and sooner or later discovers the silky texture of her hair, satin robe or blanket. So warmth, touching, smelling, tasting and sucking all promote a baby's security.

When your child attaches to a special object, then, it's usually a demonstration of his need to feel secure. The ability to attach to an object is actually healthy. When your child focuses interest on his binky, he is developing a sense of ownership. This also explains why it's so difficult for him to give up the item later.

Finding and bonding with persons *and* objects creates a sense of security. And as long as your child doesn't *substitute* an object for a person, you can even encourage attachment to loved items.

Your toddler's attachment to a transitional object doesn't necessarily mean that you're a neglectful parent. In fact, the opposite is usually true. The item your child chooses to cling to is almost always symbolic of you. A teddy bear is soft like Daddy's hugs, and a blanket may feel like Mommy's robe or gown. Your child's object choice is probably a compliment. The objects simply add to the security you've already established.

Letting go. At some point, you may be concerned with breaking these attachments (which, by the way, bother parents much more than they damage kids). Grandparents and friends criticize your child's enjoyment of his binky, so you decide to take it away. Your toddler, of course, wails in anger at bedtime. He can't sleep, and neither can you. After a short time, you relent—until Grandma's next visit. If this sounds similar to your situation, here are some ideas that might help:

Understand your toddler's sensory and emotional needs. Each child is unique. Yours may have strong sensitivities to things that stimulate his senses. He needs the reassurance that objects provide. He adapts to changes with difficulty. Any change for such a child needs to take place slowly.

Be sure your child is ready to give up the object. If he can clutch a toy, he's probably ready to begin giving up his binky or thumb sucking. Offer a toy he can grasp and put in and out of his mouth. Controlling his own playthings is a new skill that will satisfy a few more of his own needs. When he can creep about, play with toys, and focus on other people and objects, he's apt to forget his attachment object except at sleep times.

A good indication of your child's readiness to give up an object is his response to your efforts to remove it. Any attached child will fuss or whine about giving up an item. But a child who isn't ready will cry excessively for long periods. He'll look sad and show classic signs of depression—anger, unhappiness, sleep disturbances and loss of appetite. I strongly urge you not to make the breaking of attachments a cause for grief.

Make the change slowly. From years of working with children, I've learned they accept *gradual* changes most easily. Restricting the use of objects to only nap time will prepare your child for giving them up totally.

When the time comes for finally giving up that object, do so firmly. By age 3 or 4, social pressures usually demand that children, at least in public, give up their objects. However, a child may enter into a no-win power struggle over giving up an item completely. Rather than exhibiting genuine anxiety or grief, he'll act angry and become aggressive. At such a point, trust your intuition. Respond to what you believe is for your child's good—not to what someone else thinks.

If your child's object is a thumb or lock of hair, the giving-up process can be more difficult. One mother and her 4-year-old, Maria, conquered the habit by playing hide-and-seek with her thumb. Each night, Maria was determined to "win." Maria's mother tucked her in bed and sat beside her while Maria hid her thumb first under the covers, then under her pillow. Again and again she drew it out, wanting desperately to feel it in her mouth. But each time she resisted and finally fell asleep— without sucking her thumb.

Let me urge you not to be in a hurry. Be sure each of your children, individually, is ready to move away from his objects. Replace them with other things that comfort and satisfy the child's sensory hunger. With some children, chewing sugarless gum can satisfy oral cravings for a time.

And offer yourself for a few days to cuddle, rock and comfort your child through the pain of these small losses.

Effects of Sucking Habits

by Jeffrey Timm

Many parents become concerned about their child's thumb sucking or the use of a pacifier. This concern is normal. Rarely, however, does a long-term problem result from either practice.

Dental development. The structures of your child's face and jaws continue to form and take shape between the first and second year. For the most part, thumb sucking or pacifier use will do little to change this process. However, if your baby sucks almost constantly and with some force, certain changes can occur.

The most common problem is the formation of an "open bite." In an open bite, the upper and lower teeth in the front don't meet when the child bites down. The space between the upper and lower incisors corresponds to the placement of the pacifier or thumb. A child can also pull the front of her maxilla (upper jaw) forward. Both conditions are more common in children who suck their thumbs or fingers than in those who use pacifiers.

Fortunately, open bites and jaw protrusions normally correct themselves if the use of a pacifier or thumb sucking is discontinued by age 5 or 6, before permanent teeth erupt. If the condition persists after the habit has stopped, orthodontic treatment will almost always correct it.

Speech development. The main potential problem in speech development results from the presence of an open bite. There seems to be some correlation between this condition and difficulty in pronouncing certain sounds, such as "s," "z," "sh," and "ch." With an open bite, the tongue has difficulty finding the proper position for the pronunciation of these sounds. Fortunately, this problem is nearly always short term.

Social development. When it comes to babies, pacifier use or thumb sucking is seldom frowned upon. But as a child gets older and starts preschool and kindergarten, there will be increasing peer pressure to stop. Pacifier use has almost always stopped by this time, and thumb sucking is nearly always on the decline, perhaps occurring only when the child is tired.

It bears repeating that pacifiers seem to cause fewer problems than thumb sucking. Children usually will break sucking habits earlier and easier when using a pacifier. Nuk brand orthodontic pacifiers, or ones of similar design, are preferable.

Ready to Walk

by Grace Ketterman

As a mother, grandmother and physician I have observed numerous variations of "normal" child development, particularly as children learn to walk. My cousin walked well at 7 months, according to my reliable grandmother. I have known other typical children to show no interest in walking until at least 18 months. That variation averages out to 13 months of age—the time most children start to walk.

To be ready to walk, babies need:

- a strong back and neck that enables them to sit up without falling
- a good center of balance that helps them know where their bodies are in the environment
- strong arms and sturdy legs that can pull and push those bodies into an upright position and maintain that stance
- reasonably straight feet that will not trip over each other
- a safe environment that is not slippery and that has few bumps or objects over which they could trip.

There are several steps you can take to ensure that your child is ready to walk:

- Provide regular exercise for your child as early as 1 or 2 weeks of age. A few minutes a day, move those tiny arms and legs in every direction they will go. Let their fingers curl around yours, and tickle the soles of their feet. As your baby grows, extend the exercise to several times a day.
- When your baby starts to push with his feet, hold him so he can begin to push *actively* against your lap for short times. Likewise, pull him up a little bit by his arms. Do this *only* when he shows enough muscle tone to pull with you.
- Encourage your baby to roll over, hold up his head (when he is ready), and gradually sit up in a support seat or swing. Don't leave him in such a position too long; he'll tire.

When your child is able, encourage him to crawl. It's not uncommon for children to pull up and walk around furniture, missing this important stage of crawling. But movement on hands and knees is necessary to firmly establish right-handedness or left-handedness. Most babies do this naturally, but some need encouragement, even if it delays walking.

Doctors vary in recommending sturdy, protective shoes for babies beginning to walk. Have your pediatrician check your baby's feet well. If he has a special need for corrective shoes or orthopedic care, follow through with it. But most babies walk well barefoot or in flexible slippers. Buy shoes with soles rough enough to give good traction.

Be sure your home is safe. Until your baby knows how to maneuver steps, keep a safety gate across every set of stairs. Never trust a baby to play on an unenclosed stairway.

It's tempting to push children to walk before they are ready. While I recommend passive exercise and plenty of physical stimulation, avoid pushing infants too much. Enjoy your child's development. Encourage without pushing, and wait for his own developmental time clock.

When Should Toilet Training Begin?

by William Sears

The ages at which children become aware of their bladder and bowel functions vary tremendously. Instead of thinking of toilet training as an accomplishment to be mastered by a certain time, take cues from your child. Rather than "When should *I* begin her toilet training?" consider "When is *she* ready for toilet training?"

Signs that your child is ready. Most children, especially boys, do not show consistent signs of bladder or bowel awareness until after they are 18 months old. This is the age at which the nerves controlling urination and defecation become mature.

The usual indications of toilet training readiness in an infant 18 to 24 months old are: 1) a desire to imitate their parents' toilet functions; 2) signs that she about to relieve herself—squatting down, grunting, a "quiet look in a quiet place" such as a corner; 3) signs of genital awareness, such as a little boy who holds on to his penis; and 4) the after-the-fact confession.

Some toddlers go through a stage when they resist any outside suggestions to modify their behavior, especially toilet training. It is best to respect this and not frustrate everyone in attempts to toilet train during this passing stage.

How to begin training:

Give your child her own place to go. Around 2 years of age, most children begin to exhibit a desire for order. They like their own shelves for their toys, their own drawers for their clothes, their own tables and chairs, and so on. They also like their own places for their toilet functions. Place an infant potty on the floor next to one of your toilets. Rather than place your infant on her potty chair, simply place the chair alongside your toilet, and wait for your child to accompany you when you go. Most children adapt better to a child-size potty chair than to the more threatening adapter on your own toilet seat.

Teach your child words for her actions. Being able to talk about a skill greatly helps a child develop that skill. Words like *urination* or *defecation* may go beyond a child. *Go pee* or *go potty* are better. Words make toilet training a lot easier, which is another reason to delay it until your child is verbal.

Encourage a toilet routine. Some children readily accept being placed on the toilet at certain times during the day. After breakfast is usually the best time to encourage a bowel movement. Some people have a gastro-colic reflex that aids in having a bowel movement after a meal.

When your child is verbal enough to understand toilet training instructions, encourage her to respond immediately to her urge to go. Not following these urges predisposes children, especially girls, to urinary tract infections.

Use training pants. After your child has achieved daytime dryness for a few weeks, she may graduate to training pants. They resemble ordinary underwear but are padded in order to absorb occasional accidents. Do not punish for these.

Toddler Napping

by Debra Evans

As your child approaches her toddler years, you may wonder if nap times are as important as they were when he was a baby. After all, he doesn't fall asleep as easily as he used to—when you put him in bed he stays awake and creeps out of bed to play with his toys. And you think maybe if you let him skip a scheduled nap he'll sleep through the night more soundly.

Napping has restorative value for people of *all* ages. In comparison to nighttime rest, naps help us fall asleep faster and provide more efficient sleep. They're also a highly effective way to reduce stress and restore energy levels. This is as true for toddlers, whose activity levels have increased, as it is for the parents who have to keep pace with them.

Children's sleep requirements decrease with age, so the number of needed naps changes as babies grow into toddlers. While younger children usually need a sleeping nap in addition to at least 11 hours of sleep at night, older children may just play quietly in bed at nap time. Whether your child sleeps or not, a break from other activities promotes relaxation for everyone.

To reduce frustration, it pays to be flexible in responding to your child's fluctuating sleep schedules.

Sleep variations. The need for sleep varies significantly between individuals, and in the same individual at different times. The average amount of sleep required by children who are 2 or 3, for example, is nearly 13 hours daily. Yet the actual amount of sleep required by an individual child that age can range from 10 to 16 hours per day.

Physiological needs. Illness, travel and holidays can disrupt sleeping patterns as well. Observe your toddler for these signs of fatigue: fussiness and irritability, physical awkwardness (falling down or bumping into things), quarreling, whining, defiant behavior and intense spurts of physical and mental activity.

Rather than sticking to a strict sleeping schedule, make allowances for your child's physiological needs. For example, if your child sometimes naps for hours and at other times doesn't sleep at all, you may want to establish two regular bedtimes for your toddler—one for sleepless days and another for those days when he takes a lengthy nap. On special occasions, such as family gatherings, you can promote napping if you know your toddler will be staying up at unusual hours.

Lifestyle considerations. If your schedule is too busy to set time aside for your toddler's naps, encourage him to sleep or rest in his car seat, lie down beside you, or curl up with a coloring book. Parents who work full time or have hectic schedules may prefer their children take naps later in the day to allow more time together before bedtime.

Restful environment. Toddlers, who are increasingly aware of activities going on around them, can easily become too distracted to sleep. A quiet environment will definitely aid their ability to rest. Dimmed lighting and soothing music work wonders on even the most sleep-resistant kids. A bedside table stocked with books and bed toys, soft toys for snuggling and comfort, puzzles, and a music box serve as additional relaxation boosters.

If your child doesn't have his own bed or room because you're practicing attachment parenting, naps and quiet times are easily accomplished by taking time out to rest or nap with your child. Quiet time doesn't have to mean "alone time."

Most children outgrow their need for regularly scheduled naps by the time they are 5. By making midday naps and rest times a family habit, however, you can model the importance of stress reduction in an increasingly demanding world.

Preparing for a Sibling

by Debra Evans

Family dynamics shift and change to accommodate each new baby. Some children are open to this change, while others fight it. Is it possible to make the arrangement easier? Or can parents actually raise a child's anxiety by placing *too much* attention on what is to come?

A recent study at the University of Michigan suggests that when parents overemphasize sibling preparation throughout pregnancy, their child's anxiety level significantly increases. On the other hand, age-appropriate activities—especially in late pregnancy and upon the baby's arrival—can help older children feel included.

Rather than focusing on your new baby, gear activities during pregnancy to your older child. The following self-esteem builders are especially fun:

Create a picture book showing your child's growth and development. This is a great way to teach what babies can and can't do, and how a baby changes over time. Saying: "Look, Katy! This is when you were a brand new baby in the hospital. See how you liked to suck your pacifier?" teaches Katy about newborn behavior at the same time her mom is concentrating on Katy herself.

Talk about how happy you are about all that your child can do, say, see, know and be. The goal is to encourage your child to feel good about her abilities, accomplishments and personhood. When the new baby arrives, the older child will naturally compare herself to her new sibling. Knowing that you enjoy her as she is may lessen the competition.

Plan times together to build memories that last. These will bolster your child's sense of security now and pay dividends later.

Wean your older child from the high chair, crib and other baby things. Five to six months before your baby is due is not too soon to begin this process. Buying new baby equipment so the older child won't feel displaced may help.

Use simple explanations aimed at answering your child's questions as plainly and simply as possible. Providing too much information too soon is developmentally difficult for children. For instance, "Mommy, why is your tummy getting so big?" doesn't necessitate a complete run-down on gestational physiology and anatomy. Just saying, "This is where the baby is growing, in Mommy's uterus," is usually enough. Most children are easily satisfied with basic facts.

For younger children, sibling-preparation classes, children's books and "listening to the baby's heartbeat" at the doctor's office are best saved until the last month of pregnancy. Talking about hospitalization can wait until your child asks questions. If she doesn't seem interested, she probably doesn't want or need to know any more than you've told her.

Buy small gifts ahead of time for your older child to open when the baby receives gifts. Opening the baby's gifts "for the baby" may work for some children, but my kids wanted to keep some of the stuff for themselves!

Each child is special, each family member unique. The early days of life become an indelible part of a family's history, with mixed emotions, as the oldest child moves up the ladder to assume a new place within the home. The ascent need not be traumatic.

Sibling Rivalry

by William Sears

Sibling rivalry is one of the oldest family problems, dating back to Cain and Abel. The root of sibling rivalry is comparison. Comparison to others often results in feelings of inferiority, because there is always someone better than you in something. Accepting one's self is an adult goal that requires years of maturing to reach. This self-acceptance can be difficult for a child.

Sibling rivalry is a particularly sensitive problem, because a child not only compares himself to other siblings; he also evaluates how his parents compare him to those siblings.

Rivalry with a new baby. When a new baby arrives, expect some ambivalent feelings in your older child, especially if your children are spaced fewer than three years apart. Try to understand your child's feelings. Just when your 2- or 3-year-old has achieved a comfortable position in the family, someone comes along to threaten it. It's hard to sit back and watch a "stranger" become the focus of love of your parents. It hurts, especially if you feel unloved as a result of losing that attention.

When dealing with sibling rivalry, remember that you can control only your children's actions, not their feelings. Here are some suggestions for handling sibling rivalry after the new baby arrives:

Get your child involved with the new baby. Encourage her to be your little helper, changing diapers, bathing the baby, or doing similar tasks. Your older child also may become a source of developmental stimulation for your younger child. Babies often respond better to the sounds and faces of children than they do to those of adults. As a result, it is common for younger children to show more advanced development than their siblings did at the same age.

Get Dad involved. Father, make time to give special attention to your older child, who's probably feeling she's lost a lot of her mommy's prime time. You can compensate for this feeling of loss by getting involved with your older child and doing fun things with her.

As the size of your family increases, each child may have increasing difficulty finding a separate identity. Take some time every few days to do something special with each child. This helps satisfy each one's desire for equal time and gives each a feeling of individual worth.

Encourage your child to verbalize negative feelings. The more he can communicate in words, the less he shows in deeds. If he says, "I hate that baby," don't say, "No, you don't." If you deny his feelings, you're denying his right to feel emotions. It is better to express your understanding of these negative feelings. Allow your child plenty of time to approve of the new baby.

Don't condone physical aggression. Any behavior that suggests your older child is trying to hurt the younger should be dealt with immediately. Convey to the child that you will not tolerate the behavior. Not only can the baby be harmed by being hit or shaken, but this behavior models for the younger child that it is OK for an older child to hit a younger one.

Rivalry among older children. Parents of older children are often called upon to referee squabbles among their children, to judge who is at fault, and to administer appropriate punishment. Consider the following suggestions:

Encourage older children to model good behavior for younger ones. It's a fact of life that older children are expected to care for and teach younger children, especially in large families. For example, our 7-year-old Peter had a problem with patience. He was quick to lose his temper and give up on a task if it became too difficult for him. We elicited the help of 13-year-old Bobby to go to Peter at these stressful times and say, "Peter, let me help you." When one of our younger children was getting lax in his Bible reading, I asked one of our older children to engage in some brother-to-brother Bible study to model the importance of daily Scripture reading. In addition to a child's profiting from the modeling of another, it teaches family members to be concerned for and aware of the needs of others.

Pray for one another. Family devotions can encourage your children to pray for one another. In our family, each child is accountable for praying for the prayer requests of his brothers and sisters.

Encourage expressions of love for one another. Love for each other can be another focus of your family devotions. You might say, "I'm encouraging you to show acts of love for one another because this is what Christ asks his disciples to do." Consider requiring each of your children to exhibit at least one act of love a day for another sibling. Hold them accountable for these acts of love by recording them in your prayer calendar during family devotions. This will not be easy, and your children will probably forget. With encouragement, though, this can evolve into a habit that will create better feelings among siblings.

Minimize comparisons among your children. This is often the basis for feelings of inferiority, which can turn into undesirable behavior among siblings. Praise a child for her accomplishments in relation to herself, not in comparison to a sibling. Each child should feel she is special in the eyes of her parents.

Help for Older and Younger Siblings
by Clara Shaw Schuster

To help older children accept younger siblings, talk about the decision to add another member to the family for several months before the event occurs. Preschoolers need time to process events and to work through ambivalent feelings. Refer to the baby as a *baby* rather than a playmate, since it will be a long time before they can really play together.

Talk about the new child as a person. Adopted siblings should be described as well as possible, and possible cooperative activities discussed. For example:

• Younger children tend to grab toys and knock towers over. Teach patience and humor, and change the nature of the activity or goals. Set some toys apart for play when the younger child is asleep.

• Help your child see his own development progress and to participate in the development of the younger child as a helper and teacher. Share stories about the child's own younger days.

• Provide fun activities the children can enjoy together (water play, finger or pudding painting).

• Laugh at the inconveniences. Give an extra hug for good measure.

• Set clear rules about physical aggression.

To help younger children get along with older siblings:

• Teach respect for each other's property.

• Assure your child that he will gain privileges and skills with time and practice.

• Help your child identify his own unique talents and interests.

• Listen to both sides, but don't take sides. Allow children to resolve their own differences. Assist the children, as necessary, to negotiate. Help them identify problems and brainstorm options, but never solve problems for them.

• Model patience, understanding, tenderness, caring and love with your spouse. Children imitate what they observe.

Testing Times

Chapter Nine

Babies and Stress

by Patricia Rushford

Eighteen-month-old Jason hasn't slept or eaten well for a week. He's tired and cranky and this morning he threw his favorite Fruity Tunes cereal with milk across the room—after which both he and his distraught mother, Carla, threw a fit.

Upon examining Jason, his doctor assured Carla that her son was in good health and suggested that Jason might be going through a phase. "Or," he said, "it could be stress."

"Stress? But he's just a baby. How could he be stressed?"

Babies Jason's age and younger can and often do react to stressful situations. Knowing babies are susceptible to stress raises a number of questions.

What is stress? Stress is the urgency or pressure felt when extra demands are placed on one's body. These pressures include extreme stressors such as moving, a new baby, a job change or divorce. Stress can also be brought on by disruptions in a child's routine, such as holidays, birthday parties, a missed nap, persistent loud noises, visiting relatives, a vacation or even dinner out. Other stressors include those brought on by parents who nag, criticize, argue, show disapproval, and make excessive demands. Stress releases hormones into the body, which cause the heart to beat faster and the breathing rate to quicken. Too much stress can eventually lead to serious medical and psychological problems.

Are all babies affected by stress? To some degree, yes, but not all

> *Attack the sources of stress in your child's life that can be eliminated or reduced, like high levels of noise and lack of structure or routine.*
>
> *Patricia Rushford, R.N.*

179

are affected adversely. Some children, like some adults, can handle high levels of stress. In fact, some seem to thrive on it.

How can we recognize stress in babies? Signs of stress are not difficult to spot—irritability, restlessness, crankiness, whining, behavioral problems, changes in eating habits, poor sleep patterns, frequent nightmares, stomachaches, regression to earlier behavior, or excessive thumb sucking, bed-wetting or use of a pacifier. Since these symptoms can indicate other problems as well, talk with your doctor before diagnosing them as stress.

What can parents do to help babies cope with stress? Reducing or coping with stress requires thinking through alternatives and considering how to make the best of a situation. Since babies have not developed these thinking patterns, they need capable adults to help them. Children tend to mimic their parents. Consequently, one of your first steps will be to evaluate and, if necessary, improve your own coping skills.

Attack the sources of the stress in your child's life that can be eliminated or reduced: high levels of noise, lack of structure or routine, parental attitudes, negative parental reaction to stress and, to some extent, a child's environment.

If the stress your family is experiencing can't be reduced, consider ways you and your child can better cope with the stress: a restful atmosphere at intervals during the day, free time for play and laughter, warm baths, warm milk, and rocking and cuddling.

Finally, develop a strong, consistent prayer life. God is with us in all things. Knowing God can handle every situation and trusting him to do so provides a measure of security, peace and tranquillity. It is perhaps the most effective means we have of reducing stress in ourselves and our children.

Year Number Two

by Debra Evans

Consider the amazing 2-year-old: exhaustingly excitable, exasperatingly engaging, explosively emotional—and above all, endlessly curious. Put all of this energy into a small person who hasn't yet learned to wait or to control her emotions, and what do you get? A perplexed and frustrated parent.

As adults, we rationalize, complain about, and distract ourselves from destructive or negative feelings. We've also developed a certain special capacity called the ability to *wait.* We prioritize and predict, think abstractly and understand that "yesterday" doesn't necessarily mean everything that happened before today. We've found ways to delay gratification instead of always wanting it *now.* Not so the 2-year-old.

In the midst of a full-blown temper tantrum, it's natural to wonder what suddenly went wrong with this once wonderful, compliant child. How does a parent stay in control when confronted with such out-of-control behavior?

Realize that your 2-year-old is scared by the ferocious intensity of her emotions. Strong feelings are scary things for children as well as for adults. The big difference is that we're used to dealing with our emotions and have found ways to deal with them constructively. Your 2-year-old feels the same things you do—love, anger, sadness, fear, happiness—with incredible, unfiltered force.

Know that your child feels defenseless. Without the mechanisms that are learned and mastered over time, your child doesn't know how to calm down like you do. She can't say to herself, "Things will be OK tomorrow," because she doesn't have a clear concept of what tomorrow is. She won't give up easily on getting her way, because she's not even sure what her limits are until she tests them. Thus, your 2-year-old desperately needs your support, assurance and guidance to lead the way.

Don't be intimidated by momentary misbehavior. Remember that your child needs—and wants—clearly defined limits. At the same time, keep the big picture in mind: this is a *toddler,* not an adult. Then ask yourself the four basic questions: When was the last time she ate? Does she need to rest? Could she be coming down with something? Have I been too busy during the past few hours?

Surprisingly, most of the "terrible" behavior we often associate with toddlers coincides with low blood sugar, fatigue, illness or parental stress. This fact is easy to forget, but essential to remember. When a snack is more appropriate than a spanking, it's important to respond wisely, with understanding.

Avoid parent-child power struggles. When a 2-year-old acts out and acts up, it's tempting to rule by tyranny. But by understanding what your child's abilities are, it is possible to respond compassionately as well as calmly to your child's needs. Having realistic expectations about what 2-year-olds are actually like will serve both of you well.

Pray for the strength to stay in control of yourself, especially when your child is the most out-of-control. It's amazing how quickly tempers flare when both you and your child are tired, hungry, pressured or burdened. Therefore, do what you can to deal with your own fatigue and emotions; don't allow your child to become the victim of your own frustration. When you're angry, take it out on a pillow as you punch it or on the pavement while you go for a walk. If you find yourself trapped by your emotions or unable to control them, do something constructive about it: join (or start) a parent support group; talk to someone who can give you practical parenting advice; implement a plan to take regularly scheduled breaks to do something you enjoy. Above all, ask the Lord to help you be the kind of parent he wants you to be.

When They Direct Their Anger at You
by Kay Kuzma

"I hate you! I wish you were dead!" your toddler yells at you. Your first instinct may be to get angry and punish him. But he really doesn't mean what he said. He just doesn't have the words to express his real message: "Mommy, listen to me. Can't you understand that I don't like how you are treating me? What you have done has made me angry." Instead of merely punishing, it's better to teach your child a better way to handle his emotions. You must get two messages across to him: 1) What you said is not acceptable. 2) I understand that you are angry. Try the following:

Technique #1—Shock Therapy: Surprise your child as he finishes his outburst by whirling around and saying "no" in the strongest, firmest voice you have without screaming. You will startle him. Then take him in your arms and say, "You are angry with Mommy, but you may not say those words." Period. Then go on to Technique #2.

If your child is in a habit of saying these words, or if you are by nature a shouting disciplinarian, this method will not work. Go immediately to:

Technique #2—Iceberg Psychology: You recognize that your child's outburst is merely the tip of the iceberg. You must now dig for the feelings under the surface that are causing this behavior. Say, "You are angry at Mommy." (Wait for a nod of agreement.) "Mommy did something that really made you mad." (Nod.) "It makes you angry when Mommy won't listen to you—or give you what you want." (Nod.)

Your child should begin to relax at this point, because he doesn't have to fear your wrath, and because you're listening to him. When his anger is sufficiently diffused so that he can listen to you, get your two messages across. First say, "You may not say things like that to other people—it hurts them. And I cannot allow you to hurt people." Then the second message: "I will listen to you. Say, 'Mommy, I'm mad,' and I will try to solve the problem so you don't have to be angry. If I'm not listening, pull on my skirt and say the words, 'I'm mad,' again."

If your toddler is quite verbal, you can explain, "Sometimes I get so busy it takes me a while to catch on that you need me." Or: "Sometimes I get so upset myself that I don't treat you very nice. I'm sorry."

Remember, aggressive behavior is one of the easiest behaviors to model. He'll get enough from Batman and the Ninja Turtles. He doesn't need it from you too.

How to Cope with "No!"
by Grace Ketterman
• Separating from parents is all 2-year-olds' major task. This requires them to test parents' authority—it's the only way most toddlers know of to find their capabilities and understand their boundaries.

• They are compelled to explore. This urge pushes them to the top of the refrigerator to see if there are cookies in your highest cupboard. They don't intend to scare you out of your wits.

• They are possessive, grabby and selfish—not because they are bad but because they are insecure. They don't know *who* they are, so how can they comprehend what is "mine" and "not mine"?

• They retaliate by instinct. Janet bit Stephen when he pulled her hair after she grabbed his toy truck . . . .

• The most commonly used word in their vocabulary is "no!" It is their primary means of discovering new boundaries and testing the degree of their authority or power.

• They have an uncanny ability to reduce their parents to toddler behavior! Before parents realize it, they are in hand-to-hand, voice-to-voice combat at the child's own level.

Some coping strategies:
• Don't fight for power.
• Capitalize on your 2-year-old's curiosity and drive to explore. Take her out-of-doors or in your biggest roughhouse area, and help her climb safely and explore to her heart's content.
• Don't allow your 2-year-old to play unsupervised with another young child, and don't expect her to share automatically. Stay within sight and hearing so you can use any impending struggle as a teachable moment. Use "time out" to separate children, briefly take charge of toys,

183

stop fights, and instruct them how to play—separately—in one another's company.

• When another child becomes aggressive and your 2-year-old attempts to get even, firmly separate and restrain both until each gives up fighting.

• Don't worry about their use of "no!" A friend of mine simply agrees with her child. She says: "OK, Ned. Say 'no' all you like. But you'll pick up your toys anyway!" Be confident in God's wisdom and your own. Then you'll never stoop to a child's power struggle.

Handling Tantrums

by William Sears

Temper tantrums exhaust both parents and children and are one of the most frustrating of childhood behaviors. Two basic inner feelings in your child prompt most temper tantrums.

First, a young child has an intense desire to perform and accomplish, but often the desire is greater than the capacity. Facing this reality may lead to intense frustration that is released in a healthy, outward tantrum. This kind of tantrum needs loving support, gentleness, and understanding. Guide the child toward successfully achieving the activity, or channel his energy into a more easily achievable activity suited to his personality and achievement level.

The second cause of temper tantrums is hearing "no" just when a child's newly found power and desire propels him toward a certain act. Accepting an outside force contrary to his strong will is a difficult conflict he cannot handle without a fight. He wanted to be big, but his world tells him and shows him how small he is. He is upset, but he does not have the ability to handle conflicting emotions with reason, so he copes with his inner emotions by a display of outward emotions that we call a tantrum. Think of your child's tantrum in terms of his newly forming sense of self and inner controls becoming unglued. He needs someone to keep him from falling apart.

The most frightening temper tantrums are breath-holding spells. During the rage of a tantrum, a child may hold his breath, turn blue, become limp, and even faint. Breath-holding spells may resemble convulsions and may be even more alarming to already worried parents. Fortunately, most children who hold their breath resume normal breathing just as they are on the brink of passing out. Even those children who faint momentarily quickly resume normal breathing before harming themselves. These episodes usually stop when the child is old enough to more easily express his anger verbally.

Temper tantrums can be exhausting and frightening experiences for both child and parent. In more severe tantrums, a child goes out of control and does not know how to regain it, even if he wants to.

How can you handle temper tantrums? First, realize that you *can't* handle them; you can only support your child when he has one. Temper tantrums reflect your child's emotions, which *he* has to handle. Excessive interference deprives a child of the ability to release his inner tensions; too little support leaves him to cope all by himself, without the strength to do so effectively.

What is the issue at stake causing the temper tantrum? If your child has chosen an impossible task, and it becomes apparent that he is not going to achieve it but won't give up, simply be on standby. Temper tantrums bring out the best in intuitive mothering. Keep your arms extended and your attitude accepting. Often a few soothing words or a little help ("I'll untie the knot, and you put on your shoe") may put him back on the road to recovery.

If the issue at stake is a power struggle of wills (for example, he wants a toy that he should not have), then the temper tantrum should be approached with the usual firm and loving double-whammy of effective discipline: "I love you, and I am in charge."

Sometimes a strong-willed child will lose complete control of himself during a tantrum. When his behavior reaches this stage, simply hold him firmly but lovingly and explain: "You are angry and you have lost control!" (you understand his position). "I am holding you tightly because I love you. I want to help you and you will be all right" (I am in charge here).

You may discover that after a minute of struggling, a rigid child will melt into your arms as if thanking you for rescuing him. My wife ended one of our daughter's tantrums on a spiritual note with, "Now let's pray together."

Temper tantrums in public places are embarrassing, and it's often difficult to consider your child's feelings first. *What will people think of me as a mother?* is likely to be your first thought. In this situation, if it becomes uncomfortable for you, remove your child to another room where he can have his tantrum in private. If a tantrum is based upon an inner frustration, then your open arms and accepting attitude will help diffuse his explosive behavior. If the issue is one of defiance, again your authority is at stake, and your child needs to be disciplined. Sometimes a child who is crying uncontrollably can't stop when you tell him to. He may or may not want to stop, but he literally cannot get hold of himself. If he wants to stop, an offer to pray with him for help from God is all that is needed, for both of you. An in-arms prayer time is extremely comforting.

Sometimes tantrums can be so exhausting to parents that they give in; their child probably stops his disruptive behavior immediately. However, keep in mind the principle that undesirable behavior, if rewarded, will persist. In addition to weakening your authority, rewarding aggressive and violent behavior will get him what he wants.

Love and Limits

by Kay Kuzma

Parents of toddlers will be tested by their children. Unfortunately, parents too often react to a test without understanding its nature. The result is that their children feel misunderstood and continue testing, hoping that someday their parents will give them the answer they are searching for.

Because children equate love and attention, they often feel that other people or commitments requiring their parents' attention are loved more than they are. So they give their parents a "love test." They do something obnoxious to see how their parents will react. If you explode and punish, your child comes to the conclusion that she isn't loved, which can lead to feelings of jealousy and to more testing. To pass the love test, you must prove to your child that she *is* loved.

This suggestion bothers some parents, because they believe that when a child does something wrong she deserves to be disciplined; she needs to be taught correct behavior.

The problem is that there are *two kinds of tests* that toddlers give their parents.

1. The love test: Do you really love me? I don't feel very loved because you haven't given me the positive attention I need.

2. The limits test: Do you mean what you say? Do I really have to obey you?

Each test requires a different response in order to pass. If you're not careful, it's easy to confuse them. If a child gives you the second test and is asking, "Do you love me?" you have an opportunity to prove that she is loved. If she gives you the limits test and is asking, "Do I have to obey you?" you have a chance to help her know you mean what you say.

The love test is answered correctly with love. The limits test is answered correctly with discipline. During your child's toddler years, it is not always easy to figure out which test your child is giving you. To play it safe, I suggest going with what well-known child psychologist Rudolph Dreikurs suggests: Dreikurs says the number-one reason children misbehave is because they need attention—they need to feel loved. If they can't win your approval and receive positive attention for being good, they quickly turn to testing you with obnoxious behavior (the love test).

Therefore, when your toddler becomes obnoxious, your first response should be to ask yourself how much positive attention she has received recently. If it isn't much, take a little extra time to fill her love cup and see if her negative behavior fades away. This doesn't mean that, after you have given her some positive attention, you shouldn't also teach her a better way to get your attention. Say to him, "When your love cup is empty, tell me, 'Mommy, my love cup is empty,' and I'll try to fill you up so you have enough love to give away. But you may not throw things, hit me, or wake the baby."

Once you have set a limit on a certain behavior, you need to handle the behavior as a limits test if it is repeated. The best answer for the limits test is to impose a consequence. If you say, "You may not hit your sister," and he continues, separate the children. A few minutes of timeout imparts the message, "I meant what I said"—and you'll pass the limits test.

Early Discipline Strategies

by Patricia Rushford

One father recently shared a not-so-successful encounter with his 18-month-old son. Three times Jeff pulled Travis away from an electrical outlet and replaced the safety plug. Three times Travis repeated "No, no," and toddled back. The fourth time Dad tried a sterner approach. He slapped Travis' hand and said "No!" Travis frowned and slapped him back.

The need here for discipline is obvious. But when do we start reining in disobedient babies, and what are the best methods? How can we escape the guilt we feel at our lack of control, frustration and feelings of inadequacy?

Know your baby. Before we can determine when and how to discipline, we must understand how babies function. Children must accomplish certain God-given developmental tasks in order to grow and develop into healthy adults. A child's first task is to gain trust. This happens as you provide for your child's physical, emotional and social needs.

Next, babies need to develop autonomy. They learn to assert themselves, explore, climb, test, throw, feel, and become intimately acquainted with themselves and their world. In this quest for independence, they need constant support and supervision. Their "work" often leaves parents exhausted *and* exasperated.

Babies, unlike adults, think in concrete, literal terms. They have a short attention span, a narrow base of experience and a limited vocabulary. Saying "Be a good boy for Mommy" is vague and confusing. For all a baby knows, his mom wants him to be food, because at lunch she said, "Eat your squash; it's good." Knowing a child's limitations can help you develop more realistic expectations and significantly reduce your frustration.

Be assertive. In your discipline, strive for assertiveness rather than aggression. Aggressive behavior in parents does not represent control, but a lack of it. Parents who hit, yell, and frighten children have lost their ability to be effective and may cause severe emotional problems. Parents can be more effective by being firm but gentle, consistent in setting limits, and by taking time to learn how to discipline creatively.

Be selective. Avoid the pitfalls of perfectionism, high expectations and over-control. Certain behaviors are not worth fighting over; others are beyond parental control. For example, trying to force a child to eat, sleep, or go potty in the toilet is like trying to nail a raw egg to the wall—we won't accomplish our task, and we'll break the yolk trying.

Respect your child, and allow him space to explore, experiment and grow. Choose your limits wisely, and follow through on the limits you set.

Be patient. Don't take yourself or your kids too seriously. Take time to simply watch your child. Delight in the way Krysten gets her shirt on, even if it's upside down. Get down on the floor and play face to face. Listen to her. Empathize when she's tired and distraught. Don't expect your baby to meet your needs; rather adapt your schedule to meet hers. Finally, take time to take care of yourself. Your stress produces stress in your baby. Know your limits, and don't be afraid to ask for help.

~

Toddler Safety

~

Chapter Ten ———————————————

Taking Precautions

by Grace Ketterman

Most accidents happen to toddlers between the ages of 7 months and 2 years. Toddlers are curious, active and inexperienced. They love to explore. Child-proof your house, but also take time to teach your child which items and areas are off-limits. Don't leave your toddler out of your sight or hearing, except when he's sleeping.

You can't always keep your energetic toddler tied to yourself as you go about doing household tasks. The following are some suggestions to help provide safety for your child and a degree of freedom for you:

1. Invest in a playpen that is sturdy and roomy enough for your toddler to play in comfortably. He may learn to climb out, so be watchful.

2. Keep the playpen near enough so that you will be within hearing distance of each other. Talk or sing to your child so he won't feel abandoned and will know you are near.

3. Peek in on him frequently, offer a different toy, or play "peekaboo" to further reassure him you haven't forgotten him.

4. When your child gets too big for a playpen, teach him how to play. Stacking blocks, pounding a pegboard, or pulling a toy with a handle or string can entertain a toddler for some time.

5. No one enjoys stacking blocks forever, so vary your toddler's activities. He can make a drum set out of a pan and wooden spoon. Be creative in selecting safe items from your kitchen, and store them in a drawer accessible to your toddler. Other areas, of course, can be kept

> *Child-proof your house, but also take time to teach your child which items and areas are off-limits.*
>
> Dr. Grace Ketterman

safely off limits with the safety latches available in most stores.

Supervising your child's activities does not mean you must be her constant entertainer. Don't become enslaved to her every whim or even to the need of stimulation. You can create a monster out of a child who expects then demands your constant attention. Seek a balance between spending loving time with her, and some time by yourself.

Babyproofing Kitchen and Bath

by Vicki Lansky

Accidents, not illnesses, cause most child deaths—some 400 children under age 4 die of accidents each month in the United States. Most accidents in the home are preventable. What you buy, where you put it, and how you use it will determine how safe your kids are at home.

Protecting your child from harm in your home comes down to two things: 1) careful, thoughtful childproofing of potentially dangerous areas, and 2) responsible, loving vigilance.

Your object as a parent is to make your house safe for your baby to explore—that makes the learning part possible. You want to eliminate dangers without being overprotective or inhibiting your child. No parent can prevent all accidents. But as long as you've done your best, you'll have done your job.

To get you started, here are some ideas for childproofing two of the most potentially hazardous rooms in your home—the kitchen and the bathroom. Most of the safety items mentioned here are available at your hardware store.

Kitchen. Sometimes the best kitchen childproofing consists of a gate at the door, to keep your child out of the room altogether. If that is not feasible, never leave your child alone in the kitchen.

• Turn the handles of pots and pans toward the back of the stove top so your child can't grab them and pull down hot food. Fry or boil foods on the back burners whenever possible.

• Don't allow your baby to play on the floor by the stove when you're cooking.

• Buy a stove guard and knob covers.

• Use appliance latches on the refrigerator, dishwasher, microwave and trash compactor.

• Always keep the dishwasher closed. Add detergent only when you're ready to run the machine.

• Keep appliance cords short by using cord shorteners.

• Unplug all counter top appliances after every use.

• Use cabinet and drawer guard latches. Even such harmless-seeming items as toothpicks or bottle covers pose hazards to small children.

• Lock away all cleaning and other hazardous materials.

• Keep knives and other potentially dangerous kitchen utensils out of reach.

• Don't hold your baby in your arms while you cook. Never try to carry your baby and a cup of coffee or other hot liquid at the same time.

Bathroom. The bathroom is as full of risk for your baby as the kitchen. The combination of water, attractive (poisonous) substances and intriguing appliances is fascinating to a curious child looking for entertainment.

• Use a safety latch to keep the toilet lid closed so it doesn't become a place for water play.

• Get a soft spout cover for the bathtub. It will save your baby from bumps and bruises and also help avoid hot-water burns from a hot spout.

• Place childproof knob covers over cold and hot handles to prevent tampering.

• Test the bath water on the inside of your wrist before putting your baby into the tub, or invest in a bath thermometer.

• Keep the water temperature for your house set at about 120 F—hot enough to clean clothes and dishes, yet not scalding.

• Put non-skid appliqués on the bottom of the tub, or use a rubber mat.

• Never leave water in the tub when it's not in use.

• Consider using a three-legged bathtub seat to help keep your child secure during a bath.

• Never leave a child under 5 years old unattended in the tub. If you must leave the room for any reason, wrap your child in a towel and take him with you.

• Get a medicine chest that locks, or use a childproof lock on your existing cabinet.

• Be sure all medicines are in child-resistant containers.

• Don't leave a sun lamp, hair dryer or other electrical appliance where your child can reach it and pull it into a water-filled tub or sink. Unplug all appliances when not in use.

• Lock up cleaning substances and beauty aids, such as shampoo and nail polish.

Water Safety

by Debra Evans

Whether splashing in the tub, playing with the garden hose in a portable pool, or toddling along the shore of a favorite beach, encounters with water play can be one of a child's most memorable delights. By creating a secure, comfortable environment in which to bathe or swim together, you will find yourself seeing the joys of water from a refreshing perspective—your baby's. Not all babies enjoy the experience at first. But given enough time and loving supervision, every child can learn to enjoy the water.

Water play is especially beneficial because:

• Water stimulates your baby's physical and mental development. It has its own feel and texture. Water has a different taste and smell than air or food, makes sound travel in unique ways, reduces the field of gravity, and changes the surface temperature of our bodies. Water play will challenge your baby's mind and body to respond in new ways to her environment.

• Water provides opportunities for unique forms of interaction between you and your child. Because young children cannot be left alone in water, you'll need to be available whenever your baby engages in water play. Getting in the water with your baby will open up new avenues of communication, as you respond to her need for comfort and security.

• Water enhances your baby's ability to relax. Have you often found yourself rocking or walking your baby to relieve fussiness? Soothing movement is calming for both children and adults. Consequently, many babies enjoy being supported or held in water while you sway them back and forth. Also, you may have discovered that getting into the tub with your baby encourages *both* of you to relax. Touch and movement in water helps to alleviate tension. Your baby releases excess energy through water play and may be more likely to sleep better afterward.

When the weather is warm enough, there are numerous ways to provide water-play activities for your baby. An inexpensive wading pool can be set up in the backyard or on a porch. Use warm water to fill the pool, be outside with your baby whenever the pool contains water, and empty out the water when you're done. Running through the sprinkler for a few minutes or scooting down a banana slide are additional ways to get the giggles and beat the summer heat.

Remember, nothing makes a child drown-proof. When in the water, children never should be left unattended by an adult. Swimming instruction enables many younger children to feel more confident in the water, but it also may provide a false sense of security.

For a baby, however, formalized lessons introduce an additional hazard. Books and television programs in the 70s popularized the concept that babies can be trained to hold their breath to avoid drowning. Recent research suggests otherwise. *Water intoxication* is a serious condition associated with the practice of submersing babies underwater. It is caused by swallowing too much water, which produces a chemical imbalance in the baby's bloodstream. Related symptoms, which begin three to eight hours after exposure to the water, include lethargy and irritability. In severe cases, water intoxication can lead to convulsions, brain damage, or even death.

Marjorie M. Murphy, the YMCA's U.S. aquatic director, strongly urges that *swimming programs for children under the age of 3 always include a parent in the water.* She also recommends that small children *should not be placed under the water or be allowed to drink pool water.* When it comes to water play, the rule of thumb is "heads up, bottoms under," until a child matures and becomes capable of breathing correctly.

Another safety consideration concerns the body-temperature changes that accompany water exposure. Give yourself a good 20 to 30 minutes—both before and after being in the water—to adapt. Once in the water, watch for signs that indicate chilling: goose bumps, blue lips, and shivering. Have a warm, dry towel ready nearby, and limit swimming time in cooler water to less than 15 minutes.

Your baby's first experiences with sun, sand, lifeguards and chlorine provide lessons that can last a lifetime. By taking the necessary precautions, you can teach your child how to be both safe and confident around the water.

For additional reading, see: *Infant Swimming* by Cynthia Clevenger (Martin's Press). *Infaquatics: Teaching Kids to Swim* by John L. Murray (Leisure Press).

Secure Summer Environments

by William and Martha Sears

When accidents happen, moms and dads are a child's first emergency medical system. Summer weather and outdoor activities create a whole new set of accidents waiting to happen. But you can be prepared to treat these common summer mishaps.

Sunburn Prevention

Toddlers' thin skin and summer sun don't mix. Besides causing sunburn, excessive sun exposure during childhood increases the risk of adult skin cancer. Prevention is your best strategy. Here are ways to protect your child from overexposure to sun:

• Sun rays are most intense from 10 A.M. to 3 P.M. If possible, plan outdoor activities late in the afternoon.

• Cover your child with a long shirt (such as a parent's old T-shirt) and a wide-brimmed hat.

• Place your child under a sun umbrella.

• Beware of sun rays that reflect off sand and water.

• Select a lotion or milky, gel-type sunscreen rather than the clear alcohol type, which may burn a young child's skin when applied. Select a sunscreen with a sun protection factor (SPF) of 15 or more. For water play, use a waterproof sunscreen, and generously reapply the lotion after time in the water. For particularly sensitive areas, such as the nose, cheeks and ears, use an opaque zinc oxide sun block.

If your child does get too much sun, here are some treatment suggestions:

• If the skin is only slightly red and your child is not uncomfortable, no treatment is necessary. You may want to apply a nonpetroleum-based moisturizer lotion (aloe, for example) several times a day.

• If the skin is very red, immerse the burned area in cool water, or use cool water and towel compresses for 15 minutes at least four times a day.

• If the skin is blistered, it may be a second-degree burn. Call your doctor for a prescription cream.

• Give appropriate doses of acetaminophen for pain.

Insect Stings and Bites

Insects that leave their "calling card" in a child's skin can cause two potential problems: an infection at the puncture site or an allergic reaction to injected venom.

A bee will leave its stinger and attached venom sac in a sting wound. Before removing a stinger, scrape away the protruding venom sac with a knife or the edge of a credit card. If you try to squeeze the sac with a tweezers, you may force more venom into the skin. (Wasp stingers don't have an attached venom sac.) After removing the stinger with tweezers, apply ice to the sting site to slow down the spread of venom and ease the pain.

Some children will have allergic reactions to stings. If your toddler has localized swelling around the sting site, apply ice and wait before calling your doctor. If an allergic reaction is going to occur, expect it to happen within an hour. However, if your child develops swollen hands and eyelids, wheezing or a hivelike rash, take him to your doctor's office or to the emergency room.

If your child has shown any of the above signs from a prior bee sting, take this precaution: The next time he is stung, apply an ice pack and immediately go wait in the emergency room waiting room. If no allergic signs appear within a couple hours, it's safe to return home.

If your child has a history of severe allergic reactions to insect stings, discuss with your doctor the possibility of desensitizing your child to stings with a series of shots. If you are traveling and your child has had severe reactions to stings, take along a prescription insect-sting kit containing adrenaline and directions on how to administer it.

Swimming Pool Safety

Backyard pools pose a special safety hazard for toddlers. A fence and self-latching gate are required by law in many communities. But it is nearly impossible to watch a young child constantly. For added swimming pool safety measures, install safety latches on the doors in your home (so your child can't get outside without your knowledge), and never leave your toddler unsupervised around the pool. Take similar measures even if you have only a filled wading pool in your yard.

CPR classes are available through local hospitals and other organizations. All parents should take an infant CPR class. Here's a quick reminder of what you should do if your toddler stops breathing after a fall into a pool.

First, call your local emergency number. Then, begin CPR. Turn your child on his side to clear water from his mouth, then place him on his back so that his head is level with his heart. Clear the tongue from the back of the throat by lifting the chin with one hand while pressing on the forehead with the other. A child's head should be slightly tilted upward, but don't tilt the head as far back as you would an adult's. A towel rolled up under the neck usually maintains the correct position.

For infants under 1, cover the baby's mouth and nose with your mouth. For an older child, squeeze the nostrils between the thumb and forefinger, and fit your mouth tightly around the child's lips. Blow gentle puffs of breath with just enough force to see the child's chest rise. Give a steady breath every three seconds (20 per minute). Continue until the child is breathing on his own.

Check your child's pulse by pressing gently between the muscles on the inner side of the upper arm, midway between the shoulder and the elbow. If he has no pulse, begin chest compressions. Put the child on a flat surface, and place two or three of your fingers on his breastbone, just below the nipple line. Depress to a depth of one-half to one inch at a rate of 100 per minute. Give a blow of mouth-to-mouth air after every fifth compression. Continue until you feel a pulse, or until trained help arrives.

Remember that supervision is the best safety precaution around water. Maintain strict swimming pool discipline from the time your child is very young. Children should grow up with a realistic respect for water, both its enjoyment and its dangers.

Strains, Sprains and Fractures

Toddlers' unsuccessful navigation of outdoor hazards can lead to strains, sprains and fractures. The four classic signs of broken bones at any age are swelling, pain, limitation of motion and point tenderness (when the site of the fracture is tender to a fingertip's touch).

First aid for common strains, sprains and fractures can be remembered by "ICES": ice, compression, elevation and support. All four of these measures slow down continued bleeding within the joint or muscle and shorten recovery time.

Apply an ice pack to a swollen or fractured area for at least 20 minutes. Snugly—but not constrictingly—wrap the ice pack with an elastic bandage around the affected joint or possible fracture site. Elevate the limb about six inches on a pillow, or support the limb with a sling. If you suspect a broken bone, immobilize the limb and take your child to the emergency room.

Mild fractures to the midshaft of the long bone of the leg—known as toddler fracture—can occur during the frequent falls of the beginning walker. Toddlers often limp for a few hours after a fall or even from a sore on their foot or a stubbed toe. But if your child limps for more than 24 hours, seek medical attention to be sure there is no fracture or injury to the hip joint.

With proper precautions and parental preparedness, summer can be both a fun and safe time even for kids who are just starting to learn how to get around.

Poisoning Prevention and Treatment

by Patricia Rushford

Every 30 seconds a child is poisoned. Each year, over 1,000,000 cases of accidental poisoning occur in this country. Poisoning can lead to sickness, permanent disabilities or even death for thousands of children. About two-thirds of the poisonings involve children under 5 years of age. Medicines are responsible for the majority of poisonings. Aspirin and acetaminophen are the most common, followed closely by cleaning and polishing agents, cosmetics, turpentine, paints, pesticides, plants and petroleum products.

Locate the number for a poison control center in your area and list it on your phone and on an emergency phone-number sheet. Check with your local pharmacy about obtaining Mr. Yuk stickers and keep a supply on hand. Next, go through every room in your home and check for potential dangers. Attach Mr. Yuk stickers on harmful substances. Teach your child about Mr. Yuk.

Take these additional steps to prevent poisoning.

1. Keep toxic substances and medications out of reach at all times.

2. Use childproof caps on medicines.

3. Use childproof door latches to secure cupboards containing poison-ous agents.

4. Keep household cleaners in their original labeled containers. Do not transfer household products to empty food or beverage containers. Children can easily mistake them for juice or fruit drinks.

5. Never leave medicines or cleaning substances on the counter where children can reach them.

6. Keep all cosmetics, permanent wave solutions, hair colorants, drugs, perfumes, moth crystals and so on out of reach.

7. Never leave a purse within a child's reach. They often carry a wealth of treasure—a pill box, for example, may be appealing with colorful pills in different shapes and sizes.

8. Never give medications in the dark. Always read the label and check the correct dosages and times to prevent overdose.

9. Check your plants. Many are poisonous. English Ivy, mistletoe, holly, philodendron, oleander, azalea, and geranium are a few common but potentially dangerous plants.

10. Be prepared in case of accidental poisoning. Purchase a bottle of syrup of ipecac and keep it in your first-aid kit. Having ipecac at home

can save the crucial 45 minutes to an hour before you may be able to get help. It is meant to induce vomiting to keep the body from absorbing the ingested poison. Since not all poisonings require vomiting, do not give syrup of ipecac without first checking with a doctor or medical expert. Prevention is the best cure, but if an accidental poisoning does occur, stay calm and call for help.

Choking Aid and Prevention

by Grace Ketterman

Choking on a variety of objects is all too common in children. The items range from heavy mucous brought on by bronchitis to marbles or other toys.

To understand choking, you need a simple lesson in anatomy. At the back of the mouth, the throat divides into two long tubes. The one at the back is the esophagus, which directs food into the stomach. The front tube goes from the larynx (also called the voice box or the Adam's apple), into the windpipe (the trachea), which allows air to get into the lungs. A muscle shaped like an inverted V where the esophagus and larynx meet separates food from air and covers the larynx to keep food from going "down the wrong tube."

Almost everyone has had the frightening experience of getting a bit of popcorn or a fish bone caught in that trachea. The cough to get rid of such an object is almost strangling itself. But it's the cough that finally brings up the item that's been caught.

If the object is big enough, it may block the opening to the larynx and windpipe. Choking tends to lodge it even more, and unless someone is available to help, a child can die. During a bout of vomiting, a child can try to take in a deep breath. If the substance is at that crucial point of the V, you can see how it may be drawn into the windpipe, where it may cut off the flow of air.

To remove objects from a young child's throat, simply turn the child upside down, extend the neck slightly, and pat the child firmly on the back. If necessary, gently, yet firmly squeeze the chest. This forces air out of the lungs, pushing the lodged object ahead of it. A fairly rapid squeeze will lend greater force to the dislodging process.

If such a maneuver is not successful, get the child as quickly as possible to an emergency room. For choking, CPR is not useful, since it cannot remove the object from the windpipe. Gentle artificial respiration, however, may help by at least partially removing the foreign object, allowing some air into the lungs.

Keeping small objects from young toddlers is the best choking prevention. Many toy companies are now extremely careful to make toys safe for specific age groups. Read labels carefully and heed their advice. Small pieces of hard foods, such as nuts, fruit peelings, or raw vegetables, are also dangerous if given to a child before he can chew very well.

If your older children have toys that could choke a small child, teach them to keep the toys out of reach. A toddler puts everything she can hold into her mouth. It's an instinct. So it's up to you to protect her. Childproofing your home can be, and often *is*, life saving. Childproofing is a continuous process—keep a constant lookout for pieces of anything your child could choke on.

Just use good common sense, be there, and in a crisis, keep your cool!

CHAPTER ELEVEN

Early Childhood Health

Common Ailments

by Grace Ketterman

There's nothing more frustrating than a child who's in pain but can't tell you where it hurts. Here are some common ailments of babies and toddlers, and what you can do about them:

Upper-respiratory infection (URI) and the **common cold.** In cold climates, babies may have runny noses and hacking coughs most of the winter. These are more annoying and ugly than dangerous, but they may be complicated by a severe cough and/or earaches. Treating a mild cold is simple. An occasional dose of children's analgesic and simple antihistamine at naptime and bedtime will alleviate the symptoms.

Over-the-counter medications are usually fine and inexpensive. Ask your doctor or nurse about brands and dosages. It's also smart practice to give your child vitamins once a day unless she eats a lot of fresh foods—most 1-year-olds don't.

An old adage asserts that a cold, when treated vigorously, lasts about a week; when ignored lasts about seven days. Though true, treating a cold properly can help your child feel better during the get-well process.

Most medical professionals agree on three basic medications:

• Decongestants such as antihistamines and/or ephedrine help to dry mucous and make breathing easier. Toddlers dislike nasal sprays and drops, but these are reliable and instantaneously open stuffy noses.

• Aspirin-free pain relievers such as Tylenol help children to be less grouchy. Ask your doctor about appropriate dosages, because the recom-

————— ∼ —————

There's nothing more frustrating than a child who's in pain but can't tell you where it hurts.

Dr. Grace Ketterman

————— ∼ —————

207

mendation on the bottle may not be right for your child.

• Cough medicines can make the difference in whether your child is able to sleep or is kept awake. Once again, ask your medical advisor about the kind and dosage.

Vaporizers and properly elevated beds are also helpful. Most parents prefer cool-stream humidifiers, because these don't run the risk of making the delicate tissues of the respiratory passages tender, as hot-steam humidifiers do. Neither do they present the danger of burns. Propping up the head of your child's bed and providing a firm pillow will help him breathe more easily. This position can be achieved easily in a crib by adjusting the mattress. In an older toddler's bed, wood blocks, old books or magazines under the head of the bed will work. Two or three inches of elevation are enough to make a big difference.

One possible complication of a URI is an ear infection. Be sure to call your doctor if you think your child has an ear infection. Antibiotics are usually necessary to clear up this problem.

Croup. This is a scary illness caused by swelling of the vocal cords, usually from the virus that causes a cold. Your child awakes at night with a barking, seal-like cough. Breathing is labored, and she may look a bit pale or even bluish around the mouth. At first, most parents dash to the nearest emergency room. Usually, a quicker (and less expensive) remedy is a trip to the bathroom. Let your baby breathe in the steamy mist created by a hot shower—this should ease the symptoms. A dose of cough syrup and sips of cold fluids also help.

Earaches. These may occur from being outside in cold weather without adequate covering. But they are usually caused by a cold that has spread from the upper throat and nose into a child's middle ear. The swelling and fluid block the tiny tube which connects the ear and throat, allowing pressure to build and causing sharp pain.

Repeated, severe earaches can rupture the eardrum and cause hearing loss. First, give your baby a pain reliever (acetaminophen), then visit your doctor for evaluation and thorough treatment.

Falls. Almost all babies have one or more falls that are worrisome. Watch your child carefully and set strict boundaries for climbing. If your child does fall, check her carefully before picking her up. If she's crying, be grateful! Look for any deformity of arms and legs. Check for bruises and bleeding. With a flashlight, look at the round, dark center of the eyes (the pupil). It should get small when the light shines in it, and enlarge in the shade.

Danger signals that follow bad spills include pupils that do not react to light, vomiting, going limp or losing consciousness. If you have any doubts, take your baby to the nearest medical resource. Fortunately, most falls result in little or no injury, and children are up and running soon!

As your baby grows and learns to communicate, her ability to tell you how she's feeling will help you deal with these common ailments.

When to See the Doctor
by Patricia Rushford
Sniffles and sneezes are prevalent in small children, and parents frequently wonder when a visit to the doctor is necessary. Call or see your doctor if:

- Cold symptoms persist longer than a week or two
- Symptoms intensify
- There is persistent sore throat, increased redness, swelling and pain in neck glands or nodes
- Fever over 101°F lasts more than two days, or there is sudden reappearance of fever
- There is ear pain, loss of hearing, or drainage from ears
- Thick green or yellow discharge is present in the eyes, nose, ears or throat
- Shortness of breath or wheezing occurs
- There is productive cough (spitting up phlegm) with fever or chest pain
- Severe headache, stiff neck, lethargy, extreme fussiness or irritability occurs.

Illness Prevention
by James Judge
What can really help keep your baby out of the doctor's office? As usual, the answer is to get back to basics.

Wash your baby's hands frequently. Illnesses are infectious diseases transmitted from person to person. Viruses and bacteria are most readily transmitted when an infected person coughs, sneezes or wipes her nose without the aid of a tissue and then touches you. When you rub your eye or touch your nose or mouth, you've completed the circuit. Your 1- to 2-year-old's behavior is very oral; she considers no interesting object fully investigated until it has spent some time between her gums. So get neurotic about hand washing. Take advantage of her dedication to routine, repetition and inborn fascination with water play—make regular hand washing a part of your baby's daily routine. If a sibling has an active cold or flu, increase the frequency of hand washing even more.

Avoid places where infections are likely to be transmitted. You know the spots: cramped, crowded rooms filled with coughing and sneezing people. This is a pretty accurate description of many play groups and daycare situations (not to mention physicians' waiting rooms). Unfortunately, many parents may not be as conscientious about bringing children with "a little runny nose" to these places as you are. Try bringing your baby's own toys from home. Ask the child-care provider not to allow other children to play with them, and vice versa.

There will be times, especially at the height of the season, when you may have to ask parents not to bring their sick children to the nursery. If that doesn't work, try making arrangements for your child to be cared for elsewhere. Or you might want to be part of another solution: In many cases, one more adult volunteer may allow sick children to be separated from the healthy ones.

Keep your baby's immune system working at peak efficiency. Stress, whether physical or emotional, dramatically increases the likelihood that your baby will get sick. A tired, stressed-out, picky eater is an easy target for the next virus that comes her way. Be sure your baby gets plenty of rest, follow your doctor's advice regarding vitamin supplements and nutrition, and discipline yourself not to over-schedule your life or your baby's. All are important factors in keeping your child's immune shields up and working.

Fever Treatments

by William Sears

You will probably spend more time parenting your child through fever than treating any other single childhood symptom of illness. Parents need to understand what fever is and how to treat it.

What constitutes a fever? A rectal temperature greater than 100.5°F may be considered a fever. Most children have a "normal" oral body temperature of 98.5°F, but normal temperature varies among children, from 97° to 100°F. Many children show normal daily fluctuations in body temperature. It may be lower in the morning and during rest, and a degree higher in the late afternoon or during strenuous exercise.

What causes a fever? A fever is a *symptom* of an underlying illness, not an illness itself. Normal body temperature is maintained by a "thermostat" in a tiny organ of the brain called the hypothalamus, which regulates the balance between heat produced and heat lost in the body. A fever occurs when more heat is produced than can be released, thus raising your child's temperature. Germs from infection within your child's body release substances into the bloodstream called pyrogens (heat producers), which cause fever.

Any time there is a change from normal body temperature, the thermostat reacts to bring the temperature back to normal. For example, when your child is cold, he shivers to produce heat. When your child is warm or has a fever, the blood vessels of his skin become larger (as evidenced by his flushed cheeks), and his heart beats faster. These mechanisms allow more blood to reach the surface of the skin, releasing the excess body heat. A child with fever also sweats to cool his body by evaporation and breathes more quickly to get rid of the warm air. In addition to these general signs of fever, a child may have headaches, muscle aches and general fatigue.

When to worry about fever. Two kinds of infections cause fever: viral and bacterial. Viral infections are usually less worrisome and show the following features: The fever comes on suddenly in a previously well child; the fever is usually high (103° to 105°F); the fever is usually brought down by the methods outlined below; a child seems to feel better when the fever is brought down. When their children have viral infections, parents often say, "I'm surprised the fever is so high, because my child doesn't look or act that sick."

In a bacterial infection, the temperature may not be as high as that of a viral infection, but the fever does not come down as easily with the methods recommended for treating your child's fever. Also, when your child has a bacterial infection, he acts as sick as the high fever indicates.

When to call your doctor about fever. Remember, your doctor is more interested in how sick your child looks and acts than in how high your child's temperature really is. If your child does not act particularly sick, administer all the recommended methods to lower his temperature before calling your doctor.

How your child responds to temperature-lowering methods is one of the doctor's main concerns. The younger the infant, the more worrisome the fever. Any fever in an infant less than 4 months old should be reported to your doctor. If your child's temperature can't be lowered by using the methods suggested below, and if he is rapidly becoming more ill, call your doctor.

How to treat your child's fever. Medications can lower your child's temperature. The medications will reset the body's thermostat so that when the child's temperature is lowered by cooling (in a tepid bath), his body will not react to produce more heat. The most commonly used medications for lowering a child's temperature are aspirin and acetaminophen. In children, acetaminophen is safer and as equally effective at lowering fever as aspirin.

In addition to using acetaminophen to reset your child's thermostat, the following methods will remove excess heat from your child's system:

• Undress your child completely; at most, dress him in light, loose-fitting clothing. This allows excess heat to radiate out of his body. Avoid the tendency to bundle up your child when he has a fever; this will only cause his body to retain heat.

• Keep your child's environment cool. Decrease the temperature in his room, open a window slightly, or use an air conditioner or nearby fan to remove the heat that is radiating out of his body. Yes, your child may go outside when he has a fever. Fresh air is good for him.

• Give your child a lot of extra fluids when he has a fever; excess body heat has a dehydrating effect. Frequently give your child cool, clear liquids in small amounts.

• Give your child a cooling bath. If, in spite of all these other measures, your child's temperature remains over 103°F, or if he continues to be uncomfortable with the fever, place him in a tub of water and run the water all the way up to his neck. The water temperature should be warm enough not to be uncomfortable but cooler than his body temperature. Keeping your child in the cooling bath for 20 to 30 minutes should bring his temperature down a couple of degrees.

Remember, because a child with a fever is often uncomfortable, keep his body quiet and his soul at peace. Pray for your child, asking God to relieve his fever and the illness producing his discomfort.

Breathing Aids

by William Sears

Because the nasal passages are relatively small in a baby, even a slight amount of stuffiness can result in uncomfortable breathing. In an infant and child, the nose is like the front porch of a house: If you keep the nose clean, the rest of the breathing passages are likely to stay cleaner too. In fact, one of the best ways to prevent colds in your child is to keep the nose clear. Here's how:

Keep your child's sleeping environment free of allergens. The same little fuzzy things that keep your child cozy at night also spew allergens out into the air. Defuzz your child's sleeping environment. If your child wakes up every morning with a stuffy nose, chances are he is allergic to the dust collectors in the bedroom, such as stuffed animals, feather pillows, wool blankets and down comforters. If your child is highly allergic, try an air purifier in the bedroom. The HEPA type of air purifier is best.

Add moisture to the dry air in the bedroom. Breathing passages are lined with tiny filaments, called cilia, which support a layer of mucous. This protective system acts like a miniature conveyor belt that removes lint and other particles from inhaled air. Dry air, in effect, stops those conveyor belts, resulting in swollen, clogged airways.

Giving your child extra fluids during the day and running a vaporizer while he's sleeping helps thin secretions, making them easier to sneeze or cough out. Also, steam opens clogged breathing passages and helps drain secretions. Take your baby into the bathroom, close the door, turn on the hot water in the shower, and enjoy a steam bath together.

Maintaining the proper humidity in your child's sleeping environment will give the breathing passages the moisture they need. Humidity levels can be checked by using a hygrometer (available at hardware stores). A room humidity of 30 to 50 percent is ideal.

Choosing and using a vaporizer. Humid air is produced in three ways: shaking the water (ultrasonic), blowing it (impeller type), and boiling it (a vaporizer).

Humidifiers produce a *cool* mist. The newest are the ultrasonic type, which use high-frequency sound to break up water into mist. New studies reveal that ultrasonic mist may also contain the pulverized impurities in mineral-laden tap water. These minute particles (such as asbestos, lead and other minerals) can be breathed into the airways and may irritate the lower breathing passages. This potential danger can be minimized by using distilled water in an ultrasonic humidifier with a built-in particle filter or changeable demineralizing cartridges.

The main problem with impeller-type humidifiers is that they are likely to harbor bacteria and spew these germs into the air. I discourage the use of older rotating drum- and furnace-mounted humidifiers that hold a pool of stagnant water, though some do come with filters.

Vaporizers produce a *hot* vapor and deliver a more concentrated amount of mist over a smaller area. Because the water is boiled, bacteria and molds are killed, and minerals never leave the machine. Vaporizers are preferable to humidifiers for delivering moisture to breathing passages.

Tips for using vaporizers and humidifiers:

• Because vaporizers produce hot mist, they pose a burn hazard. Be sure to place the vaporizer out of your baby's grabbing distance.

• Clean vaporizers and humidifiers according to the manufacturers' suggestions at *least* once a week. Rinse well after cleaning.

• Change water daily and dry the vaporizer between uses.

• Use water (either distilled or tap) according to the manufacturers' suggestions.

• Place the vaporizer about two feet from your infant, and direct the jet across his nose to deliver concentrated humidity.

• Unless advised by your doctor, it is unnecessary to add medicine to the vaporizer water.

Unstuffing little noses. Babies can seldom blow their own noses. Here's how to "hose the nose" for them: Purchase saline nasal spray (a specially formulated salt-water mist solution available over the counter at a pharmacy). Hold your baby upright. Squirt one spray into each nostril. Next, lie your baby down for a minute with his head lower than his body. This allows the salt water to loosen the thick secretion and will stimulate your child to sneeze it to the front of the nose, where you can remove it with a nasal aspirator.

You can also make your own salt-water nose drops. Put a pinch of salt (no more than one-quarter teaspoon) in an eight-ounce glass of warm tap water. With a plastic eye dropper, squirt a few drops in each nostril. Be careful not to release the dropper bulb while it is still in your child's nose—doing so allows nasal secretions into the dropper or bottle, which contaminate the fluid. However, over-the-counter nasal spray is kinder to the lining of the nasal passages than homemade nose drops.

To use a nasal aspirator, squeeze the rubber bulb, then insert the plastic or rubber tip into the nose firmly enough to form a seal. Slowly release the bulb, letting the suction draw out the mucous plug. Do this two or three times in each nostril. After each use, suck soap and water into the aspirator and rinse well with plain water. Various shapes of nasal aspirators are available at your pharmacy.

Teach your child to blow his nose. You can begin to teach your child to "blow" at age 2 to 3. Teach him to blow out a candle, and then show him how to do it with his nose. Then blow your nose while your child holds a tissue for you. Next, let him do the same, and then blow noses together.

Blow gently. Blowing or sniffing too hard may drive secretions into the sinuses and prolong a cold. In fact, some nose specialists believe that it's better for a child to gently sniff the secretions back into the throat and expel them than to blow mucous into the sinuses.

Get to know your child's nose—what irritates it, what stuffs it. A clean nose increases your chances of having a healthier and happier child.

Treating and Preventing Ear Infections

by William Sears

Because of the frequency and severity of ear infections in young children, I want you to have a full understanding of their causes and treatment.

Children harbor germs to which they have not yet become immune in the secretions of their nose and throat. Because of the proximity of the nose and throat to the ears, germs commonly travel up the eustachian tube into the ear during a cold.

The eustachian tube in children often functions inadequately. The eustachian tube has two main functions: It serves to equalize the air pressure on both sides of the eardrum, allowing the eardrum to vibrate freely and produce sounds, and it drains the middle ear of the fluid and germs which may collect during a cold.

A child's eustachian tube is short, wide, straight, and sits at a horizontal angle, allowing germs to travel more easily from the throat up into the middle ear. As your child grows, the eustachian tube becomes longer, narrower, and sits at a more acute angle, thereby making it more difficult for germs and fluid to collect in the ear.

During a cold, fluid accumulates in the middle ear. If the eustachian tube does not function properly and the fluid remains trapped, germs may cause an infection of the fluid within the cavity of the middle ear. The infected fluid accumulates behind the eardrum, applying pressure on the eardrum and producing intense pain. If the pressure from the trapped fluid builds up too much, this fluid may rupture the eardrum, and you may notice drainage of the fluid outside the ear canal. This fluid resembles the secretions of a runny nose.

It is important for parents to be vigilant about recognizing the signs of a ruptured eardrum. The pressure is released when the eardrum ruptures, making a child *feel* better. But this is a false improvement; the infection still should be treated to allow the perforated area of the eardrum to heal. Continuous scarring of the eardrum can result in permanent hearing loss.

Ear infections often bother a child more at night than during the day. When she is lying down, the fluid presses down on her eardrum. Parents will often notice that their baby feels better when held in an upright position or allowed to stand up in her crib.

How to recognize an ear infection in your child. An older child can tell you when his ear hurts, but it is often difficult for a parent to recognize an ear infection in a pre-verbal child.

Here are some general signs of ear infections in a young child: Your baby starts off with a clear, runny nose but is reasonably happy; the nasal discharge progresses from runny to thick, and your child's behavior moves from happy to increasingly irritable.

Teething may be confused with ear infections, but when teething, your child should look generally well, and his throat and nose secretions should not be persistently yellow or green. The combination of a discharging nose—with or without yellow drainage from the eyes—and increasing crankiness should alert parents to the possibility of an ear infection. If you suspect an ear infection, consult a doctor.

Sometimes the fluid that builds up in the middle ear does not become infected and may not produce significant pain. This fluid will restrict movement of the eardrum, thus diminishing your child's hearing. Even if only fluid is in the middle ear and there is no infection, most children show some change in behavior as a result of their diminished hearing. This behavior may be the only sign to alert you of a middle-ear problem.

How to prevent ear infections. Most children, because of the eustachian tube structure, will have occasional ear infections. The following suggestions may help lessen the severity of these infections:

• Breastfeed your infant as long as possible. Breastfed infants have fewer ear infections.

• Control allergies. Allergies often cause fluid to build up in the middle ear, which can get infected. Food allergies (especially those caused by dairy products) and inhalant allergies (especially those caused by cigarette smoke and dust collected by items such as stuffed animals) are the most common.

• Observe your child's "cold pattern" and treat these colds early and appropriately. If your child has had previous ear infections and the usual sequence of events occurs—first a runny nose, then a snotty nose, then crankiness—it may be wise to seek medical attention. Do this at the snotty-nose stage—before the cold settles in your child's ears.

• Some medications prevent the frequent occurrence of ear infections. Your doctor can recommend what is best for your child.

I cannot overemphasize the importance of being vigilant in treating your child's ear infections. Recurrent ear infections usually occur during a stage of speech development. If a child's hearing is lost periodically during these formative years of speech development, he may show some speech delay and some permanent hearing loss.

Even more noticeable are the behavioral problems that occur with chronic ear infections. And poor school performance is a common result of chronic ear infections in the older child. Remember, a child who feels right usually acts right.

Smart Reactions to Allergies

by William Sears

Children with allergies frequently get down in the dumps. They wonder: "Why am I always sick? Why am I different? Why do I need all this medicine?" Sometimes a child feels his whole life revolves around his allergies.

The term *allergy* means "altered reaction": Something gets into your child's body and causes an unusual reaction. The offending substance, called an allergen, may be something in the air, something that touches the skin, or a certain kind of food. In this chapter, I will primarily discuss airborne allergens.

Allergens enter the body through the skin, the gastrointestinal tract or the respiratory tract and stimulate the immune system to produce antibodies. The presence of the allergen and the antibody in certain tissues, such as the membranes that line the respiratory tract, stimulates the production of substances called histamines. Histamines cause the blood vessels to dilate, which leads to redness of the skin, hives, excessive mucus secretion, runny eyes and nose, a cough, and the accumulation of fluid in the middle ear. Histamines also make the muscles around the breathing passages contract, causing wheezing and asthma.

How can you tell if your child is allergic? Here are the most common symptoms:

- runny nose (with clear secretions), watery eyes, seasonal sneezing and wheezing
- chronic cough
- circles under the eyes
- constant sniffling
- frequent colds and/or ear infections
- frequent skin rashes, such as eczema or hives
- night coughs and stuffy nose in the morning
- coughing during exercise
- diarrhea, abdominal pain and bloating
- lots of intestinal gas
- fatigue, behavior problems and headaches.

Treating allergies. Try to strike a balance when deciding about treatment of a child's allergies. Help your child understand that he has a medical problem and that most people have problems. You and he together are going to figure out how he can learn to live with it. He'll still be able to have a lot of fun.

If you can determine what things trigger your child's allergic reactions, you can remove many of these things in his environment. Common inhalant allergens include grass, trees, ragweed pollens, house dust, feathers, mold, mildew, tobacco smoke, wool, animal dander, cooking odors, deodorizers, air fresheners, fireplace smoke, house plants and aerosols.

Tracking down hidden inhalant allergies begins by "defuzzing" your child's bedroom. If your child has a lot of nighttime symptoms or awakens in the morning with a stuffy nose, it's possible that something in his bedroom is to blame. As much as possible, try to maintain a dust-free sleeping environment. Try the following:

- Use the bedroom only for sleeping. Dress, study and play in another bedroom.
- Keep the door to the bedroom closed.
- Use foam-rubber, non allergenic pillows. Avoid feather pillows.
- Cover mattress springs with dust-proof covers. Seal the zippers with tape.

- Purchase a non-allergenic mattress.
- Avoid fuzzy bedding and wash the linens frequently.
- Avoid wool blankets and down comforters.
- Remove fuzzy stuffed toys from the crib and bed. If your child is highly allergic, you may have to put all the fuzzy toys in a garbage bag and temporarily store them. Synthetic nylon toys stuffed with foam rubber tend to be less allergenic than others.
- Remove all clothes, books and toys from the bedroom. Or store clothing in a tightly zippered garment bag.
- Move house plants to an area in your home where your child spends little time.
- Remove paints, such as those used to decorate models, from areas where your child spends any time.
- Look for molds and mildew that collect in damp places. Mold may collect in the bedroom if you use humidifiers or vaporizers frequently.
- During pollen season, your child may collect pollen in his hair. Washing his hair nightly before going to bed may minimize reactions.
- Avoid using wall-to-wall carpet in your child's bedroom. Use washable throw rugs on wood or linoleum floors. If this is not possible, get carpet that is less likely to collect dust, and vacuum it daily. Do not vacuum while your child is in the house. Vacuum cleaners spread tiny dust particles into the air.
- Replace dust-collecting drapes or blinds with washable cotton or synthetic curtains or pull-down window shades. Remove upholstered furniture from your child's bedroom. Use wooden chairs or furniture with removable foam cushions and smooth, washable covers. Certain kinds of boards used in the construction of beds are made with formaldehyde. This is a highly allergenic material that should be removed from the bedroom of an allergic child. Any remodeling or redecorating should be done while your child is away—at summer camp or visiting Grandma.
- Clean and replace air filters frequently, especially if you have a forced-air heating system. You may need to place accessory filters in the registers of your child's bedroom. Highly allergic children benefit from electronic air filters. (The cost may be covered by medical insurance.)
- Furry or feathered pets should be kept out of your child's bedroom and preferably out of the house. Most children, given the choice, will elect to keep a pet despite allergic symptoms. It is wise to be sure that your child is not allergic to an animal before that animal becomes a

permanent house guest.

Allergists usually have free booklets on how to create a livable dust-free environment. Most parents find they do not have to take all of the above steps for their allergic child to improve.

Allergy shots. Allergy shots gradually build up your child's tolerance to an offending allergen. In deciding whether or not to recommend allergy shots for your child, a doctor considers whether the child is likely to grow out of his hay fever, or if there is a risk of the child developing more severe allergies. This risk must be weighed against the discomfort and inconvenience of several years of weekly or twice-weekly injections—with no guarantee that they will work.

Allergic Tendencies
by Audrey Hingley

The tendency to become allergic to typically harmless substances is usually inherited. Although children are not "born with asthma" or "born with allergies," they *are* born with a *tendency* to become allergic or asthmatic.

What a person becomes allergic to depends in part on what he is exposed to, as well as to the amount of exposure. A child who has inherited allergic tendencies may become sensitive to cow's milk shortly after birth, or to dog hair at age 6 after getting a pet dog. Throughout life, he may develop new allergies as he undergoes new exposures, and previous allergies may remain or fade away. For physicians as well as parents, diagnosis sometimes is difficult.

The first step to treating allergies is to detect which substances your child is allergic to. Close observation, elimination of suspected allergens for a trial period, and skin testing are the most commonly used methods. In a skin test, an allergist pricks or scratches the skin with an instrument containing a suspected substance, and observes the child's reaction to it (redness, swelling, and so on).

Once allergies are discovered, treatment may consist of removing the offending allergens when possible, medication and attempting to build up the child's resistance to allergens by allergy vaccine immunotherapy (allergy shots). Removal of the allergens is the preferred method if it can be carried out in a practical matter.

A number of different medicines are used to treat allergies and/or asthma. Antihistamines and decongestants are used for nasal symptoms of sneezing and itching. Bronchodilator drugs, such as beta agents and theophylline, are used for asthma sufferers. Bronchodilator aerosols, or inhalers, may also be prescribed. Inhalers are fast acting and tend to cause a minimum of side effects, but they do have abuse potential. To prevent abuse, follow this simple rule: If wheezing fails to respond significantly to the inhaler, or the effect is less than four hours in duration, call your doctor or visit the emergency room, depending on the severity of symptoms.

When you're looking for an allergist, seek qualified help. Sarah E. Kaluzny, communications coordinator for the American Academy of Allergy and Immunology, suggests you locate an Academy board-certified allergist. To determine if physicians are certified, "Just ask them," Kaluzny recommends. She adds that some allergists list their board certification in the Yellow Pages of the phone directory.

For more information or referral to a board-certified allergist in your area, call the Allergy Information Referral Line at their 24-hour, toll-free number: 800/822-ASMA. Or contact The American Academy of Allergy and Immunology, 611 East Wells St., Milwaukee, WI, 53202. 414/272-6071.

Common Vision Problems

by Grace Ketterman

Bryan was born with a blocked tear duct in one eye. This meant that the fluid that normally washes the eye keeping it healthy and clean could not flow properly. He often had infections requiring medication and causing considerable discomfort. Fortunately, when Bryan was about 3 months old, the problem corrected itself.

Other eye defects are not so easily cured. A common, generally inherited problem is strabismus, or "crossed-eyes." This condition occurs when a set of muscles on one side of the eye is shorter than the set on the other side and consequently pulls the eye inward or outward. While this defect does not seriously impair vision, it is considered unattractive, and most families choose to have it corrected by surgical means. This surgery is delicate but not dangerous and can make the eyes focus correctly. Your doctor can help you decide at what age this should be done.

Another birth defect involves eyelids with weak muscles that allow the lid to droop over the eye. This hinders good vision by acting like a curtain that covers the pupil, through which light and images reach the retina and sight center of the eye.

More serious defects involve the lenses, which diffuse light rays to the retina and create a clear image. At times a lens is cloudy or malformed at birth—a condition called "congenital cataracts." Most of these problems can be remedied by surgery, but timing is important. Consult your doctor.

Blindness at birth is rare, fortunately. It may be caused by a serious illness early in pregnancy, or it could be an inherited condition. It may involve the entire eye, the lining of the eye (retina), or the optic nerve, which collects all the fibers from the tiny cells in the retina and sends their messages to the brain for interpretation as vision. Rarely, if ever, can blindness of this sort be corrected.

Eye infections are common in young children. They are usually caused by viruses or bacteria. The eyes turn red, there is crusting of the lids, and usually discomfort results. Little children have a tendency to rub their eyes, which aggravates the irritation. Medication to treat any serious eye infection must be prescribed by your physician.

Steps to Good Foot Care

by Grace Ketterman

Recently I observed my 20-month-old grandson at play. He was running, climbing, and stretching up on his toes. His chubby legs are straight and his feet are aligned perfectly—he is a well-coordinated child.

But not all children are as blessed. The grandson of a dear friend is an example: His toes turn inward so much that he tends to stumble over his own feet. Other children have flat arches, and their toes may turn outward. These most common defects of children's feet are congenital— that is, children are born with the problem.

Bone specialists tell us that these foot conditions are created by the twisting of one of three bone structures: the femur (thigh bone), the tibia (the large bone in the lower leg), or certain metatarsal (foot) bones. Serious malformations may require surgery to make the twisted bone straight. After surgery, a cast is applied and worn for several weeks.

Few deformities, however, are so severe. Most feet become reasonably straight as growth occurs. By early adolescence, these children are nearly as adept as their peers.

No one knows for certain what causes these mild defects. One theory is that the position of a baby in the uterus before birth may cause them. Other factors, such as heredity, may be even more important.

Orthopedic doctors usually recommend careful diagnosis but little treatment. They have studied children who have worn corrective shoes and had intensive treatments—such as wearing a cast. In most cases, these children seemed no better by adolescence than those who had received no special treatment. There are, however, some helpful measures you may wish to try. I always feel better when I'm putting some effort into correcting problems, even though a perfect outcome is not guaranteed.

Here are my suggestions:

• As early as you are aware of a deformity, gently but firmly massage those feet in the direction opposite to that in which they turn. Do this several times daily for a few minutes. When your baby is asleep, turn her feet (or foot) outward or inward, whichever is appropriate. Feet will hold that new position for only a short time, but it may help.

• As your child begins to sit up, do not allow her to sit cross-legged ("Indian style") for any length of time. Teach your child to turn her feet as far as possible in the direction opposite the defect, holding them that way for as long as she can comfortably do so.

• Be certain your doctor investigates the degree of the problem and its tendency to correct itself. If your doctor believes surgical correction is necessary, seriously consider cooperating with the recommendation so that your child's correctable problem will be solved.

Skin-Care Strategies

by Grace Ketterman

The skin often is overlooked as one of the most important parts of the body. Yet proper care for your infant's skin will prevent serious problems. Here are five fundamental guidelines:

1. Keep it clean. Millions of tiny openings in the skin lead to oil and sweat glands and hair follicles. In babies, body hair is usually so fine and light that it can hardly be seen, so we tend to overlook those tiny pores through which germs may enter. Clean your baby's skin daily with mild soap and warm water.

2. Keep it soft. Babies start to form perspiration at about 3 weeks of age. If their outer layer of skin (the epidermis) is dry, the oil and sweat secretions cannot flow out of the pores to the surface of the skin; they will cause tiny, white bumps to form on your child's face. These bumps, called "milia," often are a source of needless worry. Daily use of a mild baby lotion will help soften the epidermis so that it becomes soft enough to allow secretions to escape. Don't use baby oil, because bacteria can actually feed on it and cause infections.

3. Keep it dry. When babies stay in wet diapers too long, they may suffer serious diaper rashes. Disposable diapers usually have liners that help prevent such irritation. Excessive perspiration also can cause irritation, so keep your baby cool. Sponge off the skin occasionally, and apply powder or kitchen cornstarch generously.

4. Keep it free of infection. Skin infections are common in babies who are handled by many people and who crawl on the floor where there are germs. Generally, the above care will result in healthy skin that resists infection. Watch any red areas or yellow-headed pustules (pimples) carefully, but don't bother them. If they spread or don't begin to heal in a few days, call your baby's doctor. In the summertime especially, skin infections can spread quickly and become serious infections.

5. Take special care of the scalp. Many parents are concerned about care of their baby's hair due to the "soft spot" (fontanel). On the top and front of infants' heads is a spot where the bones eventually will join together to form the strong, protective skull. Since babies need to grow, however, these bones are separated for several months, leaving only a thick skin (scalp) to cover the brain. You need not be afraid of gentle, thorough cleansing of baby's scalp, because it is strong enough to take such handling.

Regular shampoos with mild soap, brisk rubbing with a towel, and careful brushing or combing will prevent the irritating collection of oil on your baby's skin. Use a mild baby lotion after shampooing to prevent drying and clogging of those pores.

Understanding Childhood Obesity

by William Sears

If your child's weight is 10 percent greater than the average weight for his sex, height and age, he is overweight and potentially obese. If your child weighs 20 percent more than his ideal weight, he is fat or obese.

Ten to 20 percent of all children are obese.

But what the mirror shows and what your child feels are often even more important than what the scales or growth charts say. That is why the amount of excess fat your child has means more than his actual weight.

Why they become overweight. The fat-cell theory postulates that fat tissue increases by the size or number of fat cells. During a child's first two years, the critical period for fat-cell development, his fat cells increase in number. Lesser spurts in fat-cell number occur at about 7 years of age and again during adolescence. After growth is finished and a person has reached adulthood, his fat cells do not increase significantly in number. Thereafter, any increase or decrease in fat tissue results from a change in the size of these cells.

If a child is overfed during infancy (or middle childhood or adolescence), the excess calories he ingests may produce an excess number of fat cells. Continued overfeeding will cause these fat cells to get larger. This results in a tendency toward obesity, which simply means that a person has more fat cells to get fat. This theory gives rise to the concern that a child who has an excessive number of fat cells may have to watch his weight all his life.

Perhaps the most important determinant of childhood obesity is the body type of his or her parents. Heredity plays an important role in one's tendency toward obesity. According to statistics, overweight parents produce overweight children. Because of hereditary factors, some children have a higher obesity potential than others. But whether or not they actually become obese depends on many environmental factors.

Calorie balance. Weight control requires a balance between the number of calories a child takes in and the number of calories he burns up. Children need calories for three basic purposes: to maintain bodily functions, to grow, and to obtain fuel for exercise. Adults' caloric requirements change only with exercise, whereas children's caloric requirements are greatest during periods of rapid growth. If a child consumes more calories than he needs for growth and exercise, the excess calories are deposited as excess fat.

Appestat. Appetite control, or "appestat," means a child consumes just the right number of calories for his needs and has an appetite that adjusts to his changing needs. There are many factors that affect a child's appetite control, and it is not completely known why some children cannot control their appetites.

Early feeding practices. It is possible that early feeding habits may affect a child's ability to control his appetite. One of the early feeding habits that may effect eventual appetite control is breastfeeding.

Whether or not breastfed infants are less likely to become obese than formula-fed infants is controversial. In my opinion, though, breast-feeding does lower the risk of obesity for the following reason: Breast milk changes to accommodate the changing needs of an infant. The fat content of breast milk changes during each feeding and also at various times of the day, usually being higher in fat in the morning and lower in the evening.

A nursing infant initially gets foremilk, which is low in fat. Continued sucking rewards him with the creamier hindmilk that is high in fat and calories. When the infant has obtained sufficient hindmilk, the high-calorie milk *may* signal his appestat that he is full, so that he stops sucking when both his sucking needs and his appetite are completely satisfied.

It is often difficult for a mother to tell whether her baby is hungry or thirsty. When breastfed babies are thirsty, they may suck a shorter period of time and less vigorously to obtain the foremilk. The bottle-fed baby, however, does not enjoy the advantages of different milks for different needs. He gets the same high-calorie milk whether he is thirsty or hungry, and the same high-calorie milk at each feeding.

As an infant grows older, he needs fewer calories per pound of body weight. Therefore, breast milk gradually decreases in fat and calories accordingly. Since there is a general agreement that obesity is not healthy, it seems logical that the changes in caloric content of breast milk are in accordance with God's design for preventing obesity in his children.

Some breastfed babies do appear to be very fat during their first year, especially those babies who nurse "all day and all night." but nearly all of these babies lose their excess fat by the time they are 2 years old.

Another early feeding practice that may contribute to obesity is the early introduction of solid foods. This also is controversial, but the high rate of obesity in certain cultures that introduce solid food at early ages suggests that this practice may lead to obesity in some children.

Temperament. A child's temperament is also a factor in obesity. Children who have quiet, placid personalities—those who enjoy more sedentary activities—have a high obesity potential. A vicious cycle can develop: The less active a child is, the fatter he becomes, and the less interested he becomes in physical activities. Fat children do not always eat more than lean children, and some may even eat less. But fat children do eat more than their level of exercise requires. Children with normal weight and appetite control reach a balance between exercise and appetite. As they exercise less, they eat less, and vice versa.

Obese children, however, do not achieve this balance. As they exercise less, they do not eat proportionally less. This imbalance between calories and exercise is an important concept in appetite control. I believe more childhood obesity is caused by too little exercise than by too much eating.

Digestive Troubles

by Grace Ketterman

Stomach trouble in a child younger than 2 is always a matter of concern, but rarely panic. Vomiting, the forceful emptying of the contents of the stomach by a reverse motion of the stomach muscles, is usually preceded by a sense of nausea, paleness of the face or about the mouth, and a "sick" look and feel. Often a baby won't want to eat or drink, letting you know her stomach needs to be at rest.

After a bout of vomiting, wait until your child acts thirsty, and then offer her a small amount of a clear, carbonated drink, such as ginger ale or lemon-lime, diluted half-and-half with water. Only half an ounce at a time is needed. If your child keeps this down, wait 20 to 30 minutes and try another half-ounce or ounce. Increase the amount if your child wants more and can keep it down.

If the vomiting lasts longer than two feedings, or if your baby cannot keep down the clear liquid after several hours, call your doctor. He will probably recommend a formula called Pedilyte. This is specially prepared to replace salt and other elements important to preventing the complications of stomach upsets.

Feeding your sick child. Other liquids that may appeal to your baby include liquid fruit-flavored gelatin, weak tea and diluted fruit juice (such as apple juice). Avoid solid foods and milk for a day or two. Also avoid ice cream and any rich or fat-laden foods. These are hard to digest and may prolong the illness. Gradually return your child's diet to its normal routine, starting with weakened formula and adding starchy foods, applesauce or apples, bananas, cereals and other foods. Watch for the return of her appetite and general sense of well-being.

Causes of diarrhea. Diarrhea, the excretion of bowel movements that are "loose" or watery and frequent, often involve cramping and pain during and between the movements. This may be due to some food intolerance, but more commonly it is due to an infection of the lining of the intestinal tract. In temperate climates, the usual cause is a virus, and the duration is a few days or less. In warmer climates, especially when sanitary conditions are poor, bacteria may be the cause. Bacterial infections are more serious and usually require antibiotics.

For milder infections, the clear liquid diet listed above will usually be enough. *Should the problem last more than two days, however, or if your child shows evidence of dehydration, be sure to see your doctor.*

These are the signs of dehydration:

• Scanty urine output—your baby's diapers are dry for longer periods of time than usual.

• The mouth is not moist and the tongue is dry.

• The skin is not as elastic and soft as normal. It feels "doughy."

• The eyes appear sunken a bit.

Do not wait for these signs to become marked. If you see one or more of them in the course of prolonged or severe vomiting or diarrhea, go at once to your doctor's office or an emergency room.

It is common for diarrhea to follow several days of treatment with antibiotics for an infection. This is due to the destruction of the normal, healthy bacteria in the intestinal tract. Usually this will correct itself in a few days. Giving a child a concentrate of healthy bacteria in cultured buttermilk, yogurt or cheese will help reestablish normal "flora" or bacterial growth, and the diarrhea will stop. If this continues, however, be sure to call your physician.

Treating Constipation

by William Sears

Annette became concerned about 1½-year-old Kimberly when the child started hugging her legs to her chest and getting red in the face. Afterward, Annette would find stools in Kimberly's diaper that resembled rabbit droppings. As her mom discovered, Kimberly had constipation—a highly treatable condition.

Constipation refers to the consistency of stools and the difficulty in passing them, not to the frequency of bowel movements. Some infants and small children normally have bowel movements only once every three to five days. If your child does not appear uncomfortable, she is not constipated. If her bowel movements are three to four days apart (or longer), but are reasonably soft and are passed without difficulty, she is not constipated. A constipated infant draws her legs up into her abdomen and becomes red in the face as she strains to pass hard, pellet-like stools.

Since an infant's rectum is often small, the passage of a hard stool may cause a small tear in the wall of the rectum. This is called a rectal fissure. It may produce a few streaks of fresh blood in the stool or a few drops of blood on the diaper. Rectal fissures can start a vicious cycle of constipation in an infant, because it hurts to pass a hard stool over this tear. Your baby may voluntarily hold onto the stool, creating more constipation. If your child has a rectal fissure, apply a small amount of glycerin over the area to soothe it and ease the passage of stools. Persistently black, tarry or bloody stools indicate bleeding in the intestines. Notify your doctor if this occurs.

Constipation in infants. Breastfed babies are rarely constipated, although after the newborn stage they may go several days or a week between stools. Constipation can be a problem for babies who have started solids, and also for formula-fed infants.

Rice cereal, bananas, apples and carrots are all constipating foods. Stay away from these if constipation is a problem for your baby. Instead, encourage her to eat foods that have a laxative effect, such as prunes, pears, apricots and peaches.

Babies usually accept diluted prune juice; start with one tablespoon a day and work up to eight ounces. Your baby might like prune purée, or you may have to disguise it by mixing the strained prunes with another favorite food. Try to give your constipated infant two or three tablespoons of strained prunes daily.

Offer your child water frequently between meals or, if she is exclusively formula-fed, between feedings. Smaller, more frequent feedings may also help lessen constipation in a formula-fed infant. You may want to experiment with different kinds of formula to see if another type makes bowel movements easier. Too much cow's milk may produce constipation.

Adding fiber to your infant's diet will help with constipation. Fiber softens stools by drawing water into them. It also adds bulk to stools, which makes them pass more quickly through your child's intestines. Bran cereals, graham crackers and other whole-grain breads and crackers are good sources of fiber for babies.

When your infant is having difficulty passing a stool, insert a glycerin suppository or liquid glycerin from a dropper high into her rectum. (These are available at drug stores and don't require a prescription.) Inserting the glycerin is especially helpful if she has a rectal fissure. For a tiny baby, you may have to cut the suppository in half and insert only the pointed top end. Hold the baby's buttocks together for a few minutes so that the glycerin will dissolve.

If diet changes are not effective in resolving your baby's constipation, your doctor may recommend a stool softener such as Colase, Maltsupex or Metamucil. Mineral oil, one tablespoon a day until the stools soften, may also be helpful.

Constipation in the older child. In addition to the kinds of diet changes suggested for infants, the older child needs some other measure to resolve constipation, since she can now choose whether or not to respond to the urge to defecate. Sometimes older children who are chronically constipated will soil their pants. The soiling is due to the leaking of stools from the lower intestinal muscles that have been weakened by chronic constipation.

Teach your child to respond immediately to the urge-to-go signal and not to hold onto her stools. Explain that not paying attention to the signal weakens the "doughnut muscles" around the rectum and that this will eventually cause her to have pain when she has a bowel movement. Tell her to "go when you have to go."

In addition to the high-fiber foods mentioned for infants, your older child's diet should include fiber in the form of green leafy vegetables and raw fruits. Potentially constipating foods for the older child include rice, cheese, bananas and chocolate. Encourage your older child to drink lots of liquids, at least four eight-ounce glasses of water daily.

In addition to the stool-softeners mentioned above, older children may use laxatives. Sometimes prescription laxatives may also be necessary. If the above measures fail to produce normal bowel movements, you may need to start your child's treatment/regimen with a clean slate by giving her an enema.

How to give an enema. In babies, use a Fleet enema specifically formulated for infants. Apply petroleum jelly to the tip of the syringe. Gently insert the tip into your baby's rectum (as you do with a thermometer), allowing it to seek its own path. Then squeeze gently. Remove the syringe and hold your baby's buttocks together. Give the enema three to five minutes to work before you let go.

In a child over 3, you can use an adult-type Fleet enema. For a 30- to 60-pound child, use half a dose; over 60 pounds, use a full dose. Place your child on her side and flex her upper leg toward her abdomen. After you have inserted the enema, hold the buttocks together for 10 minutes, if possible, and then place your child on the toilet. An enema can be repeated after an hour if necessary.

CHAPTER TWELVE

Nutrition and Dental Care

Sorting Out Sugars

by William Sears

Infants and children are sugarholics—they come by it naturally. Fifty percent of the calories in human milk—the nutritional standard—comes from sugars. And in a healthy diet for infants, half the daily calories are from sugars.

Kids crave sweets because they need a lot of energy—mental and physical. Sugars are the body's main fuel. Each molecule in sugar is like a tiny power pack, energizing cells to do their work. Sugars come in two forms, simple and complex, and each type behaves differently in the body. Nutritionally speaking, there is no such thing as a bad sugar. It's how it is processed and packaged that determines whether it is good, better or best for your child.

Which sugar is which? Good sugars, or refined sugars, go by the names of *glucose, dextrose* and *sucrose*. This is the sweet-tasting stuff in the sugar bowl, in candy, icings and syrup. Because it is cheap and sweet, this is the sugar most often added to commercial foods. A small amount of these sugars won't harm a child, but too much of these good sugars can become bad.

Take a ride with refined sugars from mouth to blood stream, and you'll see how they behave in the body. These simple sugars contain only one or two molecules—they require little or no intestinal digestion. So when a spoonful of sugar hits the intestines and immediately enters the blood stream, the roller coaster ride begins.

> *Infants and children are sugarholics . . . because they need a lot of energy.*
>
> Dr. William Sears

High blood sugar that comes from the rush of eating a doughnut or a piece of cake triggers the release of *insulin*—a hormone needed to escort these sugars into the body's cells. The initially high blood sugar is tackled rapidly, causing the sugar level to plunge to a sugar low (also known as "hypoglycemia" or "sugar blues"). This low blood sugar triggers stress hormones that squeeze stored sugar from the liver, sending the blood sugar back up. The ups and downs of the blood sugar level and the hormones scrambling to smooth the coaster ride also result in roller coaster-like behavior in a child.

Check out alternatives to refined sugars. For instance, replace a cup of sugar in an apple pie with fruit-juice concentrate or honey. These are healthier, because they contain *fructose* and small quantities of vitamins and minerals. When substituting for sugar, use half the amount the recipe calls for. (Avoid giving honey to infants before they're 1 year old because of the risk of botulism.)

Fructose sugars are obtained primarily from fruits. These sugars taste sweet, but less so than the syrups and frostings made with refined sugars. We call these sources of quick energy "better" because they do not excite the hormone roller coaster as do their sweet relatives in the birthday cake. Blood-sugar swings and consequent behavior swings are less drastic under the influence of an orange than a candy bar.

Milk sugar, or *lactose,* also behaves better in the body, because it doesn't rush into the blood stream as fast as the refined stuff. Another plus for fructose and lactose is the company they keep: Unlike the megadoses of concentrated sugar in granular sweets, the fruit, vegetable and milk sugars enter the intestines with other nutrients, so the rush into the blood stream is not so fast.

The best sugars are complex polysaccharides, better known as starches. These include pasta, peas, potatoes, grains, rice, soy beans, millet, beans, lentils, seeds and nuts. These nutrients enter the intestines like a long line of simple-sugar molecules holding hands. During digestion, they enter the blood stream one by one, a time-released energy capsule that provides slow, steady energy and prolongs the feeling of fullness.

Shaping young tastes. Infants who enter childhood with sweet, fatty or salty tastes in their mouths are likely to continue these cravings into childhood and probably also adulthood. Infancy is the only time in your child's life when you can completely curb the candy.

Years ago I had a theory that if during the first two years you exposed young taste buds and developing intestines to *only* healthy foods, your child would refuse junk foods later.

My wife and I tried this experiment with our children. For the first three years we gave our babies only healthy food. We kept out of our diet added salt, table sugar and unhealthy fats. Our sixth child, Matthew, was really junk-food deprived. What happened when Matthew went out into the sugar-coated world of birthday parties and candy giving? Of course he had sticky fingers and icing on his face, but he did not *overdose*. Halfway through the mound of icing or chocolate delight, Matthew would stop and convey the "I don't feel good" signs of sick tummy. Now our children know to scrape off the frosting and just eat the cake.

Even as young as 3, children make the food connection: I eat well—I feel well; I eat poorly—I feel poorly. Health-food-primed babies seldom overindulge—that's the best we can hope for in raising a healthy kid.

Cholesterol Concerns

by Karby Allington

Your doctor wants to do a cholesterol test on your 3-year-old. Is this necessary at such a young age? What if it's high? Does the doctor really expect you to get a 3-year-old to follow a diet that most adults can't stick to?

Your physician reminds you of your family's history of heart disease. Prevention can't start too soon, so you have the test. The results? Normal. But the doctor says a low level now doesn't guarantee a low level in 10 years and recommends checking this regularly.

Whether or not your toddler has a cholesterol test, and regardless of the results, keep in mind that there is no immunity to heart disease. However, you can give yourself some peace of mind by starting a heart-healthy diet now—not just for your child, but for the whole family. Since your toddler gives you enough "nos" during your day, these suggestions focus on what you *can* do for him.

Choose healthy fats. Fats from nuts and from olive and canola oils actually reduce your blood cholesterol. Nut butters (such as peanut and almond) *in their natural form* (meaning they don't have added fats) make great sandwiches. Snack on peanuts and raisins. Canola oil can be substituted for any vegetable oil, and olive oil is wonderful in salad dressings and spaghetti sauces.

Take advantage of fat-free products. Ice cream, sour cream, cheese, salad dressings, yogurt and mayonnaise are only a few of the many products available in fat-free form. Beware of products that claim to have a fat-free *percentage,* such as "96 percent fat free." This misleading claim often portrays a product as less fatty than it actually is.

Add fiber to your diet. Certain types of fibers also promote a reduction in cholesterol levels. You can replace a half cup of flour with oat bran in almost any recipe. Serve steaming oatmeal sweetened with apple butter for a hearty breakfast.

Introduce your family to dried beans, a great finger food for toddlers. The canned variety is convenient and highly nutritious, as opposed to most other canned foods. Carrots and apples (though not their juices) also supply this type of fiber. If these are new foods for your family, add them gradually. Children's bodies especially need time to adjust to an increased fiber intake.

Replace convenience and fast foods. Much of the fat and cholesterol in your child's diet may be "hidden" in packaged and processed foods. Bake wedges of pita bread until crispy to replace fatty crackers. Serve pretzels in place of chips. Make a delicious smoothie with tofu, banana and frozen apple-juice concentrate for a snack or a meal on the run. This same mixture can be frozen on a stick to replace ice-cream treats.

In six minutes, you can bake a potato in the microwave and replace a frozen dinner. Top it with non fat cottage cheese or fat-free sour cream. Keep a "veggie grab bag" in a plastic container filled with water in the fridge. Stock it with your child's favorite vegetables, cut up and ready to eat. (Be sure to change the water daily.) This will be especially appealing if it's something your toddler can get to on his own.

The goal for you and your child is to develop a heart-healthy diet over time. Don't expect immediate perfection. Your chances of success are much greater with slow, gradual changes that the whole family makes together.

Fast Snacks for Healthy Eating
- Celery sticks with fat-free, soft cream cheese
- Fruit salad: a crunchy combination of chopped bananas, apples, grapes, oranges, melons and berries tossed with lime juice and a little honey
- Grape-Nuts and vanilla yogurt
- Baked potato (zapped in the microwave for two to three minutes)

topped with bacon bits, chives, salsa, chopped broccoli, shredded mozzarella cheese, low-fat sour cream, and so on.

- Apricot halves and cottage cheese
- Quickie shake: Low-fat milk blended until frothy with one-quarter cup berries or half a banana, a dash of spice (cinnamon or nutmeg) and vanilla, sweetened to taste
- Tuna or chicken salad on crackers or Melba toast
- Dairy booster: Use low-fat milk to make instant pudding, tapioca or baked custard
- Refried beans spread on fresh corn tortilla triangles, sprinkled with salsa, shredded low-fat cheese and seasonings, heated until cheese melts
- Cranberry spritzer: two ounces of cranberry juice mixed with eight ounces of sparkling water in a tall glass with ice and lemon slices
- Mozzarella sticks and pre-peeled baby carrots
- Pita bread stuffed with leafy lettuce, tomato and green pepper slices, sprouts, shaved turkey, and thinly sliced provolone
- Apple slices and sugar-free fruit-flavored yogurt

Identifying Food Allergies

by Karby Allington

Parents seeking to prevent allergic reactions in their children may become frustrated by conflicting information. Many food intolerances, such as food poisoning, headaches or digestive difficulties, are wrongly classified as food allergies. In reality, food allergies promote reactions that involve the immune system. They are generally reflected in the skin (as a rash or hives), the gastrointestinal tract (as a swollen tongue or diarrhea) or the respiratory tract (as watery eyes or wheezing).

In spite of the confusion, there are some practical things you can do to detect, treat, and even prevent food allergies in your children while they are still babies.

Know your risk factors. The most common allergens (foods that cause an allergic reaction) are milk, soy, eggs, fish, nuts, wheat, citrus and chocolate. If you or your spouse have food allergies, or if your baby has asthma, your baby has an increased risk for allergies. If she is at risk, delaying the introduction of these foods may prevent the onset of an allergy.

Be an allergy sleuth. Allergic reactions may be immediate, or they may develop over time after repeated exposure to an allergen. A written food log can help link your baby's reactions to specific foods. For example, if your baby breaks out in hives after eating french toast, you might assume an egg allergy. A food log that tracks all foods may prevent the onset of an allergy.

To pin down a suspected food, eliminate it completely from your baby's diet for one to two weeks. (It's unlikely that a nutritional imbalance will result in this short time.) If symptoms subside after the elimination diet, reintroduce the food. Reappearance of symptoms confirms the allergy. *A word of caution:* If your baby's reaction to the food was severe, consult your physician before reintroducing the food.

The more information you gather before visiting an allergist, the more helpful your session will be. In addition, write down and ask every question that concerns you. If the answers are highly technical or evasive, don't be afraid to seek a second opinion.

How to treat confirmed allergies. The only way to treat a food allergy is to avoid that food completely. If your baby is still nursing, you should eliminate the allergen from your own diet as well. Learn all names for the food. For instance, a food that claims to be "non-dairy" may contain casein, which is derived from milk.

If your child's reaction is severe, keep epinephrine on hand to treat an accidental consumption of the food. Instruct care givers on which foods to avoid and how to treat emergencies.

Hopeful allergy facts. Although children are the largest population affected by food allergies, only seven-and-a-half percent actually have them. The majority of children grow out of them, leaving only one to two percent of adults affected. The earlier you detect an allergy, and the more rigorously you adhere to the elimination diet, the greater the chance that your child will outgrow it.

Once you get down the facts, allergies are not difficult to understand. As an informed parent, you can take concrete steps to identify possible allergens and prevent their symptoms.

The Truth about Milk Allergies

by Karby Allington

Amber was a thriving 2-year-old who loved milk. But her mother sometimes worried. Amber was prone to ear infections, and some friends had suggested dairy products were the cause. Julie wondered if she was "poisoning" her child.

Dairy products are often blamed for runny noses, intestinal disorders, ear infections, diabetes, anemia and even behavioral problems.

Because food allergies are difficult to diagnose, research findings are controversial. Studies show milk products are among the most common allergens for children. Diagnosis is difficult and should be a continuous process. However, kids often outgrow dairy allergies. The allergic 3-year-old may become a healthy, milk-imbibing 4-year-old.

Some research indicates a link between ear infections and milk consumption in sensitive children. This is substantiated by parents who have been able to avoid surgery or decrease use of antibiotics by removing dairy products from their child's diet.

Overconsumption of milk (one quart or more per day) puts your toddler at risk for anemia because it replaces iron-rich foods.

The relationship between milk and other ailments is not well documented at this time. But the majority of 2- to 3-year-olds receive more benefit than harm from dairy products due to the nutrients provided.

Parents who feel they need to eliminate dairy products from their toddler's diet also need to compensate for these nutrients:

Calcium. Calcium is so vital that the body will sacrifice the bones to keep a constant supply in the blood stream. Osteoporosis (brittle bones) does not appear until years after it is possible to remedy it. One- to 3-year-olds need two-and-a-half cups of milk per day to get their recommended 800 milligrams of calcium. To get the same calcium from non-dairy sources, you would need six cups of broccoli, 14 oranges or one-and-a-quarter pounds of tofu. Vegetable sources of calcium are also bound up in chemicals called oxalates and are not as well absorbed by the body.

Protein. Experts now agree that the required amount of protein for 1- to 3-year-olds is about one-third less than previously thought. It used to be difficult for toddlers to get the necessary protein without milk, cheese or yogurt. Today, if your child is dairy free, he can meet his daily protein need with two ounces of meat, four tablespoons of peanut butter, two eggs or one cup of dried beans.

Riboflavin. Milk products are also an excellent source of riboflavin (vitamin B-2). A toddler must eat large amounts of eggs, meat and dark leafy greens to get enough riboflavin without milk. This nutrient is important in the body's ability to produce energy.

If you suspect your child is allergic to dairy products, work closely with your doctor to diagnose the problem. Make a list of symptoms that appear related to milk intake. Then eliminate all dairy products for two or three weeks. Continue to keep a written account of symptoms. Then reintroduce the dairy products. If allergic symptoms reappear, your child is probably sensitive. Unfortunately, more objective tests for food sensitivity are not reliable.

Eliminating all dairy products while still ensuring adequate nutrition will be easier with the help of your doctor or a registered dietitian. For the allergy-sensitive child, it's well worth the effort.

Vegetarian Options for Babies

by Karby Allington

"A vegetarian diet is unsafe for small children. Animal products ensure proper development."

Do you agree with this? Research has shown that, overall, a vegetarian diet is cheaper, better for the environment, and promotes a longer life span with fewer chronic diseases. Wouldn't our babies benefit from such a diet?

Subtle differences. Most of the six to eight million vegetarians in the United States fall into one of two categories: *Lacto-ovo-vegetarians* consume eggs and dairy products, but not animal flesh. *Vegans,* or strict vegetarians, don't consume any animal food. (You'll hear other terms: macrobiotic, fruititarian, live- or raw-foods diet; but the above really sums up most vegetarians.) Despite their differences, most vegetarians agree that their choice involves more than just not eating meat. They're striving for a diet of wholesome foods that haven't been overly processed.

Nutritional impact. Both types of vegetarians end up with a diet that is higher in fiber and lower in fat and calories than the average American diet. Although this is desirable for adults, babies' nutritional needs are slightly different.

Because growing requires a lot of energy, babies actually need more calories per pound of body weight than adults. This, combined with a baby's small and sporadic appetite, makes it important for vegetarian parents to emphasize higher-calorie choices in their baby's regimen.

The vegetarian emphasis on whole grains may provide too much fiber for a baby's immature digestive system. To prevent undue stress, add refined grains to your baby's diet.

If you choose a lacto-ovo vegetarian diet for your baby, the eggs and dairy products will usually provide adequate nutrition. As with any baby, allow your doctor to monitor your baby's iron stores and growth during routine checkups.

A strict vegetarian diet, however, requires careful attention to the key nutrients your baby needs. Deficiencies of calcium, iron, vitamin B-12, riboflavin and protein can be related to anemia, neurological damage or cracks on the sides of your baby's mouth. Growth and bone development may also be affected. It is possible for committed vegan parents to raise a healthy baby. By working closely with a knowledgeable physician, you can monitor your baby's nutritional parameters and the potential need for supplements.

Making a choice. The best diet for your baby is the one that works best for your family. Although a vegetarian lifestyle requires more effort on your part, recent evidence about the relationship between diet and disease may influence you to go the extra mile.

Whether you adopt a strict vegetarian diet or not, including vegetarian cuisine in your baby's early diet is beneficial. Growing accustomed to the taste and texture of dried beans and grains at an early age will broaden your baby's tastes and possibly promote a healthier adult diet.

Allow flexibility within your boundaries. Even strict vegetarians recommend avoiding power struggles over meat. Rigid diet rules may backfire, whereas allowing a little experimentation even with "off limits" foods may diffuse the issue. Work with your child as you can, and continue to model the diet to which you are committed. Your child's nutritional status must take precedence over indulging your child to keep him happy, or complying with a certain set of rules. Whether you have a vegetarian baby or not, strive to have a healthy baby.

Get the Most from Your Veggies
by Kim Townsel
We don't have much control over nutrients in our food being lost via processing and transportation. However, there are steps we can take to ensure that those valuable nutrients get into our (and our *kids'*) bodies.

• Surprisingly, sometimes frozen or canned vegetables actually retain more nutrients than fresh ones. Certain nutrients, like the B-complex vitamins, are quickly lost when the vegetable is overly exposed to heat and light after picking. Produce that is quickly canned or frozen may lose fewer nutrients.

When choosing canned or frozen vegetables, opt for those with less salt and other additives. Eventually, your family can be weaned from a salt addiction. Avoid dented cans or packages of frozen foods that feel mushy or appear discolored. Store canned products in a cool, dry place, and keep frozen foods in a freezer with temperatures consistently under 30 degrees.

• When possible, avoid adding butter, margarine or other fats to vegetables during cooking. Fat-soluble vitamins (A, E) prefer to reside in fat and will leave the veggie to cuddle up with the margarine. When the cooking liquid is drained off, so is much of the vitamin content. If necessary, add fat after the liquid is drained.

• To preserve even more nutrients, use as little cooking liquid as possible. Water-soluble vitamins abandon their resident veggie for pure water, so when we cook two cups of green beans in three cups of water, we lose vital nutrients. Remember to recycle that liquid in soups and stews!

• Use as short a cooking time and as little water as possible. Many of us grew up in households where veggies were boiled in a lot of water for a long time. We were conditioned to shrunken green beans and soft, gummy carrots. Kids prefer veggies with some resistance, so cooking produce to death isn't required. Ideal methods include pressure cooking, microwaving and stir-frying.

Selective Eaters

by Karby Allington

About 25 percent of all children have some type of eating problem that makes mealtimes challenging. If your baby is one of them, you know it! Like other parents of fussy eaters, you've tried everything to get them to eat. And nothing works.

You can give a baby food, but his temperament will affect his approach to it. Your selective eater is probably cautious. He may equate "trying" a new food with merely looking at it. If you continue offering him a variety of foods (preferably identical to the rest of the family's) and allow him to proceed at his own pace, he may accept more foods. Allowing him to remove distasteful food from his mouth (rather than insisting it be swallowed) makes it safer for a child to try new things.

Temperament aside, 1- to 2-year-olds strive for independence by testing limits and exploring. These developmental tasks, along with a diminishing growth rate, can decrease even a "good" eater's appetite.

It's important to make sure that your fussy eater can manage the size and texture of the food you give him. In spite of the mess, most finicky babies will eat more when allowed to feed themselves. As you encourage his autonomy, yet remain supportive and involved, you establish a positive feeding relationship between you and your child. This is far more important than getting in a few more bites at a meal.

Continue to structure meals and snacks in spite of your baby's resistance. As with discipline at this age, consistent limits (for example, eating only at the table) provide security. Your baby will also relax if you direct more of your attention to him rather than to what he puts in his mouth.

Relax, it's not your job! The hardest part of feeding a finicky eater is letting your baby decide how much to eat, and if he eats at all. *Your* primary job is to provide nutritious food at regular intervals in a positive, supportive way.

Although it's scary to let go of trying to make your baby eat, hanging on will usually squelch your baby's appetite and leave you discouraged. A supportive feeding relationship teaches a baby to be comfortable with his own eating. You can teach him to tolerate the presence of a disliked food, or to pick it out of a mixed dish. Your baby won't learn to handle his own finickiness if you short-order cook or force offensive food on him. Remember, your reaction to his eating influences his nutrition more than the actual food you give him.

Another part of your job is to assess your baby's eating. View his intake over several days. Is he drinking too many calories in milk or juice between meals? Is an underlying family dynamic affecting his eating? Are you and your spouse unified in your approach to feeding? Some of these questions require gut-level honesty. A helpful resource is the book *How to Get Your Kid to Eat . . . But Not Too Much,* by Ellyn Satter (Bull Publishing Co.).

If your baby's growth is poor, the temptation to "take over" his eating will be strong. If he's small or below the 5th percentile for his age, discuss his eating habits with your physician. They may be normal for your baby.

If growth is a problem, check for underlying disease or eating problems. Having a trained health-care professional observe your feeding interaction can be an invaluable tool in this process.

As you feed your finicky eater, avoid catering to him, but work to respect and cultivate his individual taste sensitivity.

Baby-Bottle Tooth Decay

by Jeffrey Timm

Do you frequently give your baby a bottle of fruit juice, sweetened liquids, milk or formula? When your baby is ready for a nap or to go to bed, are any of these liquids in her bottle? If your answer to these questions is yes, your baby is at risk of developing baby-bottle tooth decay. This form of tooth disease can destroy the teeth of a baby or a young child. While all teeth are susceptible, the upper front teeth are most likely to be damaged, which will affect the baby's smile.

Even though a baby's permanent teeth aren't in, your child needs healthy primary teeth to learn to speak correctly, chew food properly, and guide the permanent teeth into place. That's why it's important to take proper care of your baby's teeth, and to understand the potential problems associated with this disease.

Causes. Baby-bottle tooth decay is caused by the frequent exposure, over time, of a child's teeth to liquids containing sugars. The sugars contained in milk, formula, fruit juices, pop or any sweetened liquid can cause the bacteria in plaque to produce acids. The acids then attack the tooth enamel, leading to decay.

Every time your child drinks a liquid containing sugars, acids result which attack the teeth for at least 20 minutes. So not only is the liquid a factor, but the frequency and duration of contact with your child's teeth are equally important.

For example, it is not a good idea repeatedly to offer your child a bottle containing these sweetened liquids as a pacifier. And allowing your baby to fall asleep at nap time or at night with a bottle of anything but water can be harmful to his teeth. The flow of saliva decreases during sleep, allowing liquids in the bottle to pool and remain concentrated around the child's teeth over extended periods of time.

Prevention. A number of years ago, baby-bottle tooth decay was quite common. Subsequent education and the use of fluoride caused the incidence of the disease to decrease, but for a number of reasons it is on the increase again. The following steps will help you protect your baby's teeth from the disease:

• If you suspect your baby has dental problems, take the child to see a dentist as soon as possible.

• Your baby should be getting fluoride supplements. If your local water supply does not contain the correct amount of fluoride, your dentist can prescribe it.

• Never allow your child to fall asleep with a bottle containing milk, formula, fruit juice, pop or any sweetened liquid. Between regular feedings, during naps or at night, give your baby a bottle filled with cool water, or provide a clean pacifier.

• Clean your child's teeth and gums after each feeding. You can wipe them with a damp washcloth or gauze pad. As soon as your baby's first tooth erupts, begin a regimen of brushing with a soft toothbrush.

Baby-bottle tooth decay can easily be prevented. But if you suspect its presence, have the condition treated as soon as possible to help assure that your child has a mouth full of healthy teeth as he grows older.

Dental Care

by Jeffrey Timm

Because children ages 3 to 5 are becoming increasingly independent, we sometimes let them brush their teeth without much supervision, not always detecting inadequate jobs. However, it's during this time that brushing must be emphasized even more. Other than strictly forbidding any sugary goodies, there are ways to teach our children proper dental care and reasonable snacking.

Care for little teeth. At this age, brushing is of primary importance; flossing follows closely behind. Choose a soft-bristled toothbrush with a small head that will fit into all areas of your child's mouth. All of the tooth surfaces must be brushed—chewing surfaces as well as inner and outer sides. Show your preschooler how to brush in a semicircular motion over inside and outside surfaces, and in a back-and-forth motion over chewing surfaces. Your child should brush her tongue as well.

A timer can help your child know how long to brush. Place it in the bathroom, and start it when she begins brushing. One minute is sufficient. Your preschooler should brush a minimum of twice a day (in the morning and at night before bed), but three or more times a day when she eats more sugary snacks than normal.

Almost any fluoride-containing toothpaste is fine for children. Find one with a taste they like and stick with it. I recommend not giving your child tartar-control toothpastes, since they tend to have too strong a flavor. Careful, frequent brushing should minimize tartar. A fluoride mouth rinse, used once a day after brushing, also helps protect young teeth.

If your child's teeth sit closely together, floss them several times a week. Preschoolers have a tough time flossing, so I recommend that parents help out. An easy way to floss your child's teeth is to have her lie down with her head in your lap, making it easier for you to see and floss.

If your child usually brushes by herself, monitor her brushing and check her teeth periodically. If plaque is forming, you may need to step in and help out. For example, she can brush for 30 seconds, then you brush for 30 seconds. Be creative.

Monitor the sugar. Many children suffer from an increase of canker sores when their sugar intake increases. Any over-the-counter remedies should help. Ask your dentist or pharmacist which he recommends, especially if your child has several sores, or if the sores interfere with her ability to eat or drink.

If it will be a while before your child can brush her teeth after snacking, have her rinse her mouth out with water. This dilutes the sugars and acids that lead to decay.

Cutting back on sugar in recipes and limiting sugary snacks are two ways to reduce sweets. Substituting healthier snacks such as cheese and crackers, vegetables and fruits is another way. Give your child choices. Help her understand why too many sugary treats aren't good for her teeth or health.

Tooth Brushing Tricks

by Laurie Winslow Sargent

Do you have to pin down your 2-year-old to get a toothbrush into his mouth? Baby teeth *do* need to be healthy, to make way for healthy permanent teeth. Dentists suggest brushing with the bristles held at about a 45 degree angle to the teeth, and to brush for *at least* one full minute. Impossible with toddlers?

The following creative tricks encourage cooperation while you brush your toddler's teeth and thoroughness when she learns to brush on her own. Rotate ideas as needed.

Serenade Mom. While your toddler sings "Aaaaaa," brush her back teeth; "Eeeeee" gets the front.

Meal review. You: "What did you eat today?" Child: "Ummmm, a hot dog!" You: "OK; ten for the hot dog. One, two, three . . . . What else did you eat?" (My 2½-year-old loved this—often *over*-extending tooth brushing time to " 'member everything.")

Synchronized brushing. Brush together, looking in the mirror. Then you finish hers—and let her finish yours. Emphasize growing up: "What a big girl you are, with all those teeth! We'd better take good care of them!"

Toothbrush tunes. A child who usually brushes for only a few seconds may brush for the full length of a song (as you sing it to him). Reserve a fun song for tooth brushing time.

Gimmick toothbrushes. Try a brush in a favorite color or with a cartoon character on it or a jingle in the handle. Your toddler's brush may become so beloved that he won't let go of it.

Real choices. Increase cooperation by offering choices: even between two activities a kid hates! "Do you want to go to bed right now, or brush teeth first?" sent my son running for his brush. Avoid fake choices, like "Brush them right now, or go straight to bed!" That's a threat, not a choice. If your child chooses bedtime, so be it (but offer different choices tomorrow). Avoid questions ("Want to brush your teeth now?") unless you can accept "No!"

To be firm, but fair, try:

Time warnings. "You have five more minutes to play, and then it will be time to brush your teeth." Even we adults appreciate a little time to switch gears. Although a toddler's concept of time is vague, a warning will help him begin detaching from his current task.

Setting routines. Verbally emphasize that tooth brushing will always be an expected part of daily living. "We always brush teeth after story time and before bedtime."

Goal-setting. To establish consistency and the habit of brushing, a goal-oriented child can work to earn a prize for consistent cooperation. For instance, each cooperative episode can earn her a sticker; 14 stickers earn rental of a favorite movie.

We often underestimate our toddler's abilities. A 2- to 3-year-old can begin understanding that food, especially sugar, sticks to the teeth. If not brushed off, it can make holes that can hurt. Once your child comprehends why brushing is necessary, it will help build a habit of teeth care.

Baby's First Dentist Visit

by Jeffrey Timm

The thought of taking your child to the dentist for the first time may bring back unpleasant memories of your own first experience. But with today's innovations and the use of fluoride, a child can look forward to his first visit to the dentist. Here are some of the most commonly asked questions regarding a child's first visit to the dentist:

When should I first take my child to the dentist? The answer to this question depends upon the reason for the visit. If your child is having a dental problem of any kind or you suspect something is wrong, see your dentist regardless of your child's age. If your child is not having any problems, age 3 is a good time to begin regular dental treatment. At this age, most children understand what is being done and why. Maturity levels vary greatly—take that into account when scheduling that first appointment.

What can we expect during the first appointment? Depending on the reason for the appointment and the age of your child, several things can happen. The key is not to frighten or push the child beyond his limits of comprehension and patience. An exception to this is an emergency visit involving pain or swelling.

Most dentists follow a "tell-show-do" approach. The child is told what will be done in terms he can understand. Then he is shown the instruments that will be used and is allowed to touch and hold them before the procedure begins.

During the routine first visit, the dentist performs a complete exam. Teeth are checked for decay and proper alignment. All soft tissues, including the tongue, soft palate, lips and cheeks, are checked for abnormalities. X-rays may also be taken. The teeth are then cleaned, polished, and given a fluoride treatment. Most preschoolers have no problem with these procedures and look forward to coming back.

How do I prepare my child? This section could more accurately be titled "What *not* to say about going to the dentist." It seems every child has a brother, sister or friend who can tell some horror story.

It can be helpful to let your preschooler "practice" going to the dentist. He can lie on the couch and you can practice counting his teeth. You may even want to brush your child's teeth while he is in this prone position. Let your child hold a mirror and watch while you do this. You can explain in simple terms that the dentist will count the teeth and will use a "special toothbrush" to get the teeth "super" clean.

Try to avoid any comments with negative connotations such as "The dentist won't hurt you." This only makes the child wonder why the dentist *might* hurt him. Approach the upcoming visit in a positive way, and your child should have a pleasant and rewarding first experience at the dental office.

Play-and-Learn Ideas

Chapter Thirteen

Why Play?

by Laurie Winslow Sargent

Do you ever have to *make* yourself play with your kids? You may find it a relief to know you're not alone. It's a myth that all parents know how to play (or always want to). Our ability to play is affected by:

• Limited energy and time. Housework. Volunteer and church work. Outside jobs. Multiple children of different ages—who all want us at the same time. Whew!

• Struggles with high perfectionism and low spontaneity.

• Lack of familiarity with play for parents who didn't come from playful families.

• Behavioral problems in some children.

• Personality differences and interests between parent and child.

Is parenting fun? Or mostly work? What about the joy God desires for us?

One recent evening, my husband, Gordy, leapt from the dinner table mid-bite. Turning up the stereo, he began conducting with a fork. Aimee and I left the table to jitterbug. Tyler donned dark glasses and lip-synched into a carrot. Five minutes later we were back to eating—but that little bit of goofiness had pulled our family together.

Sometimes it takes effort for me to be playful. The child in me may want to jitterbug, but the grown-up wants to scold, "No, no, sit down! Eat before your food gets cold!" The more stressed out and pressured I feel, the more the grown-up side takes over. How about you?

> It's a myth
> that all parents
> know how
> to play
> (or want to).
>
> Laurie Winslow Sargent

Why Play?

• Play adds intimacy to your relationship with your child. An adoring look, spontaneous hug, or a blurted "I love you, Mom!" is more likely to occur during play than when you're forcing your child to clean his room. Daily doses of play also help decrease whining and defiance.

• Play helps your child learn or improve motor skills, social skills, problem-solving, reading and speech. If your child is delayed in any area, your interaction may be crucial.

• Play creates a more fun job for yourself as a parent. Is there a better reason?

Let's look at seven keys to nurturing playfulness in you and your children.

1. Acknowledge parenthood stress.

I overheard Wilma Flintstone say something like this: "Between Pebbles, the dishes and laundry, nothing's ever dry at the same time." Constant demands rob parents of time and energy for play.

Recognize your own high-stress times. Try to change those patterns. In my case, I'm wiped out by 5 P.M. Making dinner while kids fight for attention drives me crazy. For less stress, I try cooking in advance, so at five we can relax in the recliner with story books.

If you're overextended, try to prioritize your activities. Let go of some. Give yourself permission to play without feeling guilty. This can actually help *decrease* stress.

2. Grasp the simplicity of play.

Short is often very sweet and uncomplicated, as in a 30-second "I'm gonna get you!" with a giggly preschooler. Or a corny knock-knock joke with a 3rd grader.

Try these simple ideas:

• Make mundane chores fun. Sometimes I pull clothes from the dryer out and yell, "Warm laundry alert!" My kids fling themselves on the floor, oohing and aahing as I sprinkle warm clothes on them.

• Explore simple five-minute games that require neither materials nor planning ahead. Play word games on the way to the dentist, like "Dress the Bear." (Take turns dressing an imaginary bear without repeating articles of clothing or colors.)

• Don't shy away from activities which require materials yet are still simple. Try making "goop" (cornstarch mixed with water). Is it a solid or liquid? Two-year-olds, 7-year-olds, even 30-something-year-olds find this stuff fascinating.

3. Stop. Look. Listen.

• Appreciate personality differences. See negatively viewed traits in a positive way. Is your child "hyper" or "enthusiastic"? "Picky" or "thorough"?

• Explore your interests and your child's. If you love to bake and she loves math, can she measure for you? Can you learn new activities together from library books or classes?

• Observe your children closely at least five times a day—to see *them*, not just their noise or their mess. Notice your son's beautiful long lashes. Listen to your preschooler talk. You'll want to stop and play. Quick— before they change.

4. Learn.

• Learn about child development. When your child reaches milestones, play will be more fun for you, because it's exciting to see changes.

• Learn about giftedness or learning disabilities if these apply to your child. Some games or toys may frustrate her. Others may help her overcome learning problems or challenge her.

• Learn more about your children's interests, which may then interest you too. After reading books on salamanders, feeding them and holding them, I find them less slimy and more cute.

5. Watch your interaction with your child as you play.

• Sit back. Watch your urge to control the game and be a cheerleader instead. You might be amazed! At age 4, my son taught me a dozen games to play with blocks—without building anything.

• Be sensitive to pitfalls of perfectionism. Most play doesn't have to be "done right."

• Be aware of too high (or too low) expectations. When preschoolers use glue, it will get on the table. Let your child's developmental age (and your own tolerance for mess) guide choice and time length of activities.

• Sometimes it's OK to say, "I'm not crazy about playing that. Let's do something we *both* like." But often a child feels well loved if you do exactly what he wants. He may allow some variations: When I tired of telling *Goldilocks and the Three Bears* every night (aaaargh!), the story gradually became Phonylocks and the Mare, the Bear and the Hare.

• Doing chores together can bring togetherness. But be honest. Can you wash the car and give your child focused attention at the same time? Your child may not see it as play.

• Often your child doesn't want toys. She wants *you*, made by God, batteries not included. (Sometimes I wish they were!)

But playing with toys *together* can connect you and also interest your child more in playing independently. And you can regenerate your child's interest in old, forgotten toys by playing with them yourself. Scattered Fisher-Price people come to life again when your child sees you pretend with them in a squeaky voice.

• Your child will not always thank you for playing. When he cries "You never play with me!" you may throw up your hands in despair, reminding him of the two hours you spent yesterday making pirate maps.

The accumulation of your time together is molding your relationship and your child's character. I doubt I thanked my own parents as a child. But I praise God for them now—for the legacy of playfulness they passed down to me.

6. Prioritize play. Set goals.

• What are your life goals? Is one to raise confident, loving, bright children? Then even if dirty dishes pile up in the sink while you play, remember that you are working toward an important goal. The results are not as immediate as clean dishes, but there will be positive, long-term results.

• Get organized to free up more time for play. Try reading Gwen Weising's *Making Time for Family Fun* (Revell). But do use that time for play.

• Make play dates with your child. This works well when a child whines for attention while you try to work. Let your child know when you'll be available (for example, when "Mister Roger's Neighborhood" ends, or when the oven buzzer rings).

At the appointed time, stop and play—hard. Many children are satisfied with a mere 10 minutes of concentrated attention. Set your timer before you begin playing. When it buzzes, it will be the bad guy, making you go back to work.

Plan further ahead for longer play dates, especially with older kids. To really honor your child, let an answering machine take your calls. Get a sitter for little sister, or play while she naps (a real sacrifice if her nap time is your work time). If someone comes to the door, tell her you have an appointment and can't talk.

If older siblings compete for attention, arrange play dates with each. When they know their turn will come, they're more likely to leave you and your "date" alone.

7. Strive for a playful, positive attitude. Practice spontaneity.

Play is more an attitude than activities.

• Choose to be cheerful. Despite all the modern hoopla about positive thinking, remember that the concept originally came from Proverbs 17:22: "A cheerful heart is good medicine, but a crushed spirit dries up the bones."

Do a personal Bible study on joy. Try reading *Laugh Again* by Chuck Swindoll (Word). A joyful Christian offers a more powerful witness to unbelievers than a down-in-the-mouth one.

• Is it difficult for you to be spontaneous? To learn how, simply watch and listen to your kids. Let them disrupt your plans sometimes—and go with the flow.

• Be playful with your spouse. Pinches, tickles or a long, mushy kiss in front of our kids guarantees giggles in our home.

• Spend time with friends who possess a sense of humor—limit time with those who constantly complain. Both are contagious.

• Consciously seek the potentially funny side of situations. Fortunately, my husband often does this when I'm stuck in the daily grind. One week, after I'd finished the laundry and taken the clean clothes upstairs, I heard hysterical laughter. Gordy, Tyler and Aimee paraded downstairs, arms linked, wearing—just underwear. Underwear as underwear. Underwear as hats. Underwear as masks.

I caught the underwear family on videotape dancing on the bed to D.C. Talk. It got even funnier when my husband frantically tried to hide from the camera.

It may not be one of "America's Funniest Home Videos." But it will be a precious reminder to us (and our children) of playful, joyful family times.

A Father's Little Playbook

by Kirk Livingston

Dad-play can serve a greater purpose than just keeping kids occupied. Your time together will stimulate your kids, your own creativity, and give you rollicking, memorable fun.

Dad-play can be wacky. At Marty's house, silly, spontaneous games are the rule. He looks forward to the games that spring from the mind of his 3-year-old daughter, such as pretending to be a pancake: "I'm ready, flip me!"

Recently left alone for a few hours with five kids under 3 (his own kids and a friend's), Marty filled the hours with role-play. He became a housecall doctor; the kids were patients and hosts. To the kids it was a game, but they were learning hospitality.

Dad-play connects kids to the outside world. A child identifies the world outside home with Daddy, says fathering author Gordon Dalbey. Anything that lets you talk about God and the adventures of everyday life strengthens your child's connection to the outside world.

Take your child to the hardware store, or make arrangements for him to visit your workplace. Rich, a physical therapist, sets aside two appointments per week that his 4-year-old daughter can attend. These visits help her see how the Word of God is bound to her dad's heart through acts of mercy and compassion.

Dad-play is unique. Jim found freedom when he realized that he didn't have to mimic his wife's way of playing with their kids to be a good dad. He started playing in ways more natural to himself, alternating between teaching about electricity and chasing the kids through the house like a wild beast. "I let go of what I thought I *should* do," he said, "and did what was natural and fun for me."

Dad-play draws kids to God. Knowing about God's rules can be the first step to knowing God. But kids need the movement behind the rules. "My daughters' relationships with their heavenly Father is based on what they see in me," says Marty.

Rather than Dad the policeman, or Dad the comatose TV-watcher, you can be Dad the adventurer—on a journey deep into the mysteries of God, willing to bring your curious children along.

Benefits of Infant Stimulation

by William Sears

What are the benefits of stimulation strategies for you and for your baby? First, *you really can enhance your child's intellectual ability*. According to Dr. Michael Lewis, director of child development at Rutgers Medical School, the most important factor in increasing a child's intellectual development is the responsiveness of the mother to the cues of her infant. Another benefit is that when parents and their baby spend more time doing things together, *the baby also develops the parents*. The more you interact with your baby, the more you know and appreciate your infant's capabilities and preferences at each stage of development.

Dr. Susan Ludington, founder of the Infant Stimulation Education Association, defines the goal of infant stimulation as "A well-rounded, well-balanced baby: one who is equally comfortable and competent in mental, motor, social and emotional skills."

Dialogue with your baby. During the first six months, talking and listening to your baby is one of the most stimulating activities you can do. The ability to hold each other's attention is one of the most important goals of infant stimulation. Singing stimulates more of a baby's brain than simply talking. When you sing to your baby, the lyrics impact the left half of the brain, while the melody affects the right.

Choose age-appropriate and stage-appropriate toys. Take into account what babies enjoy and are capable of doing at each stage of development. Babies seem to relate best to contrasting stripes, dots, bull's-eyes and checkerboard patterns. For infant stimulation, black and white is in; babies do not seem to show a preference for colors until after 4 months.

Babies relate best to objects that are round, soft, contrasting dark and light and ever-changing. Consequently, the familiar faces of Mom and Dad are still the most powerful infant stimulators. Because of this fascination with familiar faces, we placed an eight-by-ten black and white photo of my wife and me beside our baby's bassinet.

Choose toys for your baby that provide a reaction in response to his action. For example, kicking or batting at a dangling object or shaking a rattle produces both movement and sound. Soon a baby learns cause-and-effect and develops a feeling of competence.

Try to change toys frequently. Babies tend to get bored with the same old toys. Toy bears have regained popularity in recent years. Because of the light-dark contrast, panda bears are often the preferred choice. Around 3 months of age, the simplest and most educational toy is a red rubber ring three to four inches in diameter. A baby can do a lot with this simple, inexpensive toy.

Individualize. Learn the facial gestures, tone of voice and toys that are pleasing to your baby. Learn what your baby is capable of doing at each stage of development and what he or she likes or dislikes. Rigid play programs deny your baby's individuality. Be more oriented toward what your baby *enjoys* than what he can *do*. A baby still has plenty of time to make his debut into a performance-oriented society.

Watch for "stop signs." Just as babies show "engagement cues" (smiling, making eye contact, hands-out gesturing) they also show signs of "disengagement" (vacant staring, averting hands and eyes away from your face or a toy, furrowed forehead).

Fathers often take longer to recognize baby's stop signs than do mothers. Because of their eagerness to play with baby, dads sometimes may *agitate* more than *stimulate*. Fathers are seldom allowed the luxury of long periods of unscheduled time with their babies, so they are prone to over-stimulate, to rush in to initiate playful interaction. Infant-stimulation classes teach fathers to approach babies in a more baby-oriented manner: First, elicit eye contact, then talk to baby, and *then* pick up baby for play.

Interactions initiated by your baby and subsequently reinforced by you are most beneficial to your child.

Stimulation Strategies
by Grace Ketterman

Evaluate your child's basic energy level and tolerance for stimuli. Some babies are calm and sensitive and need only gentle input to meet their needs adequately. Soft colors, low sound levels and gentle handling suit them perfectly. But be certain they have enough visual, auditory and tactile (touch) stimuli to make them alert and help them develop. Many quiet babies, however, need louder sounds, brighter colors and more active handling to meet their needs. High-energy babies need stimulation in more subtle ways. Such babies need the calming effect of rocking instead of jiggling, pastel colors rather than bright ones, and low sounds that will not startle.

Just as calm infants may do better with low-level stimuli, active babies may need high-level input to avoid frustration. Learn to observe your baby's responses to louder sounds, brighter lights, and intense physical activity. If she is enjoying these, does not become nervous or irritable, and eats and sleeps comfortably, you will know what her individual needs and tolerances are.

Assess your energy level as a parent. We know that many parent-child conflicts originate with a marked difference between temperaments in parent and child. Do not exhaust your energy reserves in trying to meet your child's every little need.

Stay in charge. Play with your baby at your convenience as well as at his desire. If he cries a bit while you finish a task or catch a 10-minute rest, that's perfectly OK. Calming yourself will allow you to give the best possible care to your baby.

Recognize that your baby's needs for stimulation will vary. If she is not feeling well or had too active a day the day before, her needs will be less. Spend a little time studying your baby: her facial expression, quality of crying and body movements will help you understand what she is feeling, and therefore what is needed.

Avoid over-stimulation. Babies need to learn some self-gratification, so too much attention may actually prevent enough growth of independence. Alternate times of isolation with times for play, cuddling, or simply being near each other. If *you* are enjoying your child, she will learn to have fun with you—and that sort of love is the best stimulation of all!

Creative Play Ideas

by Laurie Winslow Sargent

Your 1-year-old is on a search-and-destroy mission. Assignment as follows:

1. Knock phone off hook and press redial (long distance).
2. Take videotapes from cabinets. Pull out those neat ribbons.
3. Throw unpaid bills in garbage.
4. Swish toothpaste tube in toilet.

With a vocabulary limited to bop-bop (bottle), meow and other short words, it's tough to figure out what she's thinking. It's actually pretty amazing what goes through that little brain. Has she seen *you* toss junk mail, or rinse off the toothpaste tube in the sink? (Sink, toilet—what's the difference?) Babies are great imitators, *always* learning more than we think we are teaching them.

Surprises like these make parenting exciting. Your baby will learn so rapidly it will take your breath away. Keys to keeping those surprises coming are stimulation and expectations.

Stimulation. Playing with, talking to, and reading to your baby comes naturally for many parents. You might spontaneously grab a cup of pretend tea and sip it with your baby, asking, "Mmm, did *you* make this? It's so *good*!" Worn out knees in your pants reveal that you spend as much time on the floor with your baby as you do on your feet.

However, you may be less comfortable with play and rely more on toys. You may feel awkward chatting with a baby whose words are so limited. And parenting is so exhausting—just keeping her messy trails picked up takes time and energy. Add diapering, meals, siblings . . . .

Most likely, you fall somewhere in between the playful parent and the preoccupied parent. But the more interaction you have with your baby, the more stimulation she's likely to get. Gab while you do the dishes. Have her "help" you sort laundry.

Consistently offer your baby a bit more than what you think she'll grasp. Expose her to words, pictures, colors, textures, music, hugs and kisses.

Expectations. Avoid setting up expectations for your child to learn specific things by certain times. Examples: "If I describe the colors in her clothes, she'll know her colors before she's 3 years old," or "If I read to my baby, it will make him an early reader." This puts extreme pressure on your child or leads to disappointment on your part—or both.

Instead, maintain the expectation that your baby will learn something from anything you do together. Talk with her using as many "big" words as you would with anyone else. Assume that she understands at least a bit, if not all, of what you're saying.

Your baby won't always learn what you set out to teach her. That's OK. This simply reveals the unique personality God has given your child which is separate from your own. By stimulating your child and assuming that she is intelligent, you teach her new things about her world. What things? Just sit back and wait. Expect surprises.

Baby-Play Essentials
Birth to 5 weeks:
- Contact with people—physical and visual
- Nurturing (essential to a baby's survival)
- You, not toys: Babies enjoy faces and voices most of all.

5 weeks to 3 months:
- People-contact: cuddling, the chance to study faces and watch the world
- Opportunities to focus his eyes and recognize things by appearance
- Objects strung across the crib or stroller: These provide interest, as do happy faces (black-on-white background) and textured toys.

3 months to 6 months:
- Things in a variety of shapes and colors to look at and hold
- Physical play (rocking, bouncing, stretching, and listening to new sounds)
- Interaction with the environment through physical activity (discovering where the body ends and the outside world begins)
- Safe toys in bright colors that make neat noises: bean bags, fluffy balls, and rattles; soft plastic rings, squeaky animals, and fleecy bears.

• A bouncer for jumping, and your lap as an exercise floor.

6 months to 1 year:

• Everyday household objects, which take on new meaning as a baby's world expands and require close supervision

• Interactive and imitative games (peekaboo, daddy's helper, Old MacDonald) that demonstrate how actions bring about effects and build on the bond you share

• Repetition, which teaches new skills and lets a baby imitate the way you do things

• Toys to pull, balls to bounce, things to take apart, sounds to make— any items that can be squeezed and shaken safely.

• Personal possessions—such as books, dinnerware and photos.

Bath Time

by Laurie Winslow Sargent

A fun alternative to using a baby bath is to take your infant in the big tub *with* you (after the umbilical cord has fallen off). You both get squeaky clean and enjoy intimate playtime together.

For safe, hassle-free bathing, follow these steps:

1. Fill the tub (safety mat in place). Water temperature must be cooler than a normal adult bath to avoid overheating your infant, who has thinner, more sensitive skin.

2. Place all bathtub goodies—baby shampoo, soap, washcloth—beside the tub. Once you're stuck in the bath, infant on your lap, the shampoo in the cupboard will seem a million miles away.

3. Set an infant seat beside the tub, and put your baby in it.

4. You get in first. Sit in the tub, legs together, knees bent.

5. Lift your baby out of the infant seat onto your thighs, resting his head on your knees. As he lies against your warm skin, give him a gentle, soapy massage. After shampooing his hair, rinse with a few handfuls of water.

Dr. David M. Lush, family physician, says that "little children in a big tub are less likely to be fearful of the water if a parent is in with them." Once you feel confident bathing your infant, let him experience the pleasure of floating and kicking (as you support his upper body). Immersing his ears is not recommended because of the potential of ear infections.

6. Set your baby out first, into the infant seat. Wrap his towel around him for warmth. *Never* climb out holding your infant, lest you fall.

7. After you're out and dry, finish drying your child. Wrap him in your bathrobe, next to your skin, to give him an extra cuddle before you get dressed.

You may be concerned about spreading an infection (such as yeast) to your child. Lush states that in 20 years of experience, he has never seen infection spread from parent to child via tub water. Yeast, a dry plant, is not waterborne. Bacteria are usually bound and killed in hot, soapy water. However, staph or venereal infections *can* spread from skin to skin contact (in or out of the tub). If you have open sores associated with these infections, consult your doctor before bathing with your child.

Lush reminds parents that faucet water is considered sterile, but routinely disinfecting your bathtub is important. He also cautions against using bubble baths and perfumed soaps when bathing with your baby.

A perfectly legitimate worry is that your infant might defecate in the tub with you. Avoid this by timing your bath according to your infant's schedule, not yours. The best time for a bath? *After* a messy diaper change! I've managed well over 50 fun baths with my children—all without incident.

Parents who prefer showers to tubs can still enjoy splash times with their baby. Showering with a slick baby is tricky (a towel wrapped around him provides a better grip). You might skip shampooing, since you have only one free hand.

How long should you bathe with a child of the opposite sex? What do you do when he stares and pokes at you with interest? Consider more privacy when your child passes late toddlerhood. Respond to questions with appropriate terminology and without embarrassment. Most children find naming private parts no different from naming elbows and toes, and soon turn back to playing in the tub.

Soapsud Safety

Your bathroom presents four hazards you need to safeguard your baby from: the *tub, toilet, electrical appliances* and *poisonous substances*.

Never leave your baby alone in the bathtub. As unlikely as it seems, a child can drown in a couple of inches of water in just a few moments. If you need to leave the room during your baby's bath, wrap her in a warm towel and carry her with you. When bath time's over, empty the tub immediately so you won't forget about it later. Because your toilet also presents a drowning hazard, put a safety latch on the lid and keep it closed when not in use.

You can prevent accidental scalding by turning down your hot water heater thermostat to 120°F and putting childproof tub knobs over the handles to guard against tampering. Place a soft spout over the faucet to save your baby from painful bumps and bruises. (A rubber mat or no-skid appliqués work great for this purpose too.)

To guard against electrocution, don't use appliances, such as a blow dryer, if you have water in the tub. Store electrical appliances unplugged and beyond your baby's reach.

Place perfumes, mouthwashes, aftershaves, hair products, nail polish and remover, cosmetics, cleansers and disinfectants in a locked cabinet along with any medicine. Be sure all drugs and vitamins are stored in child-resistant containers. In cabinets your baby can open, towels and tub toys work great for amusing your little one when you're busy in the bathroom.

Playpens and Creativity

by Elaine McEwan-Adkins

We started shopping for nursery furniture as soon as we got the exciting news that we were going to be parents. One item in particular engendered quite a bit of heated discussion between my husband and me— a playpen.

My husband insisted that no child of his was going to spend time imprisoned in a playpen. I wasn't so sure. After all, what do you do with the baby when she isn't in her crib or highchair? Since I lost the playpen argument, I soon found out. At 5 months of age, Emily was rolling everywhere. She seemed able to cover vast territories in only minutes.

Early one dark fall morning, she cried out in her crib, signaling the beginning of another active day. I was weary from a late night. My husband was sleeping soundly in a warm mound next to me. I rose silently, feeling tempted to wake him to join our "fun." But I let him slumber on. After changing her diaper and dressing her in a clean sleeper, I carried Emily out to the living room. I placed her in the middle of the floor on a blanket and lay down on the sofa to watch her play.

Moments later, I awoke with a start. While I had drifted off to sleep, Emily had rolled across the room. In that brief span of time, she managed to pull over a potted plant, tear several leaves from its branches, and scatter dirt everywhere—all from a prone position. I silently berated my husband for his shortsightedness. It was very well for him to ban playpens from the household, but he was enjoying a blissful sleep while I was vacuuming up vermiculite and potting soil.

As Emily grew and become more mobile, we got rid of our plants. We removed the Limoges pottery from our coffee table. We placed our magazines and books on top of shelves. I had taken five years to decorate our home; in one month our decor went from fashionable to practical.

I didn't realize early on that the simple decision to bypass the purchase of a playpen was one of the most important decisions we could have made as parents. Dr. Burton White, director of Harvard Preschool Project and author of several books on child development, says that "to bore a child on a daily basis by the regular use of a playpen is a very poor childrearing practice, in terms of the child's educational needs" (*The First Three Years of Life,* Prentice-Hall).

The higher levels of intelligence are built on a child's sensorimotor explorations, which take place during the first three years. When a child is confined to a playpen, highchair, crib or jump seat, he is less likely to be engaged in active learning explorations.

Children involved in active learning are challenging to supervise and care for. But the stimulation of their minds and bodies must take precedence over our personal desire for structure and control. Childproofing your house becomes essential, and constant vigilance is necessary. When children are free to move about and make decisions about what they want to do, however, you'll find that your need to entertain them diminishes.

Perhaps you'll purchase a playpen for those moments when you absolutely can't supervise your child—for a quick telephone call, a trip to the basement to get laundry, or an uninterrupted moment in the bathroom. But use good judgment about the amount of time your child spends in it.

Derailing the Superbaby Express

by Patricia Rushford

Glenn Doman, known as the grand guru of baby building, began the Better Baby Institute in 1977. He has written such classics as *How to*

Teach Your Baby to Read, Teach Your Baby Math, and *How to Multiply Your Baby's Intelligence.* Doman claims, "Tiny children believe that it is their job to grow up. They know instinctively that learning is a survival skill. It's adults who want to keep children children; during the period they learn the most, we treat them like chowderheads."

It's true—babies do learn at an early age. But I worry that this push-and-shove mentality to get them to excel will create in them stress, frustration and feelings of failure. Yes, babies do learn more in their first few years than in the rest of their lifetimes. But think about the vast amount of knowledge that has to be absorbed by that "little sponge" in so short a time. They must learn about life and how to survive in it.

Realistically, even the best sponges absorb only so much. Are we trying to fill our babies up too much too soon?

Babies are born with some primitive instincts, such as the rooting and sucking reflex, which helps them find food. From the time they are born, babies must learn where food comes from, and more important, how to let someone know they're hungry. They must learn how to ask their parents to change their diapers and how to get someone to cuddle them. They must determine who's who in this family they've been plopped into. Babies must learn how to hold onto things and how to let go. They must learn adult-speak as well as teach their parents how to understand baby talk.

Another interesting thought is that children want to please their parents. They learn rules by watching how their behavior affects their mom and dad. Good behavior is associated with smiles, hugs and kisses, while no-no's are met with frowns and punishment.

Babies have a lot to learn without the added pressure of flash cards.

While love may be the motive for wanting your children to excel, a child often considers that his parents' pleasure in him is in direct proportion to his academic performance. My concerns for the future of these Superbabies is shared by many experts in the field of child development. In fact, psychologist Lee Salk says: "This pressure for high achievement really sets children up for failure. Love should be unconditional where children are concerned; it should not be based on IQ."

According to Dr. Raymond Moore, a noted developmental psychologist, children who are pressed to read at an early age often develop reading problems and, more seriously, sight impairment later on. Child educators are seeing more and more children experiencing burnout by the time they hit second or third grade—some even earlier.

While trying to saturate those "little sponges" with knowledge, parents fill them with the stresses and strains so prevalent in our hectic, grown-up world. It's bound to cause problems. The development of a Super Baby may have been born out of love and desire for the child to have the very best life has to offer. But it also may be born out of the parents' desire to be successful in all areas—including parenting.

We live in a success-oriented culture where material wealth and social-ladder climbing has become an obsession. Competition and grooming the "successful" child can take its toll on any young, impressionable body. Maybe it's time to count the cost.

Learning through Art and Play

by Allen F. Johnson

Play and art are crucial to the life of any preschool-age child, including children with special developmental, emotional or physical needs. Education through art and play is one of life's most enjoyable and enriching means of learning.

The following are benefits of play and art for any child. These creative endeavors:

• nurture and teach
• enhance a child's feelings of self-reliance, self-esteem, spontaneity and creativity
• give a child opportunities for social interaction
• cause a child to use his intellect, emotions and muscles.

A child's play is the cornerstone of his learning. The more preschoolers are exposed to problem-solving activities in play, the more they will learn about cause-and-effect relationships in the world about them.

It is true that play and the arts are not the same, but creative activities often parallel play. Creative, expressive play can best be represented in the arts—finger painting, modeling with clay, and similar activities.

When utilizing play as a creative art form, you will find many avenues open to your child for experimentation and making connections between cause and effect. As you structure art-play experiences, keep in mind these suggestions:

• Remember that the *process* by which a child creates the art is as important as the final "masterpiece."
• The final creation may be crude, so try not to compare it with

another child's art, since each work is special in and of itself.

• Accept a child's art as an expression of his self, and reward the expression with hugs.

• When you ask a child what the meaning is behind his art work, try not to give your own opinion of what it might be; let the child's own imagination determine the work's "meaning."

• Join with your child in your own creative expression of art even while he is busy at work. This shared time will help him associate creative activities with togetherness and closeness.

Often a child with special needs is unable to participate in play or activities like he wishes to because of the limitations of his disability. For example, the child in a wheelchair might assume that he cannot engage in games such as baseball or basketball. But what he often forgets is that there are many nondisabled youngsters who cannot perform those same activities.

If you are the parent of a child with a special need, remember that there are many types of adaptive equipment which can make play accessible. If you wish to find out more about creative play and toys designed for children with special needs, call your local Easter Seal Society, the Special Olympics program, or Very Special Arts in your area. Or write for the catalogue, *Special Things for Special Kids,* from J.A. Preston Corp., 60 Page Road, Clifton, NJ 07012. 800/631-7277.

Setting Limits on "Stuff"

by Mary Manz Simon

Is the toy box overflowing? Is your toddler's closet jammed? If so, the "Stuff Monster" may have visited your house. But wait: don't blame your 2-year-old yet. Having the Stuff Monster settle in your home can simply be the result of well-intentioned giving—by you and other relatives— that's gone too far.

As parents, we want the very best for our children. We can easily justify the equation, "more plus more equals the best for my child." But more is not always better. Reflect on these points as you answer the question, "Has the Stuff Monster visited here?"

Toddlers need things. They need to touch things, turn them over, feel things, tug on things, and yes, they still might chew things. Toddlers learn from being busy with things. Two- and 3-year-olds laugh at puppets and love wearing our old hats. They add sound effects to toy fire trucks and sing lullabies to a sleeping family cat.

In spite of what toy manufacturers advertise, toddlers don't need expensive playthings. Empty margarine containers with lids, a plastic bucket and shovel, and the cardboard boxes from the grocery store can be favorites.

Toddlers need people. They need consistent care givers who will share a lap, a smile and a prayer. Toddlers need people who will describe what's going on, set and maintain consistent limits and say, "I love you." No shiny red truck or expensive doll will ever be an adequate substitute for the love you give your child.

Toddlers outgrow clothing quickly. Go through your child's closet and drawers. Pack away clothing that no longer fits, or give the items away. When the Stuff Monster took up permanent residence in our children's closets, I developed a plan for continual weeding of clothes. We store an empty box under the laundry table, and when an item no longer fits, it automatically goes into that thrift store box after being washed. I also keep a "Mom's Memory Box" for items of clothing that have special meaning for me, and someday might be cherished when my children are grown: the newborn T-shirt from the hospital, the blue romper that looked so cute on all three children, the Polly Flinders dress the girls wore for their second Easter.

Too much stimulation can be distracting. Toddlers begin to learn decision-making by choosing between two items: Do you want to wear your red shirt or blue shirt? Young children can focus more easily on the question when choices are limited. Is the number of items in your child's closet appropriate to your child's needs?

Look around your child's room. If shelves are crowded, sort the playthings into several boxes. Then rotate the boxes every week or two, or give some toys to a local charity. Review toys, books and clothing on a regular basis. What your child has should reflect what he needs.

Christmas can result in gift overflow. Celebrating the holidays with a toddler can be absolutely wonderful—it's such fun to shop for a young child! Prioritize what your child can really use, then share your list with relatives.

Your toddler is still too young to realize when to practice good stewardship, how to model self-discipline, or where to set limits on purchases. But you know these are qualities of good parenting. How you work on these aspects now can set a pattern you'll follow in later years.

Grown-Up Games for Kids

by Laurie Winslow Sargent

Your preschooler spies a shelf of table games in your hall closet. He begs, "Mommy, I want to play *those!*" Most of them happen to be geared for older children or adults. Is this a problem, or an opportunity?

Many games designed for grown-ups can be adapted for use with little ones. While playing modified adult table games, your child learns and practices complex skills—and enjoys feeling more "grown up." The key is to adapt games to your child's skill level and developmental age appropriately. To do this, eliminate certain rules or create new games with original boards and pieces. Decide on new rules ahead of time. Put game pieces you don't use out of sight.

Use the following examples of games which adapt well as suggested— or as a spring board for your own ideas.

UNO (International Games). For 3-year-olds, eliminate most of the rules. Stick with recognizing and matching colors. Instead of fanning cards in your hands, place them face-up on the table. Older preschoolers can match numbers and letters and use direction cards to learn right-left discrimination. Later, as dexterity increases, they can fan and conceal cards.

Verbalize your problem-solving thoughts to encourage creative thinking in your child. For instance, you might say, "You have 10 cards left. I have only two, so I'm winning. If you play a color card which you know I don't have, you will make me draw more cards!"

Monopoly (Parker Brothers). Start with place markers, dice and property cards only. Each player rolls the dice, counts the dots, and moves the marker the correct number of spaces. He "wins" the property he lands on. He gets to find the matching property card from the stack by looking for the correct color, and the first few letters in the property name. The player with the most cards wins. Increase the game's complexity by awarding money only for "Go" and to pay "rent" to property card owners.

Scrabble (Milton Bradley). Set out all the letters face-up. Have your child think of any word, and with your assistance, sound it out, find the necessary letters and spell it on the game board. Each new word should connect to the last. Together, make up a silly story with the words, pointing to them as you say them. As your child is able, increase complexity by dealing out random letters: Your child must think of a word starting with one of his letters. He can trade others to finish that word.

Master Mind (Pressman). This game is a winner for practicing problem-solving skills, fine motor control and hand-eye coordination. The mini version is excellent for car travel. Preschoolers love to create patterns by pushing the colored pegs into holes in the box. For a game, hide four single-color pegs. Your child will try to guess your hidden color by placing pegs the color of her guess in the first row. If she's incorrect, you give clues: "Not right yet—which colors haven't you tried?" Subsequent guesses are made in the following rows, while leaving previous rows in place.

This game teaches your child to 1) reflect back to what's already been tried and 2) use the process of elimination to come to a conclusion. As your child grasps these concepts, increase the complexity of color combinations and clues.

Take a peek at your old game closet with a fresh eye. You might just find some "new," creative games that both you and your preschooler will love.

Common Concerns

Chapter Fourteen —————————————————————

Why Kids Bite

by Clara Shaw Schuster

Biting is a normal, healthy (though socially undesirable) behavior in young children.

Children must explore to learn. Consequently, parents should let their baby mouth and bite "safe" objects. However, do not allow a child to bite people. Try to anticipate when your child will bite so you can pull her away before biting occurs. If it occurs before you can stop it, take away her opportunity to bite again by saying firmly, "No! Biting hurts." Then give your child something else to play with to divert her attention.

The child cannot stop himself from biting—he equates biting with exploring. Consequently, to punish your baby with sharp scolding, slapping or biting back will only teach him that it's bad to explore and increase his frustration. The emotional tension can lead to more biting.

Sometimes, young children bite when they are hungry. When they don't have words to say something, they use action. If teething is the problem, a teething ring is a good investment.

Some toddlers bite as a way of saying, "Hello, I like you." ("Biting feels good to me. It should feel good to you too.") They're surprised and upset when their friendship overture precipitates a bad scene. Over-enthusiastic "kisses" can be discouraged by turning your face or with gentle, loving roughhousing.

Toddlers generally bite because they are frustrated. When someone takes a toy away from them, when they can't go where they want to go,

> *Children must explore to learn. Consequently, parents should let their baby bite "safe" objects.*
>
> Clara Shaw Schuster

are sleepy, or can't do what they want to do, they get angry. But toddlers have few social controls—they act the way they feel. Since they can't stop the expression of a feeling, they bite, hit, pinch or kick the closest object or person. Since adults (in a child's mind) can make anything happen, toddlers use biting to get adults' attention or to say in the strongest way possible: "Listen to me, and do what I want! Help me!"

Since a child cannot separate behavior from feelings, when the child is punished he begins to assume that the feelings are bad and, consequently, that he is bad. Instead of punishing your child for biting, try to help him recognize that the feelings are OK and normal, but the *behaviors* are unacceptable; a toddler is old enough to begin to understand this concept in a limited way, with adult help.

The following are steps for helping a child (of any age) to understand socially acceptable behaviors:

• Acknowledge your child's feelings. "You are angry because _____, disappointed when _____, sad because _____," and so on.

• State why your child is upset. "You are sad because Sister took your toy . . . you want to go with Grandma . . . the toy won't work . . . ."

• Set a limit on the behavior. "But I can't let you bite Mommy; that hurts."

• Assure the child of your love and protection. "I love you. I won't let Sister hit you, and I can't let you bite Sister."

• Show your child an alternative behavior. "Use your words. Say 'Help, Daddy,' or 'My toy.'" Sometimes it also helps to give your child a safe object that she can bite, to get rid of the anger energy.

• Help your child experience success when she uses the alternative behavior. Have Daddy "help," or encourage Sister to return the toy.

When necessary, provide your child with a more interesting or appropriate activity that will catch her attention and reduce frustration before it occurs.

Tips to Stop the Biting
by William Sears

The tough part of coping with a biter or hitter is helping him understand which forms of communication are appropriate. But parents need to resist the temptation to reach for the muzzle and handcuffs. There are easier ways to tame a biter or hitter.

• Teach alternatives. Provide your toddler with appropriate words and gestures to express his feelings. Help him make a good social impression instead a lasting impression on your skin: "Don't bite—biting hurts Mommy!" Offer alternatives: "Hug Daddy—give me five."

• Show and tell. You don't have to bite back to let your child know that biting hurts. Here's one technique that parents have used successfully to make the point: Press your child's forearm against his upper teeth as if he is biting himself, but not in a punitive, angry way. Reinforce his self-produced marks on his own arm with, "See, biting hurts!" Administer this lesson immediately after your child bites someone.

• Consider the circumstances. Keep a diary of what situations set off aggressive behavior, such as being with too many kids in a crowded space. Is your child tired, bored, hungry or in a setting where tempers flare? Try to minimize his exposure to these situations.

• Tame the play. If you detect a "mean streak" developing in your child, you can model gentle actions and play such as "hug the bear," "pet the kitty," and "love the doll." Evidence of a developing aggressive streak is found in the child who consistently bangs toys, crashes cars or bashes dolls together. While this certainly is normal play, it's important to balance aggressive play with gentle play. Talk about the difference between "bear hugs" (good for Mom and Dad) and "bunny hugs" (good for fellow toddlers).

• Actively supervise. Keep an eye on biters and hitters in play situations, and encourage other parents to be vigilant as well. If your child bites or hits other children, separate them and isolate the offender for a timeout. Reinforce the isolation with appropriate admonitions such as, "Biting hurts, and it's wrong to hurt, so you're going to sit on the chair to think about why you shouldn't bite." If your child is verbal and understanding enough, encourage him to apologize.

• Protect your own friendships. Your biter may cost you your best friend. The parents of a biter are often embarrassed, and the parents of the bitee are naturally upset that their child has been hurt. If your child bites or hits, prepare the other parents ahead of time. Ask for their help in tempering your child's behavior.

Curbing Perfectionism

by Kevin Leman

Little Kristin, age 3½, anxiously asks Mommy what she can do to help. Mommy says, "Well, Honey, right now Mommy's busy, but maybe later you can help." Kristin whines and cries, so her mommy relents, "OK, Kristin, why don't you go and make your bed for Mommy?"

Kristin, as a wishing-to-please 3½-year-old, goes and makes her bed. Of course, the bed is going to look like a 3½-year-old made it. It's not going to be perfect; it's not going to be like a young Marine's bunk at boot camp.

Kristin calls her mom into the room. Mommy looks at the bed and says, "Oh, Kristin, thank you for helping me." But while she's thanking her daughter, Kristin's mother is smoothing out the wrinkles, turning over the pillow, and making the bed in near-perfect fashion! This discourages Kristin beyond belief.

Many times a parent's disapproval is communicated subtly by actions, rather than words. Kristin's mom didn't mean to blow out her daughter's candle, but the expression on Kristin's face tells us that's exactly what happened; she feels defeated by her mom's superior ability. It's easy to see where a defeatist rationale can come into Kristin's life: "What's the use of trying? Mommy can do so much better than I can."

Most parents probably think they're encouraging their children by pointing out to them that they could have done better. But this kind of "encouragement" really leads to discouragement, and sometimes to perfectionism.

What can a parent do to curb perfectionism in their children? The following suggestions may help:

Always assign tasks to children that they can handle. It's never good to give a child a situation that he obviously can't accomplish. Some parents choose this strategy to "motivate" their children. But it often sets a child up for the pursuit of perfectionism.

Look for the positive. It's just as easy to look for positive things in life as it is negative or critical things. Criticism is a most destructive means of communicating with a child. Constructive criticism *can* be good, of course. But when trying to help a child do something better, it's so important that we *keep the child directed at the act, rather than the child.*

Encourage your children, and give them decision-making opportunities so that they can have a means of making decisions and coping with the realities of life. *When mistakes are made, be practical and develop a sense of humor.* Spilled milk requires a rag, not a lecture. Perfectionists take such things too seriously. We need to help our children by allowing them to learn from their mistakes.

Be aware of comparisons and rivalries in the family. Let each child know that he has an individual, special place in your heart. When making comparisons about children, parents often say things like, "Oh, Harry, do you remember when Susie did that?"—and indirectly tell little Sarah that what she's just done was already done by her bigger sister, who can do things so much better than she can, anyway. We parents often are responsible for subtle put-downs without our realizing it.

Don't model perfectionism. Above all, try to curb your own perfectionist tendencies. Let your preschooler behave as a child; don't expect him to be a little adult!

Your Strong-Willed Child

by Patricia Rushford

Many of us know firsthand about the strong-willed child. They test us to the limit and sometimes make us wonder why we ever decided to have children. They make us ask questions like: Is my child's behavior normal? What am I doing wrong? What can I do to survive this behavior?

I've asked all of these questions about my own two strong-willed kids—and I've discovered some answers. If you have a strong-willed child, take heart; you're not doomed to a lifetime of parenting frustration.

Is my child normal? Probably. Your child is most likely going through normal phases of growth and development and simply has a strong propensity to do things his own way. I remember feeling exasperated when my son turned 2. Until that time, I thought I was an effective parent. I talked to my mother-in-law about how independent and stubborn he'd become. "It gets worse," she said. She was right.

It's normal for children to go through phases of crying, whining, manipulating, throwing temper tantrums, resisting authority and refusing to eat. However, some children's behavior problems may be indicative of something more serious—such as Attention Deficit Disorder. Additionally, some illnesses and disabilities can affect your child's behavior. Allergies, food additives and certain toxins have also been linked to behavioral changes in children. If you suspect an underlying problem, talk with your pediatrician or a child-development specialist.

What am I doing wrong? We parents often blame ourselves for our children's behavior. Certainly we carry most of the responsibility for rearing our children, but for conscientious parents, strong feelings of guilt inhibit our ability to parent well. We may become so overwhelmed

281

by fear or inadequacy that we fail to trust our instincts and intuition.

If you love your kids unconditionally, and if you're doing your best to meet their needs and provide a safe, nurturing environment, you most likely have no reason to feel guilty. Psychologist James Dobson notes, "The willful child can be difficult to control even when his parents handle him with great skill and dedication."

If guilt is a problem for you, write down what you feel guilty about. Ask yourself: Am I really doing something wrong? Do I have my priorities out of order? Am I hurting my children? What can I do to make the situation better? You may also want to talk with a pastor or counselor about dealing with guilt in a healthy way.

What can I do to survive my child's behavior? There are no simple answers to complex problems. But these coping strategies may help your child's behavior and make you a happier parent.

• Avoid unrealistic expectations. Loosening some of the standards we set for ourselves and our children can spare us unmerited guilt. There's no magic formula that instantly transforms us into expert parents. And rearing one child does not necessarily equip you to shape the next one with more expertise. Be patient with yourself and with each of your unique children.

• Ask for help if you become excessively angry. Most of us would never dream of abusing a child, but it's important that we mention the issue when dealing with difficult-to-manage children. The combination of stress, the inability to cope, and a child who won't cooperate can send a parent over the edge. Parents of such a child need the support of a trusted family member or friend when they're overwhelmed.

If you feel close to the edge, ask for help. Take a parenting class, talk with a friend, or join Parents Anonymous, a support group for parents who need an empathetic ear (520 S. Lafayette Park Pl., Suite 316, Los Angeles, CA 90057. 213/388-6685).

• Be objective. Respond to your child by focusing on his needs and how you can meet them. This may mean getting away from your child and your emotions. Take time to think about what's happening, and respond to the problem rationally. When we respond as emotionally healthy adults, we're able to understand, identify and meet our children's needs. The goal is to maintain enough distance from a need to satisfy it.

• Have confidence in yourself. Your child needs to see you being strong in order to feel safe and secure, though she may fight you every inch of the way.

• Be positive. A strong will is important to becoming autonomous. It's a basic tool for survival. It can help children overcome obstacles and persevere in the face of trauma or tragedy.

However, many parents tend to think of strong-willed children in negative terms. These are the kids who "have a mind of their own" or "give their parents a bad time." We talk about the "terrible twos" and "rebellious teens." We might use the terms stubborn, belligerent or argumentative. Instead, use more positive words, such as determined, persistent, imaginative, curious, motivated, dynamic, persuasive and assertive. The labels we use are important; they change how we view our children, and how they view themselves.

Catch your child doing good things, and give a lot of positive reinforcement. Some experts suggest you offer three praises for each criticism.

• Direct your child's will toward God. The will is a good thing. Bernard of Clairvaux, a 12th-century theologian, wrote, "By the will, I love and embrace God." The choices we make, however, can deter the will and bend it in the wrong direction, away from God. Our job as parents is not to weaken or break the will, but to nurture, encourage, correct and guide our child's will toward God.

• Look beyond the behavior. A child usually misbehaves for a reason. Sometimes he tests the limits you've placed on him, or he may simply be telling you he's tired, hungry or needs attention.

Consider 4-year-old Josh. His mom recently took a job outside the home. Now, getting out the door in the morning is the most frustrating part of the day. Josh may want things back the way they were—leisurely mornings with Mom at home. But he may not be able to verbalize his feelings, so he acts them out. He doesn't want to get up. He eats breakfast slowly. He pokes around until his parents finally threaten to take him to daycare in his underwear.

Instead of asking "Why is he being so stubborn?" Josh's parents may ask, "What is Josh really trying to tell us, and how can we help him?" They may get up earlier in the morning or snuggle in his bed so that he wakes up being held and feeling loved. Or they may have most things ready to go the night before so they can have time for a relaxed breakfast before they leave.

• Make your child feel valued. Children who are valued and who learn to value themselves are less likely to go along with activities or behaviors that could harm them. M. Scott Peck, author of *The Road Less Traveled*

(Simon & Schuster), writes: "The feeling of being valuable is a cornerstone of self-discipline, because when you consider yourself valuable, you will take care of yourself.... In this way, self-discipline is self-caring."

How do we affirm our children's value? We say things like: "I'm so glad you were born and that you are a part of our family." "I enjoy being with you." "You draw better than anyone I know." "You are important to me." We get to know their likes, dislikes, concerns, fears and passions.

The Ten-to-One Rule
by Kay Kuzma

Try to give your child 10 positive strokes to every negative one. Because the more difficult child is obviously going to get a few more negative strokes, you must proportionately increase the positive interactions with him in order for it to have the same effect.

For example, you might notice your child's smile, his remembering to say please and thank you, or simply his willingness to spend a few extra minutes playing with the dog. Become a master at catching your child being good.

Remember, a positive stroke doesn't always have to be given in words. Smile, wink, ruffle the child's hair—and he will get the message that you're tuned in to him and will be giving him loving attention.

• Discipline wisely. Often, in an effort to protect children or keep control, concerned parents tighten their grip, causing strong-willed kids to resist like mules.

To avoid conflict, make your rules clear and concise. Decide what's really important. Don't make demands that are impossible for your child to achieve. For example, you wouldn't discipline a 2-year-old for playing with her food or a 4-year-old for wetting the bed. Choose your limits wisely, and make certain you can follow through on the limits you do set.

Be assertive but not aggressive. Parents who hit, yell, and frighten children lose their ability to be effective. Ross Campbell, M.D., says, "Any time you start yelling and screaming, start lecturing, or become negative with your child, you are preventing him from taking responsibility."

Children, especially those 4 and older, who know the rules and yet consistently disobey need to know they have a problem. You can empathize with them and help them work on resolutions, but you may not necessarily be able to fix them. Go to your children with a humble attitude that says, "I love you and want to help—with your imagination, my experience and God's guidance, we can find a way."

• Laugh a little. One of the best ways to defuse family conflict is to find something to laugh about. Lawrence Kutner, Ph.D., of Harvard University Medical School, suggests parents and children together break the cycle of whining. For example, if your child starts complaining the moment you pick her up at daycare, you might say, "Sounds like you had a rough day, too. I think I'll whine with you." Then take turns moaning and groaning and giggling. I've done this before with my children. We ended up laughing and feeling better.

Parenting can be an exhausting job. Sometimes you'll wonder if you've made any headway at all. Then one day, your strong-willed child will wrap her arms around your neck, give you a big smooch, and say, "I love you." And you'll wonder what all the fuss was about—until the next day . . . .

By maintaining a more relaxed, positive attitude and setting reasonable boundaries, you will become more secure in your parenting and better able to cope with your strong-willed child.

Effective Discipline for Strong-Willed Kids
by Kay Kuzma

• Love unconditionally. Make I Corinthians 13:4-7 a foundation upon which you establish your rules and guidelines.

• Let your child know what you expect before you expect it. As psychologist James Dobson says, "If you haven't defined it—don't enforce it." Never discipline a child for mistakes or accidents.

• Children need consistency. Establish routines and follow them.

• Respond with confidence when your child deliberately defies you or challenges your authority. If your child kicks you, stop him immediately. Take firm hold of his foot and say, "Stop!" Then, after he's calm, ask why he's upset and explain why his behavior won't be tolerated.

• Make sure the punishment fits the crime. If a child's misbehavior warrants discipline, make certain it is just and fair. For example, discipline for harming someone should be harsher than discipline for failing to pick up toys.

• Don't argue with your child or get into deep analytical discussions about how she's feeling or why she hit her sister.

• Try a variety of child-rearing techniques. Experiment to find a method that works best for you and your child. There are no hard-and-fast rules.

• Give love and reassurance when the trouble has ended.

• Never discipline a child for showing emotions. Give your child ways to express feelings and vent anger. Have him draw, paint or mold clay. Physical activity such as running or throwing a foam ball can also help.

• Confront in a loving way with gentleness and respect.

Kids Grieve, Too

by Patricia Rushford

Children shouldn't have to experience the sad side of life. At least that's what the Johnsons thought. Andy and Sharon recently lost their infant son to SIDS. They told their 6-year-old daughter, Jamie, as little as possible. Andy and Sharon went to grief counseling and talked to one another about their feelings, but they didn't include Jamie.

Jamie became increasingly ill-tempered, whiny and depressed. The grief counselor suggested that Jamie's behavior might be a reaction to unresolved grief.

"But she's so young," Sharon said. "I just don't want her to be hurt."

"She's already hurt," the counselor replied. "Jamie needs to work through her grief as much as you do."

By working with Jamie and encouraging her to talk about her baby brother's death, the counselor discovered that Jamie's behavior stemmed from the fact that she blamed herself for the tragedy. "I told God I didn't want him," Jamie confessed. She was convinced that God had taken the baby back and that her mom and dad didn't like her anymore because of what she'd done. Her parents had no idea how Jamie felt, because they didn't ask.

As caring parents, we want to protect our children and shelter them from the hard knocks life delivers. But we can't. In fact, keeping them from facing uncomfortable, sad or painful circumstances may hurt them. We can help kids accept and grow through difficult times—here's how:

Give them opportunities to experience life as it really is. Allow Cindy to visit her cousin, Jody, who has leukemia. Encourage Michelle to spend time with her great-grandma, Annie, in the nursing home.

Open yourself to what your children can teach you. In some ways children are far more capable of dealing with pain than adults. Their honesty, sensitivity and compassion have not yet hardened to the cynicism and self-doubt we so often see in adults. When we expose our children to sadness, we may be surprised at their natural caring abilities.

Teach them healthy ways to cope with their fears, losses, confusion and grief. Children who are exposed to the effects of disease, aging and death and who are allowed to enter into and experience sadness and grief tend to be more able to deal with their own painful experiences later in life.

Be aware of your child's limitations. Some are better able to handle suffering than others.

Never force a child. Your teaching should be done by showing, not telling.

Check your attitudes. Children are intuitive and tend to learn more from what we feel than from what we say or do. If you are concerned about the way your children react, they may be acting out what they see in you.

Prepare your child. If you're heading into a situation that could be traumatic, talk about it ahead of time. There are wonderful books out about dealing with aging, illness, handicaps, divorce and death.

Don't look for trouble. Let exposure to the sad side of life happen naturally. Suffering is all around us, and most of the time we have ample opportunity to care for the sick, visit the elderly, and grieve over losses within our own families.

Accept emotions as normal. We often categorize feelings as negative and positive, as if some are right and others wrong. Consequently we feel guilty for experiencing feelings such as despair, frustration or anger. Feelings are neither good nor bad, they simply *are*. When normal emotions are suppressed, they may go away temporarily, but reappear in more severe forms, such as depression or inappropriate behavior. When we accept, express and deal with emotions, they are less likely to produce serious and wrongful acts.

Allow children to feel what they feel. In our eagerness to protect and correct our children, we often inhibit them. We may punish them when they are angry, or tickle them out of their sadness. It upsets us to see children unhappy. Some parents see a child's unhappiness as a reflection on their ability to parent well. An inner voice tells us that if we were doing our job, our kids would be living happily ever after.

Have you ever comforted a tearful child by saying, "There, there, Sweetheart, don't cry"? Instead of trying to talk a child out of being sad, empathize. Hold her close and say something like: "You seem to be feeling very sad. Can I hold you until you feel better?"

Draw them out. Unfortunately, children don't always talk about their problems. Sometimes they're not even sure what's troubling them. Even children who have a good command of language skills may have difficulty describing what's wrong. As a counselor, I've found several avenues for exploring feelings with children:

• Show by example. When you are honest about how you feel, you not only open the door for further communication, you also show your children healthy ways to express themselves.

• Name the feelings. When you sense a child is having difficulty expressing himself, help him. You may say something like, "It sounds like you're *angry*." "I wonder if you're feeling *jealous* about my holding the new baby." "You seem *happy* today."

• Visualize. Children may not always be able to express their concerns, fears or feelings directly, but they can draw, tell stories and play. We can help children deal with trauma by telling stories about other children who have had similar experiences.

Set boundaries. Venting feelings is a healthy way to deal with emotional situations. Occasionally, however, the venting can lead to destructive and unacceptable behavior. Sometimes our emotions build like water behind a dam. The dam may burst and send emotions flooding outside of established boundaries. As we allow children to express their feelings, we show them how to manage them through example and discipline.

Children will experience losses, grief and pain whether we want them to or not. As caring parents, our job is not to prevent pain, but to teach our children to manage their lives in the midst of it.

A Summary of Thoughts on Explaining Pain
by Shelley Chapin

• Be honest with your children about this world and their place in the world. We are great at giving the message, "You can be anything you want to be," yet poor at teaching them that, "In this world you will have trouble." When we emphasize the "happy" and avoid the lessons of pain, we leave our children insufficiently prepared to deal with life.

• Don't hide the reality of illness or suffering from your children. Tell them what is happening to a grandparent, or to the little boy at school with cancer, or to you or your spouse. Children know when something is wrong, and they will have fewer fears if they are included in the happenings.

• Encourage questions. If your children feel free to come to you with whatever is troubling them, they will be far more secure in the face of insecurity.

• Don't be afraid to say, "I don't know." Your children need to understand human limitations. When a child learns early that there are certain things which none of us fully understands, fear of the unknown lessens.

• Be open about your own feelings. If you are hurting for someone you love, don't wipe the tears away when your child comes into the room. Let the child see you cry and hear what those tears are about. You will encourage open communication, and you will model emotional health.

• Model a dependency upon God. As parents, we want so much to have solutions for our children's problems that we sometimes forget to let them see the One who sustains us. A child needs to learn early to depend upon God.

• Remember what Scripture teaches about pain and suffering. God uses the struggles and pains in our lives to mature and strengthen us, and to build character and faith. God will provide for your child exactly what your child needs.

When a Child Gets Depressed

by Grace Ketterman

Only in recent years have mental health clinicians understood that young children may become depressed. Children were thought to be unable to reason abstractly enough or perceive accurately enough to experience this profound emotion. We now know better.

A more accurate interpretation of childhood depression would involve the concept of grief over the many losses children endure. Recently, a baby of some 10 months of age began to change dramatically. From being alert, exploring, and charming, she became apathetic, indifferent, and refused to smile or to respond to any stimulus.

The family history revealed a tragic, sudden divorce which resulted in separation from her father, a great loss of the mother's time due to her return to work, and the absence of her older brother who had to be in daycare elsewhere. Fortunately, with help, her overwrought mother was able to create environmental changes that restored her daughter's laughter and health.

The signs of depression in very young children, beginning at 3 months of age, may include:

• A major and lasting change in mood, usually characterized by a sad expression, lowered activity level, and a loss of pleasure in life.

• Changes in eating and sleeping habits—these may be increased or decreased.

• A tendency to cry, whine or cling to parents.

• Occasionally, depressed children cover their sadness with irritability or even aggression.

When young children experience grief and depression, parents can help. Here are some suggestions:

• Consider your child's current experiences objectively to discover any losses or major changes such as an illness, a family move, the death of a pet, or loss of parents' time and attention.

• Offer your child extra affection, holding, rocking, or even playful tickling.

• Offer reassurance regarding your love and availability to your child whenever he needs you.

Preschoolers (ages 2 to 5) show depression in confusing behaviors. They often look sad, but they act mad. They are often aggressive, breaking toys and hitting friends. They may have had dreams which they can't explain. They may not feel like eating, and they sound angry when they speak.

The causes of depression in preschoolers are several. Most commonly, losses result in depression. Three-year-old Brian had a charming, compliant manner which abruptly changed to yelling, kicking and biting. He would not obey his mom and was demanding of his dad. With fairly little difficulty, his parents realized these changes coincided with the timing of a serious loss. His next-door neighbor's family moved away. Brian's long-term friend and playmate was gone. His parents had tried to prepare him for this loss and wanted to comfort him. But they didn't realize he would act angry instead of sad.

What they did to help Brian can be a guide for you if your child is depressed.

• They understood the pain of his loss, and that losses and pain are commonly covered up by anger and misbehaviors.

• They explained that it's OK to cry and even to act angry about losing his friend, but no matter what, it's *not* okay to break things or hurt people.

• They explained that his friend still loved him and remembered to show him photographs of their times together.

• They arranged some visits between the boys and helped them talk on the phone at times.

In a remarkably short time, Brian was back to being sunny and busy.

Older children may become depressed over school failures or the inability to make a team or get a part in the school play. They often feel they are not as cute or popular as other students. Not making the cheerleading team can throw a child into major depression! A broken friendship can be a devastating experience.

Never minimize your child's feelings. Listen to your child's woes with empathy. Comfort him when he will let you. Help him think out his own solutions, but only when his sadness is relieved. Don't solve his problems for him, and avoid giving out so much sympathy that he learns to feel sorry for himself.

You can not only help your children through small bouts of depression or grief, you can also teach them to cope with life. Children must learn to take what actions they can to deal with losses. They also have to face the fact that there are some things they can do nothing about. Supporting and helping our children through this frustration will give them tools to use for a lifetime.

Childhood Fears

by Kay Kuzma

It doesn't matter to a young child whether his fear is real or imaginary. If he is afraid, *his fears are very real,* and they can't be rationalized away by a well-meaning adult.

Toddlers become fearful when they perceive that they're unable to cope with a situation and feel threatened. The more perceptive a 2-year-old is, the more fears he will probably possess, because he sees more dangerous situations than others and knows he doesn't have the capabilities to cope with them.

As children grow older and more experienced, many of their fears are replaced by feelings of pleasure. For example, the child who refuses to duck his head under water at 2 years of age may be jumping from a 10-foot-high diving board three years later. The 2-year-old who screams at the sight of a dog may have an inseparable shaggy pal at 7.

Here are some suggestions on how you can help your child cope with his fears:

Be an example. Although most children are naturally afraid of sudden, unexpected happenings, such as a loud noise or falling, other fears are learned by being close to fearful people. Very often a child's fears are quite similar to his parents'. Children look to adults to learn how to behave in tense situations. When a thunderstorm breaks, how do you react? If you become upset and nervous, your children may start crying.

291

But if you seem unconcerned, it will be easier for them to overcome their fear.

Control the environment. Since a common factor in many fearful situations is the suddenness and unexpectedness of the event, prepare a child whenever possible by explaining what is going to happen. If your child is afraid of sudden loud noises, warn him before turning on the blender or vacuum. Don't deliberately expose young children to objects or animals that may move suddenly. For example, it may be better to introduce toddlers to a worm, a kitten or a caterpillar instead of a jumping frog, a snapping beetle, or even a jack-in-the-box.

Never force a child into a situation he fears. For example, throwing a child into the swimming pool won't cure his fear of water; patient teaching of swimming may.

Help your child learn to associate pleasant things with the feared object or situation. This "reconditioning" doesn't happen overnight—but it is an effective method for overcoming certain fears. For example, if your toddler is afraid of the dark, play games in the dark, or play your child's favorite story cassette while you cuddle up together.

Talk about fear. Many times, situations are fearful because they are mysterious or unfamiliar. Talking about a fear takes some of the mystery away. In fact, the more a child has been told about a potentially fearful situation, such as hospitalization, the less fearful he will be, since he will not only know what to expect but can begin to build his feelings of adequacy. Role-playing fearful situations can also be helpful.

Help your child develop a sense of trust in his parents and in God's protection. As your child develops a trust in his parents, it will be easier to trust in God. Why not place in your child's bedroom a pleasant picture of Jesus with children, or of him portrayed as the Good Shepherd? Point to that picture daily and remind your child that Jesus is always watching over his children, and repeat those comforting words found in Psalm 34:7, "The angel of the Lord encamps around those who fear him, and he delivers them."

Nighttime Fears
by Gary Oliver and H. Norman Wright
Darkness can be frightening for preschool-age kids; it generates fears of being isolated, left alone or abandoned. If your child struggles with nighttime fear, here are some ways you can help him overcome it:
• Let your child know that it's all right to be afraid. All of us have fears

at some time in our lives. A certain amount is normal, and we don't have to be ashamed when we are afraid. Share your own childhood fears with your child and let him know that they passed from your life.

• Help your child understand that being afraid is temporary. Your child may believe that he'll be afraid forever. If he (or one of his brothers or sisters) has worked through a different fear, remind him of that incident. Discuss the fear with him, how he felt before he faced it, and how he feels about it now. It's best when you do as little talking as possible. Ask your child questions, and let him talk about it.

• Let your child know that it's OK to talk about his fear. Letting your child share his fear will help keep it in perspective. Many parents find it helpful to have their children draw their feelings on paper, role-play their fantasies, or use puppets to talk out their fears.

Sometimes children have difficulty articulating their fears because they're too upset or don't have the verbal skills to express themselves. Counselors often use picture books, having kids point to what they're afraid of. You might also try the sentence-completion approach. Start a sentence, leave the ending unfinished, and let your child finish it.

• Let your child know that it's also normal *not* to be afraid. When a child observes the security of others in a situation that usually scares him, he gets the message that it's possible *not* to be afraid.

• Memorize Scripture. Memorizing God's Word at an early age is a positive step toward eliminating fears. "Fear not" is used 366 times in the Bible. Teach your child to memorize and recite Isaiah 43:1-3, I Peter 5:7, and Proverbs 3:24-26 when he begins to be afraid.

You can also share stories from the Bible to illustrate how heroes like Daniel experienced fear and found God's promises to be true. If you have some Bible-story videos, you can help alleviate fears by watching together and then saying things like, "What do you think David felt when he first saw how huge Goliath was?" After your child has identified with the emotion, it's easier to share the biblical principle that helped the Bible character get through it.

Help for Bedwetting

by Grace Ketterman

Wetting the bed (enuresis) is one of the most emotionally unsettling experiences of childhood. And the distasteful odor and persistent stains can undo any typically calm parent. While most children can remain dry by 2½ to 3 years of age during the day, nighttime dryness doesn't usually occur for another six to 12 months.

Often, parental concern about a child's bedwetting is needless and may even compound the problem by causing the child greater embarrassment. You need not worry about your child having a problem with enuresis until at least age 4. Many families have a history of delayed night-dryness. So take into account your child's family history before you make a big deal about bedwetting.

Common Causes of Bedwetting

Infections. Infections of the urinary bladder are quite common in childhood, especially among girls. The channel (urethra) that leads from the bladder outside the body is fairly short, and the opening large enough to allow germs to enter with ease. Since children may not take time to empty the bladder completely when they urinate, those germs may stay there, creating a chronic, low-grade infection. The burning sensation of such a condition is severe enough to cause the stream to stop and the bladder to stay irritated. Infections result in frequent, poorly controlled periods of urination that are difficult or impossible to control.

Physical abnormalities. While these are rare, they do occur frequently enough that a chronic bedwetter deserves a thorough examination by a doctor who specializes in such cases (a urologist).

Extremely sound sleep. Sleep patterns vary a great deal from one child to another. Some simply sleep so soundly that nothing seems to wake them. Children who normally sleep less soundly may experience unusual fatigue or an illness that results in deep sleep. We believe that, in such cases, children may dream they are going to the bathroom—only to find they have relieved themselves in bed.

Fear of getting up. Many children go through periods when they become anxious or seriously frightened by events in their lives. They may be fearful of punishment for real or imagined wrongs they have done. Getting out of bed in the dark may simply be impossible for them.

Regression to an earlier age. When a new baby is born, a family moves, or a major loss or change takes place, a sensitive child is likely to feel insecure. She may unconsciously yearn to be little again—to be totally dependent for a while. Wetting the bed may simply be an expression of such a need.

A symptom of abuse. Not as rarely as we all wish, children who are seriously over-punished or abused may wet the bed.

A family history of bedwetting. Most authorities agree that bedwetting seems to run in families. Whether this involves some unknown inherited factor or simply tolerant parents is not known. In my opinion, there may well be genetic factors.

How to Stop Bedwetting

There are no simple answers that guarantee success. Since few adults wet the bed, however, parents can rest assured that sooner or later, their bedwetting child will stop. Here are some steps to take:

1. Be sure a urologist checks your child if she has not stopped bedwetting by 6 years of age. Also be sure your doctor has ruled out any chance of infection.

2. To prevent the extremely sound sleep pattern, keep on a dim light and have a source of low-grade, monotonous sound—such as a radio—operating in the bedroom.

3. Restrict fluids for two or three hours before bedtime, especially those containing caffeine. Caffeine is found in chocolate, tea and most cola drinks.

4. If your child is old enough to cooperate, I suggest encouraging her to wait longer between trips to the bathroom. During toilet training, many parents encourage their child to urinate frequently. While this works well for daytime dryness, it may allow the urinary bladder to stay small—too small to hold a night's accumulation of urine. If you care to go to the trouble, measure the urine and rest assured: When your child can hold one measuring-cup full, she is likely to be *able* to stay dry at night.

5. If your child is afraid of the dark, it makes sense to leave on a dim light so she can find the way to the bathroom—or at least to a light switch. Some older children like having a flashlight under the pillow, and use that to light their way.

6. Some families have found a safe, electric alarm pad that is placed under the sheet useful. At the first sign of wetness, a rather loud sound awakens the heavy sleeper. This alarm may startle the family at first, but some have found it quite successful.

7. If all of these physical and mechanical ideas result in no improvement in a few weeks, I strongly urge you to evaluate possible areas of stress in your child's life. Emotional upheaval is frequently a root cause of bedwetting. Here are some common issues that trouble children and may result in bedwetting:

- a family move or anticipated move

• a new baby, or knowledge of expecting one

• any serious illness or accident affecting parents, grandparents or siblings

• repeated, intense arguments between parents

• loud yelling or angry punishment of children (not necessarily the wetter)

• real or imagined guilt—sometimes simply for not measuring up to expectations

• problems at school relating to peers

• a change in attitude or behavior around a relative or any person who might be abusive

8. Some children simply have a habit of letting their parents take responsibility for them. For such a child, I recommend your own version of this talk: "Jimmy, I realize I'm the one who has been upset about your bedwetting. It really is your problem, so I'm giving it to you. From now on, you must decide when you go to bed that you will go to the toilet by yourself.

"If you choose to wet your bed, you will need to get up a bit early so you can wash and dry your linens and remake your bed. I love you and will not be angry with you, but I will no longer be responsible for your habit."

Of course, don't do this until *after* you have had a thorough medical evaluation.

If these points of stress are assessed carefully, you may be surprised to discover how heavy a load your child is carrying. So many children have opportunities to become involved in a variety of enriching events, and they really want to do them. Before you know it, however, a conscientious child can be stretched too far; the pressure builds, and an unconscious desire to be "little" and more carefree can result in a regressive pattern of bedwetting.

As a parent, you have your *own* accumulation of stress. Being human, you may display more irritation than you realize, feeding the guilt and fear in your child or leading to angry arguments with your spouse.

When you have a strong-willed child, you are greatly at risk! Nagging or yelling may seem the only means to get your child to listen. The tension created by yelling or by your own stress can make a child so nervous that he may wet even more.

Remember to be patient. I've never known a healthy high school graduate who wets the bed!

Cures for the Chronic Bedwetter

by James Judge

Researchers agree that children bear no blame for bedwetting problems. Punishment and humiliation have no place in any treatment plan. No matter what treatment you pursue, assure your child that this is a common problem, and that no fault, laziness or sin is involved.

Treatment options fall into three categories:

1. Bladder-retention training. The majority of bedwetters have smaller-than-normal bladders. By forcing fluids during the daytime in order to stretch the bladder, a child can practice controlling the sensation to urinate. Certain exercises can also teach him to interrupt his urinary stream. Six months of effort yield improvement rates of 66 percent and cure rates of 30 percent.

2. Behavior modification/wetness alarm systems. Systems such as Wet-stop (Palco Labs) and Nytone (Medical Products, Inc.) attach sensors to a child's underwear that detect wetness. The sensors are connected to an alarm on the child's wrist or pajama collar. He soon associates the alarm with the sensation to urinate and learns to awaken before the alarm goes off. Long-term success rates of 70 percent occur after four to six months of use.

Despite being associated with the highest cure rates and lowest relapse rates, alarms are used by only 5 percent of physicians. This may reflect the time commitment required or the reluctance of physicians to go through the lengthy explanation.

3. Medications. There are currently two medications for bedwetting. The first are tricyclic antidepressants, particularly imipramine (Tofranil). This drug can be particularly toxic if an overdose occurs, so caution is imperative. Cure rates average 40 percent, but relapse rates are high.

The second medication is Desmopressin (DDAVP), a designer drug similar to a human hormone that decreases urine production at night. One hypothesis is that bedwetters lack the normal nightly increase in this hormone and continue to produce large volumes of urine at night. This medication is administered as a nasal spray and has rapid success, in many cases within two weeks. Effectiveness rates of 50 to 70 percent have been demonstrated, accompanied by a reduced likelihood of relapse if the dose is slowly tapered. Side effects are virtually absent, but cost is a drawback. A one-month supply costs about $100, and the cost for a suggested four-month initial treatment period and the tapering period can approach $1,500.

Before discussing treatment options with your doctor, ask whether this is a problem he is willing to evaluate and monitor. Many doctors simply do not have the time, interest or commitment necessary to evaluate and customize a treatment program for a particular child's needs. If your doctor demonstrates hesitancy or follows a cursory exam with a quick prescription for a "medicine to take care of the problem," seek another opinion.

Above all, remember that your child needs your understanding and patience. That mountain of extra laundry becomes meaningless in comparison to the damaged self-esteem that too often accompanies this problem.

Everything But the Truth

by David Veerman

With all the seriousness he could muster, Don looked little Donnie in the eye and said, "Lying is wrong, son. We must always tell the truth." That evening at dinner, Donnie looked at his mother and blurted out, "Mommy, you're fat!" Quickly, his father shot him a dirty look and told him to be quiet.

"Little Donnie" received mixed messages. His dad has just told him to tell the truth. Then, when he did, he was told to be quiet.

This vignette highlights a dilemma faced by many parents—how to teach preschoolers the difference between tact and lying.

The dictionary defines "lying" as "uttering falsehood, untruths." "Tact" is defined as "showing consideration for others." There is no apparent conflict between these two concepts; it should be possible to tell the truth *and* be considerate of others.

Our problem begins with a misconception of what it means to be "honest." Telling the truth does *not* mean telling *everything* one knows and thinks. Sometimes, in fact, telling "the truth" (being brutally frank) can be hateful and harmful.

Another problem is the cultural idea that to be tactful or "nice" to someone, we must lie by inventing compliments. But there are many ways to show consideration without lying. We can say nothing at all, give opinions in non-offensive terms, or, in an appropriate setting, share our thoughts in love. In other words, timing and wording are critical.

Explain this to your children to reinforce the necessity of telling the truth and to teach them to be tactful. The best method would be to explain the distinction and then talk through specific situations. The most difficult situations involve direct confrontation, in which a person asks, "What do you really think? Feel? Believe?" This is where real examples—or even role-playing—would be most helpful.

Choose situations which are realistic and relevant. You could say, "How would you answer if Jenny were to ask you what you think of her new dress, and you really don't like it?" Use multiple choice answers to make it easier and to give them the idea. Possible answers might include:

A. "I think it's ugly!"
B. "It's beautiful!"
C. "It's interesting."
D. "I think I like your green one better."

Then talk through each possible answer. "A" may be honest, but it is tactless and hurtful. "B" is a lie. "C" is an attempt to be tactful, but probably will not be helpful. "D" is true and employs tact. It tells how you feel without hurting Jenny and embarrassing both of you. The principle is, when confronted, to tell the truth *and* use tact.

In other situations, the most basic principle to share is that we must look for something positive to say to others. This reflects the adage, "If you can't say something good about someone, don't say anything at all." This does not mean that you should *never* offer criticism—but it should be *constructive* criticism. Have your child ask himself, "Will my comment help this person feel better? Do better? Be better?" If the answer to all these is no, then the best approach is silence. When teaching this principle, examples again will help. You could ask, "What would you do if Greg sang a solo but didn't do very well?" Allow your child to formulate and verbalize an answer. Whatever the response, it should be loving, truthful and helpful.

Commit yourself to teaching these concepts to your preschoolers—telling the truth and being considerate of others. Both are biblical and reflect what it means to love and to be Christlike.

Tattlers

by Grace Ketterman

What parent has not faced the problem of tattling? The annoying voice and demeanor of a child telling how bad another child is can at times annoy the best of parents!

Why *do* children tattle? There are two reasons: Some compassionate, wise children see others doing things that are wrong and hurtful. They "tell" in order to stop such actions and set things right. But other children want to feel they are accepted and that they are as good as their peers. By tattling they try to get others in trouble, thereby "proving" themselves better.

In preschool-age children, there is yet another factor. At age 4, children enter a remarkably thoughtful period of life. They have hundreds of questions about every area of life (and even about death). They become puzzled when peers do something that differs from their own familiar patterns, and this can lead them to insisting that parents keep everyone's behavior straight.

Here are the common dynamics involved in the habit of tattling:

• A child needs a great deal of adult attention and protection. He feels insecure or anxious when he is on his own.

• A tattler perceives a parent to be partial to another child. The child will "use" a problem to press the parent into giving him equal recognition.

• Being hurt by a sibling or playmate may prompt a child to tattle. The child is motivated by the desire to "get even."

• A timid child may lack the courage to get even directly with a peer who hurt him. His timidity may prompt him to try to get that child in trouble—passively—by tattling.

Now that you know why children tattle, here are some ideas that can help cure this annoying behavior:

• Pay attention to the child, and try to find out why he is tattling, or if, in fact, he is tattling at all. Sometimes a child is truly mature enough to see another child getting into a dangerous spot, and reacts out of true caring and a desire to protect.

• Stop the payoff for tattling. Even if the victim deserves punishment, make that become secondary to the act of dealing with tattling. Tell your tattler that you will not hear any more such reporting.

• Observe closely your child's interactions with playmates. If supervision is needed, step in quietly before a child feels a need to tattle.

• If one child is trying to get another in trouble because of a need to get even, find out how he was hurt. People almost never hurt someone unless they have been hurt first. It is an instinct to lash out when we have suffered pain.

- Help your child talk about his feelings and explain the situation. Comfort him, and then help him see how his habit of getting even in this passive way hurts the other person, who in turn will hurt *him* even more. The eventual rejection of a tattler is painful to see but in itself this may cure him.

- Teach him how to forgive, understand, and turn his hurts into a strong effort to stop pain, rather than inflicting more. Help him understand that he must choose whether his anger will produce more anger or stop the fight and restore fun.

- If the child tattles because of a need for attention, help him see that such attention costs too much. He is likely to lose friends and may even lose his own self-respect. Find the time to supply his needs for attention in a satisfying way.

- Tell your child there are some things he can do instead of tattling: He can handle the situation himself by helping his peers do the right thing; he can trust an adult to handle the problem in his own way and time; he can let others make their own mistakes and learn from them—unless this involves real danger. If a truly risky situation arises, your child needs to report it. Be cautious, lest in stopping tattling you inadvertently destroy your child's healthy concern about the misbehavior of his friends.

How to Talk with Your Child about Sex

by Debra Evans

Teaching children about sexuality has always been part of parenting. The good news is that it doesn't have to be a negative, confusing or embarrassing experience for you or your kids. From your children's earliest moments, you can give them the values, information and support they need to live healthy sexual lives. Teaching our kids about sex isn't separate from teaching about the rest of family life; it's an integral part of how we view and live out what it means to be created a sexual person in God's image.

Perhaps awkwardness in talking about sex with my own parents prompted me to teach my children differently. Determined to create an open atmosphere in our home where we could discuss tough topics from a scriptural standpoint, my husband and I resolved to stay calm regardless of what our children asked. For us, the question wasn't *whether* we would teach our kids about sexuality, but *when* and *how*.

When they reached the toddler stage, our kids began asking us questions—sometimes ridiculous ones. Since then, though sometimes we've been challenged by their forthrightness, we've tried to respond compassionately, if not always perfectly. From my experiences in our home, in the classroom teaching sex-education classes at the University of Nebraska, and working as a reproductive health consultant for two decades, I've discovered five principles that can help you become your children's primary teacher about human sexuality:

1. Live what you want them to learn. From the time our children are born, we parents "tell" our children what it means to be male and female by the way we stroke a new baby, tickle a 2-year-old son, or praise a 6-year-old daughter. Through what we say and do in everyday situations, our kids quickly learn how we regard sexuality. While our words mean one thing, our actions—through our tone of voice, comfort level, choice of words and style of instruction—can either confirm or contradict that meaning.

Stanton Jones, Ph.D., chairman of the psychology department at Wheaton College, and his wife, Brenna, note that the first step in teaching our kids about their sexuality is enabling our kids to give and receive love. "Which is more convincing," they ask, "distant, rigid, unemotional parents who force their children to memorize 'God is love' and other Bible verses while rarely embracing them, or loving parents who share with their children the joys of God's love while holding them and embodying that love in a vivid way?"

By using sensitivity and honesty in everyday situations, you'll teach your kids that you're comfortable with their sexual design—and your own. If your preschooler starts naming his body parts during bath time, points to his genitals, and asks, "What's this?" a simple, confident reply—"Your penis and your scrotum"—will answer his question without implying there's something bad about his body. Saying "Don't touch that!" or using slang terms for body functions and private parts, however, "says" something else entirely.

2. Be approachable and knowledgeable, and create a comfortable, open atmosphere. If your parents either skirted the subject of sexuality or didn't provide appropriate answers, you may feel uncomfortable when talking about sexuality with your own children. That's normal; *unlearning* misinformation about sexuality is often the first step in learning new ways to teach your children the beliefs, values, acts and life principles you want them to acquire.

"Many of us find it awkward to discuss sex with our children," says Marianne Neifert, M.D., professor of pediatrics at the University of Colorado and mother of five. "Yet we owe it to our children to educate them to function sexually as adults."

To overcome discomfort, start by asking other Christian parents how they handle the subject. Ask your child's pediatrician or family doctor to recommend resources. See if your church offers sexuality education seminars. Check Christian bookstores for books and videos to expand your knowledge base.

Don't worry if you still feel uneasy. There may be times when you don't know the answer to a question. It's OK to say, "I don't know the answer, but I can find out more, and we can talk about it then." When appropriate, use this as a time to learn *with* your child by visiting the library or reading a book together.

"Being able to present sexuality to your child comfortably and accurately has the fringe benefit of enabling broad communication with him in the future," notes William Sears, M.D. "It conveys to your child that you are an open, accurate and willing resource, and it sets the stage for a more meaningful dialogue by the time your child is a teenager."

3. Anticipate questions in advance and practice your answers. When it comes to talking to kids about sex, parents often worry about discussing too much too soon. But in reality, many share too little too late.

The easiest way to discuss sexuality, Neifert believes, is to begin early, answer questions freely and matter-of-factly, and offer age-appropriate information. Also, by reviewing similar information throughout childhood, at different times and in different ways, your children will absorb what they can as your explanations become more elaborate.

An honest explanation, no matter how brief, is always better than none. Avoid putting off a reply, although a specific delay—"Let's talk about that when we get home"—is preferable to, "When you're older, we'll talk about it," or, "It's not nice to talk about such things."

Answering explicit questions about sex "on the spot" takes preparation, practice and patience. On the way home from visiting her pregnant aunt, Diane's 9-year-old daughter asked, "How did the baby get in Aunt Carol's stomach?"

Although Diane was tempted to say, "God put the baby there," she was prepared to supply a more complete answer: "Aunt Carol's baby is growing inside a place called the uterus, not in her stomach. God made a husband's and wife's bodies to fit together through sexual intercourse to produce children and provide pleasure. The woman's body makes the egg, and the man's body makes the seed, called sperm, that fertilizes the egg. When the woman becomes pregnant, the baby grows inside her."

Perhaps as difficult as knowing *what* to say is knowing *when* to say it. If a 5-year-old asks the same question as Diane's 9-year-old, how much information is necessary? Most experts suggest that parents of young children are better off providing brief, basic answers and then pausing to determine if their child wants to ask anything more. Once a child's curiosity is satisfied, he'll usually go on to the next topic. As you respond to your child's developmental pace, you'll find that he'll let you know what he is and isn't ready to hear. However, you may want to initiate discussion if your child hasn't brought up the subject by age 6 or 7.

If you think about the questions your kids are likely to ask before they ask them, you'll have the opportunity to rehearse potential replies. If certain words are awkward to say, practice saying them out loud. Even though you may feel strange doing this, you'll feel more relaxed later.

4. Tune in to teachable moments. Exposing your kids to birth—both the birth of family pets and childbirth within the family—can teach important lessons about the value of life and God's design for procreation. Picture books provide a way to start acquainting 4-year-olds and older children with the facts of life.

As the years go by, draw diagrams and pictures with your child in addition to using books and other visual aids. At some point between the ages of 4 and 8, most children show an interest in understanding where babies come from. Don't wait until after your child has been exposed to others' views and values to pass on accurate knowledge about the beauty of marital sexuality.

With older children and preadolescents, avoid thinking that your child's silence means there isn't anything he needs or wants to know. In reality, your guidance is needed more than ever. Watch for openers to guide your instruction. Since children often don't ask explicit questions, it's up to you to discern their concerns.

Seize natural opportunities to talk about difficult topics as you discuss popular movies or the recent experiences of friends and relatives. If your child is older and sexuality has not been openly discussed in your home, it's not too late. Tell your son or daughter that you're aware you haven't talked about sex much, and you'd like to begin talking about it more.

Stanton and Brenna Jones advocate "inoculating" kids against destructive moral messages. This process involves "deliberately exposing kids to the arguments and pressures they'll be exposed to later in life, but in the safe environment of the family, then showing how those non-Christian influences are unconvincing, false and destructive."

For example, the Joneses suggest, "rather than shielding our children from the argument that sex is essential to really growing up, or that their hopes of having loving relationships with boyfriends of girlfriends depends on having sex with them, we become the first to tell them this argument. Then we help them reason against these destructive messages, thus inoculating them against this argument."

5. Shape scriptural values as you pray for wisdom. "Keeping the good of creation separate from sin's distortions is no easy job," admits Lewis B. Smedes, Ph.D., in *Sex for Christians* (Eerdman's). "We are to love what God has made and hate what sinful men and devils have unmade. The job is to cultivate a clear perception of what is of God and what is of sin."

Cultivating accurate perceptions of right and wrong sexual behavior is every Christian parent's right and responsibility. Our children are growing up with different pressures, in a much more deadly environment, than we confronted as young people. By describing the benefits and blessings of sexual purity—and being honest about the consequences of sexual sin—we can help protect them from lasting harm.

A Step-By-Step Plan for Teaching about Sexuality
by Debra Evans

1. Learn the facts. You don't need a Ph.D. to understand human sexuality; a medical dictionary will help you pronounce unfamiliar words. Get comfortable with terminology and become better acquainted with your own sexual design.

2. Go slowly, one step at a time. As you share information with your child about sexuality, follow a developmental method of teaching. Provide age-appropriate information your child understands. What your toddler can be taught about her body, for example, is limited to simple words; at this age, girls should learn they have a uterus and a vagina, and boys that they have a penis.

3. Follow a natural-learning progression. Each year brings new questions and your child's deepening ability to understand the answers. Answer questions as plainly as possible. Long explanations about sexuality are unnecessary—they can actually raise more questions than your child needs answered now.

4. Take each learning opportunity as it comes. Don't wait to present information about sexuality in the form of a major (and mutually embarrassing) "Big Talk." Children learn best by example and real-life situations. Each day will present you with unique opportunities to teach your children about the wonders of the natural world, including the amazing design of their bodies.

5. Don't ignore your child's sexuality. But don't go out of your way to *emphasize* it either. If sexuality is to be a private, yet natural part of life, as God designed it to be, we need to find a balance. This happens easily if your kids know they can ask you anything. They'll know this when you treat them with respect and answer questions discreetly, in a way that doesn't make them feel ashamed, silly, embarrassed or stupid.

6. Use the show-and-tell method of health education. Use resources such as books, videos and simple, hand-drawn sketches to illustrate your points. For example, to prepare your daughter for her first period, discuss and demonstrate the use of sanitary pads, pain relievers for cramps, daily bathing—even what to do with stained underwear or bedsheets. When your daughter starts her period, make it an important occasion between mom and daughter. Take her out for tea. Buy her a pretty nightgown. Later, when topics such as PMS come up, you'll want your daughter to feel good about bringing her concerns to you.

7. Include fertility appreciation along with sexuality education. By avoiding a single-focus approach to human sexuality, you will give your child the gift of appreciating the life-giving nature of sexuality and the value of human life from the moment of conception.

Sexplay and Young Children

by Heather Harpham

"Why would Michelle do something like this?" Diane asked me. "Should I discipline her? I feel like I should call the other kids' mothers, but I'm too humiliated."

Diane had unzipped a tent in her backyard to find her 5-year-old daughter and two friends, a 6-year-old girl and a 4-year-old boy, naked. When they heard the zipper, the kids jumped out from under a blanket. Michelle looked guilty and began to pull on her shorts.

I tried to reassure Diane that this was probably normal sexual curiosity, but she was still upset. I understood her feelings. The first time my son participated in sex play with a neighborhood boy, I felt confused, and I overreacted. Since then I've learned that a parent's response can easily become part of the problem.

Psychologist James Dobson, Ph.D., advises, "Parents should be careful not to express shock and extreme disapproval of this kind of curiosity." In his book, *Dr. Dobson Answers Your Questions* (Focus on the Family), he states that childhood is an important time for the formation of sexual attitudes, and adds, "Behavior during childhood is influenced considerably by sexual curiosity and interest. It is not uncommon for a 4-year-old to be fascinated by nudity and the sexual apparatus of boys versus girls."

While experts agree that sexual exploration is a natural part of a child's development, it's not uncommon for parents to experience shame, fear, sadness and embarrassment when confronted with our child's first sex-play experiences. Sometimes we simply aren't ready to see our kids as sexual beings. We may believe our child's innocence has been lost—but what's really been lost is our own "innocence" about their sexuality.

In addition, many of us bring personal baggage to this issue. Jenny, a 31-year-old mother, has vivid memories of letting a neighbor boy look under her panties when she was 5—and getting caught. Her mother spanked her and screamed that she'd done a "nasty, dirty, terrible thing!"

According to Susan Colosurdo, a child psychiatrist in Eugene, Oregon, "Our sexuality is a strong part of our lifelong identity. If you have a major shaming surrounding your sexuality as a child, it can have a big impact later." As a parent, taking stock of how you feel about your own sexuality can help you understand the way you respond to your child's.

Finally, some of our anxiety is natural concern. We want our kids to develop a healthy, moral sexuality. It's easy to panic about the possibilities of perversion. The best antidote for our fears is information. We can relax when we know what's normal and what's not.

Normal sex play. You've just walked into your 6-year-old daughter Sally's bedroom. You thought she and her friend Sarah were playing Barbies. But a naked Ken and Barbie have been abandoned, and Sarah and Sally are half-clothed, pants down, in the closet. Is this normal?

According to sex therapists Clifford and Joyce Penner, it's not only normal, it's typical. In their book, *A Gift for All Ages* (Word), they note, "Playing doctor (or other games) is almost inevitable between the ages of 5 and 7."

Patricia Rushford, R.N., describes normal sex play this way: "The children involved are similar in age and are not forced or coerced to participate. They are learning about themselves and one another, gathering information, exploring their sexuality in ways appropriate to their ages. Normal sexual responses may include excitement or pleasure."

They feel pleasure? Yes. But curiosity, not arousal, is the driving force behind most sex play with younger children. "Usually something triggers their interest in sexual matters," writes Grace Ketterman, M.D., "such as wondering what makes a girl different from a boy."

Here are some characteristics of normal sex play:

• Because children sense that adults wouldn't approve, it usually takes place in the guise of a game behind a closed door.

• The most common play is "show me yours, and I'll show you mine." "Doctor," "Mom and Dad" and similar scenarios are also popular.

• Undressing, touching and rubbing each others' genitals is frequently part of the play.

• The children know one another.

• Children may masturbate together.

• Girls playing with girls or boys with boys isn't unusual and, according to experts, doesn't indicate a homosexual tendency.

How should a parent handle normal sex play? According to Ketterman, "Condemnation pushes the child into secrecy and guilt. You don't have to accept the act, but you can accept it's natural to be curious."

It's OK to gently ask the children to get dressed and play something else. You may want to matter-of-factly tell a playmate, "We don't play like that in our home." But you don't want the kids to feel they've done something terrible.

Use the situation to guide your child's curiosity. Ketterman suggests you say, "Those parts of our bodies are very beautiful and very private, so I hope you won't take each other's pants down again. If you have questions about parts of your body, I'll be glad to talk with you about it."

You might feel tempted to stop your child from playing with the involved children. "Though this is a normal reaction," says Rushford, "it may not be a healthy one. If sexual play is within normal limits, children should be allowed together." Supervision usually prevents further incidents.

Interrogating your child about whose idea the sex play was can send the message that someone *should* be blamed, which introduces shame into the situation. Instead, you might say, "Mommy's curious about the game you and Amy played earlier. Would you tell me what happened?" You can help your child along by nonchalantly asking, "And what happened next?" Doing some small task while you talk will help your child relax.

Let the other child's parents know what took place. Keep in mind that reactions will vary. It's best to be casual: "I thought you might want to know that the kids did a little exploring today."

If *you* are the other parent, don't panic because you weren't present. Ask questions, but remember the stress this other parent may be feeling. If someone blames your child or overreacts—keep the conversation short. You might suggest, "This is hard for both of us. Why don't we read up on the subject and talk later?"

Teaching boundaries. The main purpose of teaching boundaries is to give children a defense against sexual abuse. Normal sex play isn't abuse. However, personal boundaries help kids know that they have a right to control who touches their bodies, and that they should respect the bodies of others.

Jan Hildreth, R.N., teaches human sexuality at Central Oregon Community College and is certified by the United Methodist church to write sex-education curriculum. "Even if parents feel uncomfortable talking about sexual issues," she says, "they should do it anyway. It's OK if you start out by saying, 'I'm uncomfortable talking about this.'

"Explain to the child that no one should touch her anywhere that her swimsuit covers," suggests Hildreth. "Also, she doesn't have to touch anyone else in those areas even if an adult says it's OK. Of course, Mommy or Daddy giving her a bath, or the doctor examining her are exceptions."

Parents should also explain that if anyone touches her in a way that makes her feel uncomfortable, she should say, "No," run away, and tell someone. Even small children can remember: *No! Go! Tell!*

Hildreth says boundaries should include what is OK-kissing and not-OK-kissing, as well as the difference between good secrets and bad secrets. "Good secrets are a surprise that you plan to tell later," she explains. "Bad secrets are when you are told *never* to tell something."

Reassure your kids that their bodies are beautiful things God made. Remind them that God wants touching certain areas to be saved for marriage. For now, they need to keep those special parts private.

Use specific language for anatomy, such as "vulva," "vagina," "penis" or "testicles." Depending on your upbringing, such terms may seem offensive. Many of us were taught to use less direct words, such as "wee-wee" for penis. But experts agree that this slang teaches our kids that there's something about a penis to be ashamed of.

Above all, try to speak about your child's sexuality in a way that exalts it rather than diminishes it. For example: "This part of your body is called the vagina, and it's a wonderful part. It's what makes you a girl instead of a boy."

When sex play isn't normal. Mark, 2, and Kelly, 5, had been swimming. Mark's mother, Brenda, didn't think anything when they went into the house. Five minutes later she found Mark lying naked on his bed. Kelly was bent over him, her mouth on his penis.

Although definitions of "normal" vary, there are certain guidelines, says Colosurdo. These signs could indicate when sex play isn't normal:

• There is an age difference of three or more years.

• One child coerces or bribes another to participate.

• Concepts or implements are introduced into the play that are not appropriate to the kids' ages.

• Oral sex is involved. (Colosurdo says it's possible, but unlikely, for a child to come up with this on her own.)

• Behavior is repetitive and compulsive.

• Intercourse is attempted or simulated.

• Physical damage has been suffered. For example, one child tries to shove a crayon up the other's vagina, causing bleeding and soreness.

Based on this list, Kelly was out of bounds on several counts. Perhaps she has been exposed to pornography, abused by an adult, or had something similar done to her by another child.

According to Hildreth, "It's much more common for a child to be abused by an adolescent or an adult." Though it's rare for one child to sexually victimize another, it does happen. Good families with good children encounter this problem.

What if your child is the *perpetrator?* Try to find out where he got the idea. "Have you seen this kind of game before?" Often a counselor can uncover things a parent can't. Don't hesitate to seek professional help, especially if the other child was injured or your child repeats his behavior.

According to Colosurdo, kids who victimize others have often been abused. "Abused children get inappropriately sexualized," she explains. "As a result, sometimes they become perpetrators and do to other children what has been done to them."

Explicit movies, magazines or talk can also trigger inappropriate sexual ideas. Remind your child that God didn't plan for sex to be selfish. He should never take advantage of or use another person.

If your child is the *victim,* stay calm. Colosurdo says that if your child senses you are horrified, he will feel frightened for being involved. Stress that *he has done nothing wrong,* but don't dwell on "the terrible thing that child did to you" either.

"When a child has had a victimization experience," Colosurdo explains, "the parent and family response to it is as important as the victimization."

Inform the other parents as calmly as possible about what happened. Use specific language such as, "Your daughter, fully dressed, placed her mouth over my son's penis." This leaves no room for misunderstanding. Try not to get involved in speculating about why their child did this or why your child "let" her.

In cases that could lead to intervention or prosecution (these are rare and usually involve a much older child) Hildreth warns, "Parents need to be very careful not to put any words in the child's mouth. They shouldn't ask, 'Did he do this?' Just ask the *child* to tell you what happened. Otherwise the child's testimony could be disqualified."

According to Colosurdo, this is good advice for less serious cases as well. "Parents should try to get a sense of how the child himself understood the experience. What was it like for *him?* Did *he* feel shamed? Did *he* feel afraid?" This also helps you determine if you should seek professional counseling.

If you're unsure, it doesn't hurt to wait, Colosurdo says. Sometimes rushing a child to counseling can inflame the situation. Let the child know she's safe, be available to talk, and then watch for signs of adverse "sexualization"—inappropriately talking about or doing sexual things she wouldn't have thought of before.

Other signs that a younger child may need counseling include clinging, nightmares, bedwetting, or not wanting to sleep in bed. For school-age kids, watch for lower grades, increased hostility, withdrawal, sadness, nervousness or non-compliance.

A sexual legacy. When it comes to children and sex play, the good news is that most of it is normal. We can even be glad that our kids' sexuality exists. We parents have the privilege of helping them shape a sexual identity they can be proud of, not ashamed of.

What if you've made mistakes? Take heart. According to Cliff and Joyce Penner, "Children are incredibly resilient. It is never too late to go to them and say, 'Hey, we made some mistakes. We'd like to make some changes in what we taught you.'"

As Christian parents, we can extol the wonder and power of human sexuality. We can reclaim sex from the clutches of an immoral world and return it to our kids as a good and pure gift. And since God created sex in the first place—and has yet to apologize—we can count on his applause.

Plain Talk about Masturbation
by Heather Harpham

Masturbation in children ranges from casual fondling of the genitals to more purposeful and rhythmic self-stimulation. Studies show that at least one-third of young girls and two-thirds of young boys masturbate. That adds up to a lot of concerned parents. How much is too much? Do I scold? Is this sinful? Here are some guidelines from Christian experts:

Give your child dignity. When Brenda walked past her 6-year-old son Matthew's door and saw him masturbating, she was stunned. But she didn't say anything. Later, her husband talked with Matthew about masturbation, never letting on what Brenda had witnessed.

Brenda was wise not to embarrass her son. According to pediatrician Richard Johnson, M.D., it's a mistake to catch a child in the act and then shame him. "On no account should he be scolded, frightened or threatened," he says. Instead, gently direct him toward another activity.

Give your child information. Some kids secretly worry about their masturbation and wonder if they're "normal." When Matthew's father explained that many kids do it, and that he'd done it as a boy, Matthew was relieved.

Experts recommend you approach this subject in the same matter-of-fact way you would other areas of sex education. You might say, "God made certain parts of our body to feel good when we touch them. That's called masturbation. It's something I hope we can talk about."

Give your child a moral backdrop. The Bible is silent on masturbation, and sincere Christians disagree about the moral aspects. But marriage and family counselor MaryAnn Mayo, M.A., encourages us to "view sexuality from the child's perspective; he in no way fantasizes his actions as adults do."

Children masturbate because it feels good, they're bored, or because it relieves tension and comforts them. At this age, they're not "lusting." However, you can explain that when she gets married, she'll want to save those feelings for her mate. You could also say, "Even good things can become bad if we do them too much."

Give your child boundaries. Some kids need to learn that self-stimulation isn't appropriate in public. Psychologist James Dobson recommends that you calmly explain, "There are some things that you do not do in front of other people—like going to the bathroom. They aren't evil, just private."

If your child seems intent on handling his genitals in public, psychologist Georgiana G. Rodiger, Ph.D., suggests you offer the child a substitute activity. "Shall we put LifeSavers in your pocket? Or a ring you can turn?"

By age 5, Mary masturbated so frequently before falling asleep at night that her skin became raw. Her mother's scolding her only intensified the problem.

Jan Hildreth, instructor of human sexuality at Central Oregon Community College, suggests that Mary's parents develop a new routine to help Mary get to sleep. "Perhaps they could rub her back, stroke her forehead, rock her, or play special music."

According to Rodiger, excessive masturbation is often the *symptom* of another problem. "If a child is compulsive, we have to look at the psychological causes. It reflects anxiety on the child's part. This is their way of self-soothing, to feel safe."

Johnson says that many children will stop excessive masturbation when parents initiate more physical contact. He encourages a lot of touching, holding or wrestling. Parents should also look at whether their child is getting enough exercise and stimulation, he says. If your child continues to masturbate excessively and/or in public, seek professional help.

Recognizing and Preventing Sexual Abuse

by David Peters

Experts in the field of child sexual abuse have reported that one in every four girls and one in every five boys will be sexually abused before their 18th birthday. Other recent studies indicate that the rate of sexual abuse may be even higher. Those same studies show that, contrary to popular belief, most sexual abuse takes place within the child's home or extended family. Statistically, most sexual abuse begins when children are between the ages of 6 and 9. Children in this age category are easily initiated into sexual activity under the guise of "love," and are even more easily intimidated into silence.

It has been my experience that children, even very young children, are not in the least uncomfortable being taught about what kinds of touches are good and bad and what to do about them. It's the *parent* who has difficulty dealing with such subject matter. Fortunately, a number of simple, effective teaching aids have been developed to help parents with this important task.

Since sexual abuse is a conspiracy of silence in which a child is coerced through fear, we adults must learn to recognize the signs of abuse. Early detection of sexual abuse also improves the outlook for healing once the problem is brought to light. The following are often indicators of sexual abuse in younger children:

- being uncomfortable around previously trusted persons
- sexualized behavior (excessive masturbation, sexually inserting objects, explicit sex play with other children)
- specific knowledge of sexual facts and terminology beyond their developmental age
- seductive behavior toward adults
- parentified behavior (pseudo-mature, acts like a small parent)
- wearing multiple layers of clothing to bed
- fear of restrooms, showers or baths (common sites of abuse)
- fear of being alone with men or boys
- nightmares on a regular basis or about the same person
- abrupt personality changes
- moodiness, excessive crying
- aggressive or violent behavior toward other children
- change in sleeping habits (does not want to go to sleep, seems constantly tired or has difficulty sleeping)
- clingy behavior and separation anxiety
- regressive behavior (fantasies and/or infantile behavior)
- acquisition of toys or money without explanation.

Also important to the detection of sexual abuse is the presence of physical indicators:

- pain or itching in the genital area
- difficulty walking or sitting
- vaginal discharge

- bruises or bleeding of external genitalia, vaginal or anal regions
- venereal disease
- torn, stained or bloody underclothing
- unusual and offensive odors.

If parents are led to suspect, because of the presence of behavioral or physical indicators, that their child has been sexually abused, they (one parent is better than two in such a case) should talk to their child without distractions in a setting that is comfortable for their child. It is *extremely* important that the parents talk matter-of-factly about the subject.

Should your child reveal that sexual abuse has occurred, remain calm and observe the following guidelines:

1. Believe your child! Children seldom lie about sexual abuse.

2. Assure your child that what happened was not her fault, and that you are glad she told you.

3. Tell your child you are sorry she was hurt and scared and that you will protect her from further abuse.

4. Call an agency that has expertise in the field of sexual abuse.

5. If what your child says causes you to suspect that sexual penetration or injury has occurred, seek medical attention immediately and inform the doctor of your suspicions.

6. Take whatever steps are necessary to protect your child from further abuse. In the case of incest, see that the molester, not the victim, leaves the home.

Remember, your child is counting on you. As a parent, you are responsible to prevent sexual abuse whenever possible through education, and to be loving and supportive in the unfortunate event that abuse does occur.

Learning
New Skills

Chapter Fifteen ———————————————

Talking with Your Baby

by Clara Shaw Schuster

One of the most important skills for new parents to learn is how to talk with their baby. Many people talk *to* or *at* a baby, but most do not realize that adults can and must talk *with* a baby during those crucial early months of life.

When an adult talks to a baby, he concentrates on entertaining the child. When one talks *with* a baby, however, the adult encourages the infant to become an active partner in the communication game. Both baby and adult are rewarded for participating.

True, an infant does not use words. But smiles, throat gurgles, changes in respiratory rate, hands opening and closing, and generalized body movement are all methods by which a baby "talks." Gradually, these generalized methods of attracting and keeping pleasant adult attention become more specific as neurological skills mature.

Talking does not come naturally to babies. It has to be taught by parents through an activity known as turn-taking. Initiating turn-taking games during the first days and weeks of life causes infants to be significantly more alert to, responsive with, and inquisitive about their environments by the time they are 3 to 4 months old. And they are more secure in their attachments and behaviors by the end of their first year.

Parents teach an infant to "talk," or turn-take, when they talk to their child and then pause, *giving their baby a chance to respond before they speak again.* Infants are excited by parental attention and respond with eye

When one talks with a baby, the adult encourages the infant to become an active partner in the communication game.

Clara Shaw Schuster

319

widening, hand movements, shoulder raising and vocal sounds. When a baby begins to realize that his parent will not talk again until he gives a response, he not only will respond, but will begin to "woo" the parent into interacting again. Gradually, parent and infant will have longer and longer periods of communication. If a baby is overwhelmed by too much or too loud parental talking, she will turn her head or become restless. Stop talking until the child seeks your face again.

When your baby is 6 months old, begin to imitate your child's sounds; eventually, your child will begin to imitate your specific sounds and learn language. Vocal turn-taking games eventually become nonverbal turn-taking games, such as "patting on the table" games, "peekaboo," and "fill-the-can-with-blocks" games.

Turn-taking has many significant benefits for a young child:

• The child learns he is expected to respond when someone speaks to him.

• The child learns that adults will listen to her when she "talks."

• The child learns early cause-and-effect relationships. (When I "talk," my parent responds; something happens.)

• The child's attention span increases, which is essential to learning and working.

• The child learns to pay attention to and look for interesting stimuli in the environment.

• The child learns that the parent is a friend, that the parent "speaks my language" and "goes at my pace." Children who learn this are more secure during the toddler and preschool years.

• The child learns to cooperate.

• The child learns to talk, using words at an earlier age.

• The IQ of these children will be higher at 5 and 6 years of age than those of children who did not have early turn-taking experiences.

Talking with an infant can be as satisfying as talking to an older child. But you must know your baby's "language" and go at her own pace.

Tips for Teaching Your Baby to Talk

1. When talking, speak slowly and clearly.

2. Face your baby directly when speaking.

3. Vary the pitch of your voice—babies especially enjoy high-pitched speech and music.

4. Repeat words often.

5. Respond to baby talk by listening and replying with rewarding facial

gestures and comments.

6. Give everything a name.

7. If your baby regularly stays with a sitter or other care giver, hire someone who speaks clearly and properly.

8. Speak kindly.

9. Don't pressure your baby to talk.

10. Play fun music and videos with talk aimed at babies and young children.

Speech Difficulties

by Elaine McEwan-Adkins

A child's ability to communicate makes life more interesting and less frustrating for everyone. But what happens when his speech and language development seem abnormal? How can parents know if a serious problem really exists?

Your child's ability to talk depends on two skill areas: the ability to form ideas and concepts and communicate both by speaking and understanding, and the ability to produce the correct sounds that form those words.

Give your preschooler this quick test:

• Can my child be understood by family members and by his playmates? Listen carefully to your child communicate with strangers. Do they often ask him to repeat what he says? Do they tune out your child because of their inability to understand his speech?

• Is my child producing an adequate quantity of speech? A 3-year-old should be speaking in complete sentences and have at least a 900-word vocabulary. (A 4-year-old uses about 1,500 words, a 5-year-old about 2,000 words.)

• Can my child follow two or three simple directions? For example, "First, take your teddy bear up to your bedroom. Then get your jacket and bring it to me."

Your child's ability to be understood by others can be affected by several factors: the omission of initial and final consonants, the omission of syllables, and fluency. (*Disfluency* is the official term for stuttering.)

If your child has a problem with certain sounds or parts of words, try to determine if he can be stimulated to produce the correct sounds. When you say a sound or word correctly, can your child repeat it? If so, your child probably has the ability to produce the word or sound but just needs time to mature.

Disfluency is very common between ages 3 and 5. Sometimes a child will repeat a syllable; sometimes he will be unable to utter the sound at all. If your child has a serious stuttering problem, nervous movements such as blinking or twitching often accompany the speech difficulty. Local school districts usually have preschool screenings, where your child can receive a free speech and language evaluation.

Voice disorders also cause concern for preschool parents. These disorders are caused by hard calluses, called nodules, on the vocal cords. They can make a child's voice hoarse, weak or breathy. They can be caused by vocal abuse, such as screaming, talking at the wrong pitch, frequent coughing, throat clearing, or constant and loud talking. Your child should be seen by a physician who specializes in ear, nose and throat ailments if you suspect a voice disorder.

A speech and language pathologist who specializes in working with young children is the first person to consult for advice and assistance. Seek help immediately if your child:

- uses mostly vowel sounds at any age after 1 year
- is not talking at all by age 2
- frequently omits initial consonants after age 3
- is difficult to understand after age 3
- doesn't use sentences by age 3
- frequently substitutes easy sounds for difficult ones after age 5
- demonstrates consistently faulty sentence structure after age 5
- is noticeably disfluent after age 5
- decreases vocalizing rather than steadily increases at any period up to age 7
- is embarrassed and disturbed by his speech at any age

Why All This Baby Talk?

by Faith McDonald

Baby talk is language made simple. Adults, especially mothers, often use it when talking to babies. It consists of short, simple sentences, exaggerated pitch and stress, and often includes simplified words.

Baby talk captures the attention of an infant and enables him to focus on learning to communicate. As a child learns to converse, the need for baby talk subsides. But at times, a child who has developed an adequate vocabulary and can communicate in sentences will lapse into this less mature way of speaking.

Don't confuse this with isolated speech misarticulations (like saying "frow" for throw or "wittle" for little) that your child will outgrow. I'm speaking of a noticeable reappearance of babyish behavior, which is caused by a variety of circumstances.

"Copy catting." Often, a child will copy a childish habit of a new acquaintance. All kids indulge in "trying on" behaviors. For them, exposure to a new group of kids is as intriguing as a visit to a candy store. He wants to sample the wide array of behavior he sees.

Be patient, reminding your child how much you like and appreciate *him*. Say, "I see you're acting like Jeff today. I like Matthew, and I hope he comes back soon."

Attention-getting behavior. Occasionally, a child resorts to baby talk for attention. When this happens, the less attention you draw to it the better. Exaggerated responses may encourage a child to continue acting undesirably. If you can't overlook it, try stating calmly, "I can't understand you when you talk like a baby. When you talk like the big boy you are, I'll answer you."

Compassionately respond to your child's felt need for attention by spending extra time with him later.

A sign of stress. Sometimes, return to baby talk is a cry for comfort. The child feels worried or insecure. Perhaps a new sibling arrived. Maybe the child heard frightening news on TV.

If possible, identify the cause of your child's distress and encourage him to express his feelings. Ask questions like: "How did you feel when Mommy was away?" If your child lacks the vocabulary to express his emotions, introduce him to a variety of words that give him that power. Ask, "Did you feel *uneasy* when you heard about the girl taken from her parents?" "Were you *frightened?*" "Are you *scared* now?"

Reassure your child of your constant love and protection. Pray together, asking God to comfort your child. Be patient, remembering your child will feel secure and protected eventually. Once, after I returned from a lengthy trip, my son's baby talk and crying lingered for about six weeks.

Most experts agree that the child who feels threatened doesn't revert to immature behavior intentionally. Don't give in to the temptation to treat your child like a baby. Encourage growth and independence. Remind him of his capabilities. And in all cases, continue to model good adult speech. Kids learn through imitation.

Toddlers As Helpers

by Patricia Rushford

Toddlers love to help. But all too often, toddlers who help create more work for parents. Channeling a toddler's energy and willingness to help into productive experiences is a major challenge. Here are some ideas for making toddlers' "work" a joy:

• Give specific instructions. Toddlers are just beginning to understand and take directions. Make whatever chore you want your child to tackle simple enough to understand.

• Concentrate on one task at a time. Toddlers have short attention spans and are easily distracted. Don't expect them to tackle large projects like doing dishes, setting the table, or cleaning a room. Instead, focus on specific tasks like setting napkins or silverware on the table or picking up blocks.

• Select jobs your child can manage. Muscle coordination in toddlers is not yet fine-tuned. Many tasks that seem simple to us, like folding socks, are not simple for a child whose fingers won't cooperate.

• Be patient. Toddlers take longer to get things done. If you've asked Angie to pick up her dolls, work with her. Expect distractions. A parent's impatience and irritability leads to resistance in the child and gives her a negative idea of work.

• Have fun. Play helps toddlers learn about the world around them and about where they fit into the world. Turn jobs into games when you can, or sing while doing them. One mother made up this song:
Time to put the toys away, toys away, toys away,
Time to put your toys away,
And save them for another day.

• Be generous with praise. Toddlers love to please their parents. Show your approval with hugs. Stickers are nice too. Whatever the task, however small it may seem, applaud and say, "Great job!" But don't fix up or redo work that they're proud of. Perfection usually breeds insecurity.

• Emphasize repetition and routine. These provide a basis of security. Maintain order, "a place for everything and everything in its place" (within reason). A shelf reserved for books, a box set aside for Legos, and a basket for miscellaneous toys will limit confusion.

• Stay involved. Kids love to work alongside their parents. When you give your toddler a chore, don't leave the room and expect him to work unsupervised. Stay to instruct and encourage.

• Be on the lookout for things your toddler can do. Children are spontaneous. Be ready to seize the moment. Among other tasks, toddlers can:

  – put socks and underwear into drawers while you fold clothes
  – hand money or a check to a cashier
  – be the pillow person when you make the beds
  – flush the toilet after you've cleaned it
  – take clothes to the laundry room
  – dust his table while you dust yours.

When you teach toddlers the joy of working, set aside ample time. Be creative. Loosen up, laugh and play. Experience the miracle of their growing and learning. When they are grown and really *can* manage without you, you can smile and say to yourself, "Great job!"

Learning to Empathize

by Allen Johnson

As your child begins to recognize the important role others play in his life, you should see him gradually shift away from self-interest. By the age of 5, your child should be able to be a true friend to other children and exhibit sharing and caring.

The 3-year-old often fantasizes that his wishes and desires can magically produce effects. He cannot really understand or care about how a peer feels as the object of a malicious act. Nothing matters but his own feelings. He might even take pleasure in cruel acts.

During the next two years, however, children learn how to put themselves in their friend's shoes and become aware of pain their friends feel as the object of cruel acts. Understanding other persons' feelings becomes an important factor in their ability to control their own behavior.

Encouraging a child to move from a self-centered, aggressive stance to one of love and consideration for others is, in large part, the responsibility of the parents. But a child is also influenced by others in his social environment— such as grandparents, babysitters and Sunday school teachers.

If your 3-year-old's pleasure in being naughty is not redirected by the persons he loves most, he'll find no reason to give up bad behaviors. But with their help, your child also can discover that he derives greater pleasure from receiving others' love and approval when he gives up problem behaviors. He can also discover that in setting aside attitudes and behaviors his loved ones don't like, he becomes more like *them*.

The bottom line is this: Learning to relate to others is a process of identification, hopefully with positive Christian values and morals. First, a young child develops the capacity to extend himself beyond his own egocentric boundaries so that he can imaginatively occupy the personhood of others. Second, by learning to identify with his parents and other significant role models, the child develops the capacity to incorporate admired qualities of their personalities into his own.

When a child learns to transfer love from self to others, he has developed the capacity to be a true and empathetic friend throughout his lifetime. And because he now can give his friends what he desires for himself, he has learned to love others as he loves himself—the essence of Christ's command.

Taking Turns and Sharing

by Allen Johnson

Expecting toddlers to share is one of those childhood tasks that even the developmental specialists can't agree on. So, as a parent, if you're confused, you're in good company.

One school believes that 2-year-olds are too young to be expected to share. These authorities say that such expectations come out of the parents' need, rather than the child's. Nevertheless, these professionals also think that if a 2-year-old grabs a toy away from another child, the parent should explain that he should not grab and that he must return the toy. This parent-child interaction is not based on the parents' expectations alone, but rather on the need for the 2-year-old to learn what is appropriate.

The second camp would probably agree that well-meaning parents shouldn't create expectations for their 2-year-old that are too high, but should still *begin* to teach sharing when their child turns 2. They believe sharing is not an immediately acquired developmental task.

This group suggests that the parent begin by helping the child learn to take turns. By their second birthdays, toddlers can understand that to share means to give away part of what they have, e.g., dividing a piece of cake.

But some possessions, such as a doll, can't be divided. Taking turns becomes an important part of learning to share. A 2-year-old best understands taking turns with a toy. The child can use the toy by himself or for a period of time, usually about five minutes, after which the toy must be returned. An oven timer can help the child understand how long five minutes is.

As his parents, you can be your child's role models of sharing. For example, you could start when the child is an infant to say to him that you are sharing this apple with Dad. By the time the child is a toddler, he will have heard Mom and Dad say numerous times that they share with each other, with the child, and with others—with missionaries by tithing, for example.

Growing up in a sharing home helps the child to learn the concept naturally. My parents were Salvation Army officers who worked daily with homeless men and women. My brother and I were constantly taught the importance of sharing God's love and care with those less fortunate than ourselves.

Even as a toddler I would be involved in my folks' mission work, and after the day was over, my parents would talk about how I had helped Tom or Sue that day. In that way, my small activities were remembered and identified, and they also were recognized as beneficial to others. When I said my evening prayer with my parents, we'd pray for each person by name. I could see that sharing was an important part of being a good child and Christian.

Catch your child doing something right. If the child shares small things, then the child should be recognized and complimented. The parents could say how nice it was that he shared his toy. Children love positive praise, and so they'll share more in the future to get it.

Sharing Ideas
by David Veerman and Mary Manz Simon

Teach by example. All family members—parents, grandparents, older brothers and sisters—have prized, protected possessions. Little ones learn as they watch. Ask yourself, "What does my life teach about sharing?"

Provide opportunities to be with other children. Sharing can only be learned when there are others present with whom to share; therefore, it is important for your children to play with others. "Mother's Day Out" and other daycare programs are ideal, because they provide an opportunity for children to play in a neutral setting with toys that don't belong to them. This will be especially helpful for a child who has no siblings with whom to "practice."

Don't expect them to share everything. Every child should have a special toy that can be off-limits. Make sure she knows, however, that most toys *can* be shared with brothers, sisters and friends. Also, don't expect your child to share with destructive children. If you see that a friend is banging your daughter's doll against the wall, admit to yourself and to your child that protection is sometimes appropriate.

Discuss the "whys" and "hows" of sharing. Prepare your child for potential conflicts *before* her friend arrives for the afternoon. Explain that Bonnie will want to play with her toys and that sharing is *good*. Remind her that she has played with others' toys at their homes and in Sunday school. And tell her to call you if there is a problem; yelling and fighting aren't allowed. Also, at an appropriate time (such as at the dinner table or family devotions), discuss an applicable Bible passage or Bible story.

Be a referee. When a conflict arises, don't force the issue, making one child give in to the other. Instead, talk over the situation with them and try to reach a compromise *together*. After they agree, heap praise on both parties for their great sharing attitude.

Discipline when necessary. If your child makes extreme demands, is belligerent or disobeys, step in and take action—quickly and firmly. Remove him from the room and apply the appropriate punishment with an explanation. In a severe case or a repeat performance, apologize to the your child's friend and take him home.

Recognize many ways of thinking of others. A child who begins each bedtime prayer with "Thank you, God, for the great day you gave *me* and *my family*" can be taught to include concerns for "people I love" and "hungry children in the world." Gradually, children can pray to God for and about others. For some children, offering words might be easier than offering things. After all, a 3-year-old might find it much easier to pray for "people who need houses" than to share a stick of gum with a sister. Be sure to acknowledge all kinds of giving.

Set up ways for giving to happen. "Here are two buckets. Please give one to Carlos." This offers a natural opportunity for sharing. It's also programmed to be successful so the child will feel good about giving. Once you start looking, you'll uncover numerous possibilities for encouraging giving.

Celebrate the satisfaction of giving. It's easy to forget to affirm the good that happens. Do that whenever possible. Say, "That was a loving thing to do" or "What a neat surprise that you helped Jackie pick up those toys." Call attention to the positives.

Making Decisions

by Grace Ketterman

It's breakfast time at 3-year-old Brad's house. Brad's mom wants her son to eat a nutritious breakfast. In many homes, this could be a setup for a power struggle.

But Brad's mom knows that no one likes being told what to eat. She knows that Brad responds to choices and likes to feel the "big-boy" control of making decisions. So she gives Brad a choice of two cereals, a nutritious one that she knows he likes and one that she would like him to cultivate a taste for—oatmeal.

She says, "This morning we're having cereal. Would you like Corn Whammies or oatmeal?" Brad is given a choice, based on equal nutritional value. He chooses and feels the independence and power in making a decision. Brad's mom is laying the foundation for a lifetime of making the right choices.

Preschoolers are capable of making many choices, but they need practice with small, less crucial choices, like what to eat for breakfast before they can tackle the big ones. Each time your child makes a decision and assumes responsibility for that choice, his character grows.

Two kinds of choices. Start your preschooler out with either/or choices in which there are two acceptable decisions:
- We will have either hamburgers or hot dogs. Which do you want?
- Would you rather put away your clothes first or your toys first?
- You must finish either your vegetables or your meat before leaving the table.

Then move into the more complicated when/then form of choice making:
- When you have finished your breakfast, then you may go outside and play.

- When you have finished picking up your toys, then I will help you clean the rest of your room.
- When you say, "Please," then you may leave the table.

When offering a when/then choice, always mention the less desirable activity before the more desirable.

With the more sophisticated when/then type of choice, a consequence is implied. It becomes obvious to the child that until breakfast is finished, there will be no playing outside. Whether this means five minutes or an hour is a choice the child must make.

Steps to the right decision. Here are some guidelines for helping your child learn the art of choosing:

- Collect the necessary information. Form a clear picture of the problem; for example, your daughter's room is a mess.
- List the possible options. Make a list of both good and poor possibilities—seeing poor options in writing frequently makes it easier to eliminate them.
- Make the final choice. Eliminate all the poor options to make the ultimate choice easier.
- Live with the consequences. Never rescue children from the painful outcomes of bad choices. The natural consequences of decisions will teach you to reinforce the success of wise choices or avoid the pain of poor ones. Praise your child for making difficult decisions and avoid saying, "I told you so."

Review the entire process. This helps a child analyze past choices that will enhance future decision making. Avoid lectures and condemning attitudes. Gently and clearly help your child to realize what was good or poor in his decision-making skills.

Independence and Confidence

by Debra Evans

Learning to balance parental care and protection with a child's growing need for independence is a step-by-step process. In just four years, a child moves from womb to cradle to crib to twin bed; from infant carrier to baby walker to back porch to schoolyard.

But by appropriately responding to your child's changing needs and abilities, you can nurture his independence without restricting the process of self-discipline and discovery. Here are a few ideas that can help:

Establish a healthy bond with your child. Nurturing healthy independence in children starts with a deep attachment between parent and child. When such an attachment exists, it's more likely that you'll want to foster your child's unique abilities and self-awareness.

In *On Becoming a Family* (Delacourte Press), pediatrician T. Berry Brazelton writes, "The purest sign of attachment is the ability to *detach* at appropriate stages in the [child's] development. This is critical to his ability to act for himself and to learn about the excitement of autonomy." Brazelton also says, "If he is overwhelmed even by the most caring parents, opportunities for testing out capacities in himself may be missed."

A foundation of loving care and parental supervision enables children to move beyond the security of parents and take risks in less predictable environments.

Nurture your child's sense of discovery. As you watch your child and follow cues about where he's headed, you can encourage him to move with increasing independence in new directions.

Regarding a study with mothers and their babies in Kenya, Brazelton reports that babies sat alone at 4 months, walked well at 9 months, and engaged in reaching behavior significantly earlier than babies whose motor skills were being studied in the United States. In addition, researchers noted that the African babies also displayed greater excitement upon achieving each milestone than their American counterparts did. Two years of study attributed these differences not to the babies' growth rates, but to the way their mothers subtly influenced their children's autonomy and self-discovery.

The study showed that it wasn't the mothers' verbal rewards and suggestions, but *the babies' own excitement at self-discovery* that provided reinforcement in acquiring new motor skills. When the mothers demonstrated a task, encouraged their children to do it, and then stepped back, the babies progressed most quickly.

Provide and guide. Then let your child try new things without unnecessary interference. As your child's most influential teacher, you can use silent supervision to reinforce learning and discovery. Though your preschool-age child needs to be near you as he plays and participates in the world around him, he usually doesn't need to be told what to do. In most instances, you can let him take the lead once you've demonstrated how things work in a safe setting.

Initially, your child's independent play will be fairly predictable. But

331

as he matures, his experiments will inevitably become more complex and risk-laden for you both.

Whether it's sitting up in the bathtub for the first time, learning to dress himself, or doing several laps in a preschool swim class, each new stage represents a certain level of risk. As a parent, it's your responsibility to weigh these risks against your child's maturity level and developmental capabilities.

Recently, a friend's 4-year-old son walked down the cul-de-sac by himself (with Mom watching out the window) to go play with a new neighbor. "He seemed so young to be doing that," says his dad, Brent. "Yet in just a year, he'll be getting on a bus to go to kindergarten—so I guess we need to prepare him."

Thankfully, God gives us the opportunity to guide our children one day at a time. The better we know our kids, the easier it is to make wise choices.

Use discipline to teach the boundaries that will result in your child's health, happiness and independence. The dangers kids face today are even greater than when my daughter was little. How can parents discourage streaks of independence that could result in harm to their children?

The answer is in viewing discipline as "training up" children, Proverbs-style. According to William Sears, M.D., pediatrician and author of *Creative Parenting* (Dodd, Mead & Co.), a disciplined child is one who "trusts his environment and is secure in his love-attachment with his care-giving parents; radiates both self-control and self-esteem in his desire for parental approval in an environment of mutual respect; emerges a better person for the problems he has solved and the parental input he has received; and, upon graduation from his home education, emerges a happy, feeling person, confident about the intellectual potential he has achieved, at peace with himself and society, with his actions directed by his conscience." That sounds like the type of resourceful, independent person we want our kids to grow up to be.

Sears advocates using the privilege-responsibility ratio: more privileges equals more responsibilities. He stresses that the behavior modeled by parents has a direct and lasting impact on the child.

It helps to know that parenting is a learn-as-you-go process for *all* moms and dads, no matter what their backgrounds.

"I thought I understood children before I had one," said my friend Nancy, who has a Ph.D. in early-childhood development. "But when Carl was born, life was much more challenging than I'd anticipated. Finally, I just started watching my son more and reading my books less," she said. "My education helped, but it was through my daily interactions as a mother that I learned what attachment—and detachment—actually means."

As your child reaches each new stage, you'll be required to reorganize your thinking as you adjust to his new abilities. This process will continue until he reaches adulthood.

Stay flexible—and humble—and you'll continually be amazed at your child's ability to grow into the adult that God created this little person to be.

How to Nurture Independence
by Debra Evans

• Let your child help with the housework. Teach him to work with you. Allow him to make mistakes without criticizing.

• Talk to your child about your daily experiences in words she understands. Listen actively and show your interest when she tells you about her feelings, adventures and concerns.

• Take your child along on shopping trips and errands. Explain how money works and why you choose to buy or not to buy certain items. Include cost-cutting strategies—coupons, sales and rebates—in your discussions.

• Introduce your child to your friends. Teach him to be courteous. Include him in appropriate social activities. Let him prepare for guests by fixing and serving food, setting the table, and answering the door.

• Encourage your child to show you her favorite activities and invite her to participate in yours. Jogging, bike riding, hiking, cooking, gardening and fishing are some activities that even toddlers can be involved in with parents. Use a child seat, push cart, stroller or backpack to bring your child along until she's old enough to engage in these activities herself.

• Allow your child to visit your workplace with you and see what you do there. Explain your responsibilities and show him the kinds of tasks that you perform.

• Get to know your child's friends and their parents. A play group is an excellent way for younger children to be involved in activities without a hovering parent. Give your child the freedom to play alongside others as you talk with the other parents.

Getting Dressed

by Patricia Rushford

Hannah, my charming 2-year-old granddaughter, darted into the kitchen wearing a sheer slip that reached to her ankles—and nothing else. "I dancing," she said, grinning. Her large, indigo blue eyes sparkled as she pirouetted around the room.

I was about to croon, "Oh, how adorable," when my daughter, Caryl, groaned: "That's the fourth time today she's changed her clothes. She's driving me crazy."

Why do toddlers change four or five times a day? Why do they resist wearing clothes? Unfortunately, babies don't come programmed with rules like *People don't walk around naked.* Or, *We don't wear panties on our heads,* or *Little girls don't wear their big brother's undershorts.*

Then there's the laundry problem. Clothes come off. Where do they go? On the floor, of course. As our busy child digs through drawers for something to wear, the neat little pile of socks, underwear, shirts and pants turn into a wrinkled, unidentifiable blob.

What's a parent to do? Here are some suggestions on fighting the clothes war from several battle-weary moms.

Decide which wars you need to fight. As my daughter so aptly states: "Toddlers have this radar thing when it comes to trouble. They're into everything. You have to choose your battles according to what you feel is most important. And you need to stick with your decision, otherwise you'll be disciplining them constantly."

Be consistent. If your child changes clothes every time you leave the room, don't punish her one time and laugh at her the next. This is difficult for parents. Sometimes wearing nothing is cute. Other times, like when we've got five minutes to make a doctor's appointment, it's exasperating. Try to handle problems in a similar way each time.

Choose your strategy early on. Before a problem develops into a full-scale war, consider ways to minimize it. Decide what method of discipline to use. Be certain your punishment fits the crime.

Plan a counterattack. If you can think like a child, you can outwit your toddler. Below are some field-tested techniques that may prevent the clothes war, or at least minimize it.

• Keep clothing out of your child's reach, or put a lock on the drawers. But do provide ample opportunities for children to dress and undress themselves.

• Set out two outfits and let your toddler choose her clothes for the day. Some 2- and 3-year-olds love to make choices and have definite preferences. Others aren't ready, so you'll need to choose for now.

• Try a firm approach. Calmly redress your child, restate your rule and use the timeout method whenever he opens drawers and closets or undresses inappropriately.

• Provide an alternative. Gather old, oversized clothes, hats and shoes for playing dress-up. Show your children how to put the clothes on over their own so they don't have to undress. When playtime is over, simply gather the clothes and toss them in a basket or toy box. With alternative play clothes, the family's clothes will remain neat and clean in their drawers.

With wit and imagination you can turn the clothing war into a game you both enjoy.

Bedtime Routines

by Chuck Cerling

"Eric, it's time for bed!" his mother yells from the kitchen where she is finishing the dishes.

"OK, Mom."

Ten minutes later his mom steps into the living room. Eric is sprawled on the carpet, contentedly watching TV.

"Eric, I thought I told you to go to bed. I want you to get ready right now."

"Yes, Mom." Eric groans as he struggles up from the floor and heads for the bathroom.

After another ten minutes, Eric is standing in the hall doorway, still watching TV. "Eric! Move! *Now!*"

Later, she walks to Eric's room to check on his progress. He's curled up on his bed reading. "Eric!" she screams.

"Yeah, Mom, I'm getting ready," he mutters as he jumps from his bed.

An hour later, Eric finally is in bed—and his mother is screaming mad.

Must bedtimes be such a hassle? Four principles have enabled my wife and me to avoid many common bedtime hassles. They may also be of help to you.

Put your child to bed; don't send him. You cannot send your child to bed while you work on other chores. Whenever your child sees you occupied with something other than putting her to bed, she will take advantage of your divided attention. Children know when you are weak, and they use it to their advantage.

You also should not make your child feel like she's being banished from the family at bedtime. Give her your full attention as you put her to bed, staying with her all the way.

Establish a bedtime routine. As adults, our minds and bodies operate best with a regular bedtime routine. When adults come to me for counseling about their sleep problems, one of the first things I tell them is this: "Establish a bedtime routine. It prepares your mind and body to fall asleep."

Establish a routine for your child by putting him to bed at the same time each night. You can make a small exception by using a slightly different time (half an hour to an hour later) on Fridays and Saturdays when your child can sleep later the next morning.

I also suggest different bedtimes for different ages. In the military they say, "Rank has its privileges." So give your older children a later bedtime in recognition of their age and its privileges. This also gives you special time to spend with each child.

Each night, about ten minutes before bedtime, warn your child that it's almost time for bed. This gives her time to prepare for you to interrupt her play. I don't like to be taken away from a special project without warning, and children don't either. This mentally prepares your child to quit playing and get ready for bed.

Make bedtime special. Use this time to get to know your child better. Use it to share important truths you want him to carry into life. Read a Bible story to him, use a devotional book, or read from Christian or secular classics. This not only teaches important truths, but it also allows a child to quiet down in preparation for falling asleep.

Pray with your child each night after you read to him or put him into bed. You not only can teach him how to pray, but you also can listen to him tell God about the things that concerned him during the day. Then talk with him about these concerns and include them in your own prayers, demonstrating your love for him.

Most parents object at this point, saying, "My child would talk the night away if I let him!" But I answer, "So what?"

In the first place, most children only talk too much when nobody listens to them. If you truly listen to your child, he will learn to stop talking when you say good night. Second, in the hurry of modern life there is little time to talk with your children as they grow up. If you want your child to talk with you when he's a teen, let him talk to you each night as a young child before he falls asleep.

When our children were small, we often finished bedtime with a back rub. The kids loved it (who wouldn't?) and it prepared them to fall asleep. Two usually fell asleep soon after we left the room—though one didn't.

Employ "peace aids." To prevent problems after we left the bedroom, we used three aids to keep the peace. First, we insisted that our children stay in their beds even if they didn't feel like going to sleep. There's an important principle here: I can't order my children to go to sleep because I can't *make* them sleep. My non-sleeper, Jon, often deliberately stayed awake during nap time just to prove to us that he could. But he stayed on his bed, because that was something we *could* enforce.

As our second aid, we kept a night light on in the children's rooms. When I was growing up, my father said, "You don't need a night light. You can get used to sleeping in the dark." He was right, of course; but his advice was wrong emotionally. A night light helps a child to feel more secure and less fearful of the unknown that closes in with the dark. It also means that when he gets up he is less likely to hurt himself. One mother installed night lights after her son got up to go to the bathroom, smacked his face into a door frame and blackened both eyes.

One final aid: We let our children read in bed awhile before going to sleep. As our children grew, we watched this privilege become a daily devotional habit for each of our children his or her preteen years. Each learned much about the Bible and Christian living through this practice. We usually established a half-hour limit for their reading, a concession that gave them what they wanted (reading time) and us what we wanted (sleep).

Hassle-free bedtimes are possible for your family, too. But your children must have a high priority in your eyes; if they come after housework, your job, and church duties, the system I've outlined will never work.

Bedtime Blessings
by Claudia J. Morrell

A good bedtime routine does not need to include books, although that is a tried-and-true method. The key is to use a process that is settling and soothing. More important than the actual program is a consistent and uninterrupted routine. Children vary tremendously in their needs at bedtime, and what may work for one won't necessarily work for another. By combining some new ideas with a few great old ones, even parents can enjoy their children's bedtime routine.

Sing together. Tuck your child in, darken the room and sing one or two soothing songs. You may wish to practice those songs your kids recently have learned in Sunday school.

Plan the dreams. Ask your children to tell you something pleasant that they would like to dream about. By filling their minds with positive thoughts, common fears are less likely to bother them.

Play the "listen game." Occasionally, when children are really wound up, sit quietly in the darkened bedroom for a moment. Then discuss the different night sounds your hear.

Make up a story. A story doesn't need to be a masterpiece of intrigue as long as your child is in it. My daughters love my making up stories featuring them in adventures with various "Sesame Street" characters, even though they seldom go anywhere more exciting than the shoe store.

Review the day. My older daughter seldom tells me about her day at kindergarten the moment she comes home. But she is always interested in replaying her day in great detail at bedtime.

Plan tomorrow. Variations in schedules can be better accepted by children if they understand them ahead of time. Tell your children what's planned for the next day and allow their input. You'll function better as a family than you would if you merely dictate schedules to your children.

Make a new song. Children first recognize and love the voice of their mother, whether she can carry a tune or not. Add your own words to a familiar tune, but keep the song soothing to calm active little people.

Pray together. The final bedtime prayer is an excellent way of indicating to children that the evening is concluded and it's time to sleep. Contain silliness and overly lengthy prayers by requiring that prayer be limited to special loved ones. Tell your child she can continue her prayer silently after you leave.

Bless your children. Dr. Leon Rosenberg, a clinical psychologist at Johns Hopkins Children's Center, suggests that children need a clear signal—be it a kiss and hug or a few carefully chosen words—that tells them the day is over and so is the routine. As Christian parents, it's natural that the words you use should be a blessing.

"May the good Lord watch over you and keep you safe through the night." The words work as the signal to children that there will be no more games or stories. But more than that, they instill comfort and a sense of being protected even in sleep. That, combined with a kiss and hug, leaves most children feeling content and ready to rest.

Parenting
Your Preschooler

Chapter Sixteen

Why Creative Thinking Is for Every Child

by Christine Yount

Five-year-old Topher was lost between towering stacks of sugar-coated cereals and instant coffees. Steve and Cindy frantically searched for their son, finally finding him sobbing at the front of the grocery store.

Later in the car, his parents used the incident to teach Topher more important life skills. They talked for a while about Topher's options when he was lost.

On the heels of this conversation, Topher asked, "What if I get lost in the forest?"

"Well, what would you do if you got lost in the forest?" Steve asked.

"I'd make friends with the animals," Topher decided.

"How are forest animals different from cartoon animals?" Cindy asked.

And from there the Parolini family imagined all the options Topher would have were he ever to get lost in the forest.

Many parents would have been so shaken by this incident that they would've missed the opportunity to teach their child creative-thinking skills. But Steve and Cindy understood the importance of developing Topher's imagination. One of their primary goals in parenting is to help Topher be a creative thinker.

The ability to think creatively is a crucial life skill. Anthropologist Mary Catherine Bateson of George Mason University says, "Developing our children's imagination is essential if they are going to have the skills needed to adapt to change."

> *Developing our children's imagination is essential if they are going to have the skills needed to adapt to change.*
>
> Mary Catherine Bateson, anthropologist at George Mason University

"If we teach [kids] how to think creatively, they will be better able to function in tomorrow's society," says Kimberly Wynne, coordinator for thinking skills at the Farmington Public Schools in Connecticut.

What is creativity? Many people mistakenly believe that if they can't paint or compose music, they're not creative. But there's so much more to creativity.

The God who created orchids and giraffes is the God who created us. Because we are created in the image of a creative God, each of us has incredible potential to be creative.

You may not be able to draw more than simple stick figures, but every time you adapt a recipe, stretch the budget a little further, or resolve a relationship problem, that's creativity. Every time your child makes up a story, pretends to be someone else, or spouts off a list of rhyming or nonsense words, that's also creativity.

The ability to think critically is a big part of creativity. Critical thinking includes many skills, such as predicting outcomes, drawing conclusions, devising strategies, solving problems, creating analogies and drawing inferences. Creativity also involves a passion for discovery and the freedom to express yourself.

By developing creativity in your kids, you equip them to face problems head-on, consider all the options, and choose a course of action. When my 4-year-old asks me where his milk is, I may respond with "Is it in the cow?"

"No," he giggles.

"Is it in my shoe?"

"No."

"Where is the milk, Grant?"

"It's in the refrigerator."

This silly game helps Grant think of possibilities, wild as they may seem, and broadens his thinking and imagination.

How to develop creativity. In order to develop creative-thinking skills in your child, look for his potential to be creative. Believe in your child's God-given abilities.

Use these tips in developing your child's creativity:

Be patient. Developing creative children can be messy. Creativity involves seeing things in new ways. At lunch one day, Grant held a black olive overhead on his forefinger and declared, "This is a helmet!" Rather than scolding him for the olive juice seeping down his arm, I laughed and said, "It sure is! What do you do with your helmet?"

Be childlike. Get on the floor. Wear the beat-up cowboy hat. Enjoy the pretend cookies and tea. Ask questions! Help children imagine even more of their fantasy by having them talk aloud about what they're doing. When your child goes pretend shopping, ask what she's going to buy. Pretend play enables children to "become" scientists who discover new life forms in space or translators who help world powers negotiate peace.

Use creative arts wisely. To develop critical thinking skills in your child, present him with projects that aren't counterproductive to creativity. When we say to our kids: "Here are some materials. Now make your materials look like my example," we aren't developing creativity; we're developing the ability to follow directions.

This simple art project will get your child thinking creatively: Give your child a sheet of paper and crayons. Ask her to draw a picture of a place she would like to go. After the picture is finished, ask her to explain it. Ask questions, such as "Why do you like this place? What would you do there? How would you get there?"

Allow problem-solving. When your kids have a problem, don't jump in immediately and solve it for them. Giving kids time to think through possible solutions and the consequences of each solution develops critical thinking. For instance, Tim and Sondra McKibben ran their grandfather's four-wheel scooter onto a pile of rocks and high-centered it. Adult family members refrained from intervening so that the two children would have to figure it out for themselves. It took 45 minutes, but the kids accomplished it on their own.

Give children choices. Even if the choice is as simple as whether they want two or three cookies, decision-making enhances thinking skills.

Anne Every allowed her teenage daughter to choose the colors to paint her new room. Suzanne chose lemon yellow and lime green. Anne cringed at the thought of a "fruity" room. But today, Suzanne is a critical thinker; her creative ideas have been pivotal in developing organic produce for their family farm.

Encourage perseverance. Creative people often have many ideas, but they may not pursue specific ones. Creative children may lack the self-confidence or self-discipline they need to carry out their ideas. Robert J. Sternberg, professor of psychology and education at Yale University, writes: "Almost every major creative thinker has surmounted obstacles at one time or another, and the willingness not to be derailed is a crucial element of success. . . . We need to learn to think of obstacles and the need to surmount them as part of the game."

Your teenager may want to design her own clothes, but in the process she may become frustrated with mistakes and cast aside a garment. Rather than scolding her, just encourage her to take a breather. Then go back to the project with her and help her start again. Encourage your daughter to see the value in the *process* as well as the finished product.

Experience all five senses. Help your children embrace the sense-capabilities God has given them. Point out the sights, sounds, textures, tastes and smells in daily life. Ask questions about how your child experiences these in different situations. Encourage specific answers such as, "I liked the sour taste," instead of a generic, "I liked it."

Explore with your children. Psychologist Teresa Amabile writes in her book *Growing Up Creative* (Crown): "In creative homes, parents really become intellectually engaged with their children—they discuss things, question assumptions, investigate, explore. Parents and children look closely at the world together and become excited about it."

Imagine the outcome of Topher's question about being lost in the forest had Steve barked: "That's not the issue! You weren't lost in the forest, you were lost in the store!" A creative parent recognizes those teachable moments to explore life with a child and to help him think creatively.

Creativity Boosters
by Christine Yount

Use these age-appropriate ideas to develop creativity in your kids.

Preschoolers

• Provide toys that require children to create something. Building blocks, Legos and puzzles are good examples.

• While in the car, ask your child for three items she wants to make up a story about. Then work together to weave a story. Or create new songs to familiar tunes.

• Keep a well-stocked supply of various art media. Use watercolors, crayons, chalk, tempera paint, fabric paint, glitter glue or markers. And don't limit kids to just paper; let them finger paint in the tub, create chalk drawings in the driveway, or use markers to make "rock" people.

Elementary Ages

• Play games that require thinking skills, such as Junior Pictionary or Clue.

• Encourage your children to work together to create a play. Help them think through the story line, necessary props and any required special effects. Then have them perform.

• Play "What if?" games. Ask, "What if Martians landed in front of us?" or, "What if you could go anywhere in the world just by imagining it?" Children can write and illustrate the stories in blank books. Laminate them with clear adhesive plastic.

Older Children

• Play games that stimulate thinking, such as Pictionary or Balderdash.

• While watching a movie video, stop it and discuss possible outcomes. Ask, "How do you think the character will resolve his problem?" Or, after watching the news, ask your teenager what he would do if faced with the same situation.

• Help your teenager devise a strategy to accomplish a goal, such as buying a car or getting a part-time job.

Understanding Your 4-year-old

by Debra Evans

"Really, the 4-year-old is very versatile. What can he not do? He can be quiet, noisy, calm, assertive, cozy, imperious, suggestible, independent, social, athletic, artistic, literal, fanciful, cooperative, indifferent, inquisitive, forthright, humorous, dogmatic, silly, competitive."

Sound familiar? Dr. Arnold Gessell's classic description affirms what most parents have already discovered: The age of 4 is both fun and frustrating, full of exaggeration and imagination, a year marked by both big talk and out-of-bounds behavior. Ask any parent to describe his 4-year-old; you're likely to be answered by a knowing chuckle rather than a detailed personality profile.

Four-year-olds are famous for asking about the "whys" and "hows" of things, for boasting and bragging, for making up stories and telling tall tales, for assertively wanting to do it "by myself" and acting aggressively toward others. Name-calling isn't uncommon, under provocation. Defiance often turns a simple "No" into a determined "I won't!"

It's normal to wonder if there's any hope that this often bossy kid ever will become a godly adult. Yet, considering what is happening from a child's self-centered orientation, the universe is absolutely chock-full of things to discover and experience firsthand, including rules and limits.

Parents have the privilege of setting the rules and defining the limits that provide safe boundaries for the out-of-bounds preschooler. It's not an easy task, to say the least. By keeping things in perspective, however, you can avoid being pushed beyond your ability to cope.

• Rather than viewing your lively 4-year-old as unruly and rebellious, remember that, both mentally and physically, he is in a period of disorganization and rapid growth. Set clear expectations and provide a protected environment for play and everyday recreation. Avoid expecting your child to act like an adult, but be firm with rules he can understand and follow. Establish daily routines to give greater stability to his experience of the world around him.

• Evaluate various methods of discipline, then be consistent in applying the one that works best. Spanking may lose its effectiveness for some 4-year-old children, who may respond more favorably to social isolation (timeouts or separation from the group in a nearby room) and natural/artificial consequences to their behavior. The overuse of physical discipline actually heightens a rebellious, defiant attitude in some children.

Clearly describe the behavior you expect, then stick to what you've said. Loss of privileges, cleaning up messes, and saying "I'm sorry" to the appropriate person are all ways to teach your child about the results of his words and actions.

• Affirm your 4-year-old frequently, and reward meritorious behavior. Your child needs to hear from you, to feel the warmth of your smile, to be encouraged by the positive strength of your embrace. Saying things like, "I'm glad you are you," "What you need is important to me," and "You can explore and experiment, and I will support and protect you," will send the clear message that he is a lovable and capable person.

Above all, try not to forget that the fourth year is temporary, that "the fives" will most likely bring a greater degree of organization and stability to your child's life. By then he'll reach new levels of coordination and achievement. Just when you think you may not be able to take another moment of his boisterousness, some particular nuisance behavior or irritation will become history. Looking back, you may even be able to laugh about it.

Preschoolers and Pets

by Mary Manz Simon

There are a couple ways to view pets and preschoolers:
   1. Pets and preschoolers make a winning combination. Just look

through pictures you received with last year's Christmas cards. You'll find at least one prize shot of a young child with an animal.

2. If you have one, don't have the other. That viewpoint was expressed by my husband, who might have remembered when our little Christy sampled cat food in our neighbor's kitchen.

At the same time, there are real advantages to having a pet:

• A pet can be an "always friend." A pet will never say, "Share your toys," or throw sand in your face.

• Caring for a pet can help a child develop a sense of responsibility when age-appropriate jobs are assigned.

• A child can observe firsthand the stages of life when a dog gives birth to puppies or when a fish dies.

• A child who cares for a pet has a clear niche in the home and visibly contributes to the family unit.

But before you rush to the nearest Humane Society, let's be realistic: A young child really can't handle complete pet care by himself. If you have a preschooler and want a pet, you'll need to assume responsibility for both of them. However, young children can be *introduced* to animals in several non-threatening and short-term ways. Consider these possibilities:

• Borrow an animal. Ask if your family can care for a classroom pet during the summer, or "pet sit" for a vacationing neighbor. This will give your child an idea of what is involved in having a pet, and it offers you an opportunity to observe your child with an animal.

• Sign up as a "pet parent" at a local zoo. Children and adults contribute financially to the support of specific zoo animals. Programs vary, but most zoos offer educational information on the adopted animal and schedule specific events for zoo parents. Choosing to sponsor a different animal each year is an excellent way to expand your child's horizon of the animal kingdom.

• Take advantage of opportunities to let your child interact with pets: Visit the animal barn at a fair, spend time at a petting zoo, or ask if your child can pet an animal at a local pet store.

As you introduce your child to animals, remember that one of a preschoolers' top-five fears is large dogs. Don't push your child to overcome uncertainties in this area by forcing him to relate to every tail-wagging animal. With repeated, informal contacts and increasing age, almost all preschoolers grow out of this fear naturally. Also, carefully supervise your child and animals. As you know, young children make many and sudden movements—these can easily frighten some animals. Some kids need to be shown how to approach and gently pet animals.

If your family is ready to own an animal while your child is still young, choose a pet with minimal requirements. For example, hermit crabs are fairly inexpensive, don't require a lot of space, and offer entertainment. Gerbils and guinea pigs are soft and cuddly. (But if your child is allergy-prone, avoid furry and feathered friends.) An aquarium with a few fish doubles as a night light.

The advantages of pet ownership will still be valid for your child several years from now, when he's more capable of assuming responsibility for someone in addition to himself. Pets and preschoolers? They go together most easily when a child plays with his Noah's ark set or cuddles up to her teddy at night.

Checking Out a Preschool

by Elaine McEwan-Adkins

If you've begun to wonder whether you should enroll your child in preschool—and which school is best for your child—here are some questions to consider before making your final decision:

Is preschool essential to my child's academic success? Preschools for 3- and 4-year-olds are not essential. A home play group or a Sunday school class can provide many of the same experiences. Unfortunately, many parents want more than just "fun and games" for their kids before they enter kindergarten. They want high-powered academic programs that will ensure success in later life. These parents are rushing their children to grow up quickly and to become self-sufficient.

Forcing independence on children has the opposite effect from the one most parents intend. A highly structured, competitive atmosphere can be detrimental to children; experiencing failure before they have the social and emotional skills to handle it can be devastating.

Then what is the purpose of preschool? Preschools should be child-centered and should provide activities and learning experiences. In an ideal preschool, the focus is on creative play. Stories and songs are a part of each day. There is an ample supply of arts and crafts materials, and children are encouraged to create. Preschools should give children an opportunity to play and learn with other children in a low-key and unstructured way.

How do preschools differ? Preschools are characterized by three basic philosophies:

• Traditional preschools encourage free play and discovery learning. Children make decisions about their learning, and teachers leave them free to explore.

• Academic preschools focus, through direct instruction, on the development of pre-reading and pre-math skills. Content is taught by teachers rather than being informally discovered by students.

• Montessori preschools provide students with specially developed material for learning. Children choose what they will learn from three categories of materials and activities: those to develop competence in daily activities, such as washing and sweeping; those to develop sensory skills, such as playing with blocks, beads and shapes; and those that teach the academic skills of mathematics and reading.

What should I look for when I visit a preschool? When you visit a preschool, talk with the teachers, observe for an extended period, and talk to parents of students already enrolled. If you only have time to evaluate one element, evaluate the teachers. They will be the most important part of your child's preschool experience. My grown children still talk of their preschool teacher with reverence; she made them feel special and loved. What she taught was incidental to who she was.

Preschool at Home
by Mary Manz Simon

Not all children need preschool. Four-year-olds have needs that can be met efficiently at home—but it does take planning.

Socially, a child needs opportunities to play with children her own age. She needs to practice sharing, to act out roles in dramatic play, to learn how to lose and win and to get along with others. Your child can have these kinds of experiences when friends come over to play. Also expose her to short-term programs—story times at the public library, swimming lessons, preschool fitness classes—so she will learn about being part of a group. Sunday school offers an ideal social opportunity; she'll meet other young Christians, and the curriculum usually offers developmentally appropriate learning experiences.

Emotionally, your child needs a chance to talk about her feelings, identify how she feels at different times, and be in a warm, positive environment. Feedback and experiences should produce many opportunities for her to feel good about who she is, how she is growing and what she is learning.

Mentally, your child needs exposure to many books, places, people and things. You can take your child to the zoo or fire station, both typical preschool field trips. When you go, talk about what she sees—stretch her vocabulary and creative thinking. If you see a polar bear, talk about where it lives, what it eats and what it does. Borrow a library book to learn more about it. Extend her thinking with questions: "What would you like about being a polar bear?"

Physically, your child needs opportunities to use small and large muscles. That means she should draw with chalk on the sidewalk, use her finger to write her name in the sandbox, work puzzles, put together Legos, Lincoln Logs and Tinkertoys. Play catch with her. Go on a daily walk around the block together.

Spiritually, a 4-year-old should have the chance to learn Bible stories, pray, regularly participate in worship and church activities, learn songs about Jesus, and watch you practice forgiveness.

The world of a 4-year-old can be wonderful, whether she's at home or spends some time as part of a group. Enjoy a rich year of life together, and your daughter will have a head start on kindergarten and a strong foundation for the years ahead.

Preparation for School

by Jeanne Zornes

The first day of school—it's the door opening to at least a dozen years of formal education. Yet the steps up to that door are just as important as those leading through it. Scientists say that 50 percent of a child's intellectual development takes place between birth and 4 years of age. You are your child's most important teacher before he reaches kindergarten—and after that as well.

Because parents' roles are so central to the development of preschoolers, it's important that you be aware of what you can do to help prepare your child for school. You can equip your child with many basic skills that are foundational to success throughout his school years.

Learning experts say that by the time a child meets the kindergarten teacher, he should be able to do the following:

- Write his or her first name
- Say or sing the alphabet

- Count at least to ten
- Recognize colors
- Identify major body parts
- Recognize four basic shapes (circle, square, triangle, rectangle)
- Put together a simple puzzle
- Jump with both feet
- Balance on one foot for five to 10 seconds
- Tell the left hand from the right hand.

In addition, kindergarten-age children should be taught their first and last names, age, birthday, address, telephone number, and parents' or guardians' names.

They also should know how to button and zip a coat, tend to their toilet needs, wash hands, use a handkerchief, and eat properly. Their speaking should be intelligible to an adult.

Laws require that your child's immunizations be updated. A physical exam prior to the start of school may be required too. Dentists advise a checkup.

During kindergarten registration in spring or summer, children usually meet their teachers and see their classrooms. One kindergarten teacher sets aside a day in June for all new students to preview an hour of school. They enjoy a story and craft, are shown around, then are taken out to the playground. Mothers and fathers bring their kids, but do not stay.

You can further prepare for that first day by making "dry runs" to the school grounds—either by car, if a child will be bussed, or on foot, if the school is nearby—so that streets and crossings are familiar.

One mother of three put her youngest in a stroller and walked her small family to school several times during the summer, allowing the children to play on the grounds before they returned home. "This way," she explained, "our little girl learned the route to school and got acquainted with the school grounds before the time when older children might intimidate her."

Your child will experience two divergent emotions on that first day: eagerness and fear. With kidnapping being a continuing concern, parents should teach their children how to say "no" to strangers. A librarian can recommend picture books on this subject.

You can help build anticipation for school by allowing your child to choose a new outfit for the first day. All removable clothing (sweaters, jackets, coats, boots, mittens) should be labeled with your child's name.

Your child will likely feel both eagerness and fear as the first school day approaches. A chain "countdown" calendar can help your child feel more in control during the last couple of weeks before school starts. Simply paste or staple together paper links for as many days as there are until the first day of school. Attach the chain to a picture or drawing about school. Allow your child to cut off one link each day.

Beyond the above suggestions, most preparations for school happen in the years going back to infancy. Your child will absorb spiritual values, "when you sit at home and when you walk along the road, when you lie down and when you get up" (Deut. 6:7). In addition to spiritual matters, preschool learning includes these areas:

Emotional. Nurture a healthy self-image in your child. Display his art work and mention it often. Use positive phrases like, "Thank you for helping," or "That was a good idea," instead of the self-confidence shriveling, "You're dumb," or, "I've told you a hundred times."

Listen to your child with your eyes, as well as your ears. Answer those endless questions. Let her begin to make choices—such as clothing, food, toys, gifts for others, the site of a family outing, the arrangement of her room, what stories and books to read.

Ask about a favorite play project. What may look unintelligible to you may have much thought behind it. One 5-year-old spent his afternoon using every snap-block in the box on a structure that took up most of the fireplace hearth. Then with great pride he explained to his mother the details of his "chemical plant." It stayed up for days.

Relational. If your child doesn't know any of her future classmates, invite children over to play before school starts. Throughout the preschool years, encourage playtime with others where sharing, taking turns, and cooperative play are nurtured.

Allow her pleasant experiences away from parents; Sunday school, visits with relatives, or play at friends' homes provide good training for the separation from parents at school time. Invite young singles as well as senior citizens into your home so that your child learns to relate to people of all ages.

When angry behavior erupts, teach the child to seek out the adult in charge.

Responsibility. Give your preschooler some simple chores, such as setting silverware at the table, taking his own plate to the counter after a meal, emptying wastebaskets, cleaning up his own room or play area, and caring for a pet, even if it's only a goldfish. Instill respect for neighbors' yards and possessions. And help him learn to follow directions cheerfully; one family's code of conduct is "IBGT"—"I'd Be Glad To."

World awareness. Help your child foster an interest in her environment. Let her play with sand and water. Go for walks and talk about whatever she sees—soil, water, flowers, weeds, animals, birds, clouds, trees. Take her through the barns, crafts and horticulture displays at fairs. Whenever possible, include preschoolers in adult activities, like cooking and yardwork.

Art appreciation. Sing to your child from infancy on. Make sure he has his own tapes and a tape recorder he can run himself. Use classical music as a background for play or mealtimes. Take him to concerts and ballet productions. Even if you live in a small community, there are recitals and student concerts to attend. Hold family dramas by re-enacting well-known children's stories. One father delighted his children with "Goldilocks and the Three Bears" by donning an old fur stole and playing "bear."

Let your child cut, paste, color, paint. Give him blank paper to create on, rather than confining him to the lines of coloring books. Help him make his own birthday cards, thank-you notes, or picture-letters for friends and relatives.

Reading readiness. Read, read, read to your child. Make it a routine activity before naps or bedtime. Nothing can better prepare her to read. Ruth Love, once superintendent of Chicago's public schools, said, "If we could get our parents to read to their preschool children 15 minutes a day, we could revolutionize the schools."

Elaine McEwan-Adkins, M.Ed., author of *How to Raise a Reader* (LifeJourney Books), also stresses reading aloud. "Children always have the time," she says. "If we do not fill their early days with the printed word—Bible stories, outstanding children's literature, poetry, and the classics—then television will step in as their primary teacher. As for me and my house, I'd rather they read."

Make library visits as much a survival routine as buying groceries. Let children choose some of the books; pick others yourself, with the help of reading guides. Ask the librarian about winners of the Caldecott Medal, an award given each year's best picture book.

Read with expression to your child. Ask him questions about the pictures and about the story, when you are done. To further prepare him for reading, help him direct his eye movement from left to right by moving your finger along the words.

Finally, be sure your child really is ready for school. Boys typically are half a year behind girls in their maturity. Boys and girls who turn 5 the summer or fall they start kindergarten may lag along not only that year, but throughout their school careers. An extra year at home often helps.

Learning goes on all our lives, but that big door called kindergarten must be opened at just the right time. And remember, there are two hands on the door to your child's future—one small, but one big.

First-Day-of-School Jitters

by Allen Johnson

Do you remember your first day of school? For many of us starting school was a fun experience. The idea of learning new things sparked our curiosity. But for some children, the first day of formal school can be an anxiety-laden experience.

You may have noticed that when your child feels fearful about a new experience, such as starting school, he may behave in the same way he did when he was much younger, such as by clinging to you, or resuming thumb sucking. During these anxious times in your child's life, he will ask for extra attention or reassurance that everything will be OK.

Since beginning school can be such a big event in your child's life, try to keep other changes to a minimum. For instance, if you have been planning to redecorate your child's room, wait until she has settled into the school routine before making the change.

Encouraging a child to talk about what she may be thinking or feeling is one of the best ways to help her cope with these new experiences. If you can remember how you positively dealt with these same worries, share it with your child. We all feel better when we have some alternatives at our disposal to cope with challenges when they arise. They seem much less threatening to a child after she has thought them through with a loving parent.

Here are some additional suggestions:

• Have your child play with other children starting at the same school. Suggest that they play "school" together. When children play about fearful future experiences, they often feel less anxious about the new events as they occur. And typically, a more positive child will pass along better attitudes to a worried child, rather than the other way around.

• Compare the similarities between attending Sunday school and attending regular school with your youngster. For example, although he may have felt scared on the first day of Sunday school, he came to enjoy it and to learn a great deal. His teacher and classmates were new to him then, but they came to be his friends. Reassuring him that the same will happen in kindergarten will be helpful.

• Prepare your child for learning new rules and ways of working differently from the way it is done at home. For instance, a new rule might be that you must raise your hand to talk. Explain to your child that these differences are OK. Because he may feel embarrassed when scolded by the teacher for disobeying the rules, your prior explanation will help him be less upset when it happens.

• Parting with "I love you," "Have a good day at school," and, "God bless you" is much more beneficial to your child's sense of well-being than the command, "Be good."

• Your child will want to tell you about his first few days at school. Set aside time after school to hear about his escapades. These talks should focus on the good times as well as the scary ones. Siblings can be invited to listen, but they must let the new student talk for his allotted time.

• Finally, a brief prayer after your child has told you his school adventures can become a special time of sharing. Thanking God for the good times and praying for his help during the scary and difficult times is most reassuring.

Reading Readiness

by Elaine McEwan-Adkins

Perhaps you have already succumbed to the pressure created by the "whiz kid" mentality that pervades our society today and have purchased flash cards, cassettes, and computer programs that promise your child will learn to read in 30 days or fewer. Or you may be hesitating, not sure if you have the time or talent to take on such a challenging task. In either case, you are concerned about getting your child off to the best possible start in school.

I was no different as a preschooler's parent. As a former teacher, I was well aware of the importance of reading in a child's academic career. When my daughter Emily moved through the early years, I attempted to "teach" her some reading skills. A comic strip in our local newspaper provided drills and practice on the rules of phonics. But she would have none of it.

You can imagine my surprise when Emily came home from kindergarten in early October to announce that she had learned to read that day. After much persuasion, she demonstrated her "newly learned" skill. She could indeed read. And she believed she had learned in just one day. But I knew better. The preparation for this moment had been five years of continuing conversation, incessant questions, endless repetitions of nursery rhymes and poems, and the reading aloud of hundreds of her favorite picture books.

Some researchers, fascinated by children who come to school already knowing how to read, interviewed parents to discover what elements those homes might have shared. There were four:

1. Reading took place regularly in the home. Parents read to children routinely. The parents themselves read. Reading was part of the family lifestyle.

2. A wide range of printed materials was available in the home. Magazines, books of all kinds and newspapers were part of the interior decorating scheme.

3. Children had lots of contact with paper and pencil. Children were able to produce their own scribbles and scrawls and do their own "writing."

4. Finally, all of the adults in the environment responded to what the child was trying to do. They took seriously his attempts to make sense out of the written and spoken word.

You may have noticed that formal reading instruction was *not* on the above list. But reading aloud to your child daily, from early infancy on, is one of the most important gifts you can give your child. Reading aloud takes time, patience, involves one-on-one parent-child interaction, and requires a sensitivity to the needs and interests of your individual child. It is quiet and unhurried. The rewards are definitely long term, and there are many detours and side streets before you reach your destination.

My advice is that you toss out formal programs of instruction and visit your church and public libraries. Stop *teaching* and start *sharing*, introducing your child to the richness and variety of both Christian and secular literature.

Parents engaged in teaching their children to "read" frequently become caught up in the importance of letter names and sounds. Time spent in talking about a story or laughing over some jokes and riddles will be far more beneficial to your child's development than drilling on an isolated "skill bit." A child also benefits by having a chance to learn about human emotions, other kinds of people and places, Bible stories, trucks, trains, animals, plants and famous people.

For many parents, there are two important reasons for reading aloud: You'll have fun while developing a close relationship with your child, and your child will grow up to be a reader. But for the Christian parent, the reasons for reading aloud are even more compelling. We have been challenged in the Scriptures to raise our children in the ways of the Lord. In order to nourish his faith in God's Word, the Christian must be able to read.

Tips for Making Reading Enjoyable
by Kevin Leman

• Make reading a game. Once your child has learned his ABCs, you can have fun playing "The Alphabet Game," especially during long trips in the car. Compete by looking for letters on billboards, highway signs, store windows and marquees. First you find an A, then a B, and so on. The first one to get through the alphabet is the winner.

• As your child learns to read simple words, let him read to you. Chances are he'll enjoy this role reversal, especially if you show genuine interest in what he reads. When your child stumbles over a word, you may be tempted to immediately tell him what it is. Instead, let him try to figure it out himself. If your child just can't seem to get it, you have at least encouraged him to use his brainpower. To let him struggle further would only frustrate him. Make an agreement with your child that if your can't figure out a word in three tries, you'll tell him what it is.

• Encourage your older children to read to younger siblings. This is an excellent way to involve an older child in the life of his younger brother or sister. It gives your reader a chance to practice, teaches the children to cooperate, gives parents a break, and sparks younger children's interest in reading.

• Record favorite stories on cassette tapes. This way, a child as young as 3 or 4 can "read" to himself as he plays the tape and looks at the words and pictures. An even younger child may memorize a book and pretend he is reading.

• Show interest in books your child brings home. Pick them up. Look at them. Ask about them. If possible, sit with your child and either read the book to him or have him read it to you. Hold your child close, with plenty of body contact, as you read to him. This develops both good self-esteem and positive feelings about reading.

• Take him to the library as often as possible. Young children love to go to the library and pick out their own books, because this makes them feel "big." It's a good idea to explain how the library works, and introduce your child to the librarian.

• Finally, let your child see you read. As he watches you choose and read books yourself, you become a powerful model of what you hope to teach—that reading is important and enjoyable.

Why Math Skills Count

by Elaine McEwan-Adkins

There are a lot of books about the importance of language development and reading for your preschooler, but only a handful emphasize math.

Mathematics instruction is changing in schools, and you want your child to be ready to enjoy the fun. Educators are realizing that there is more to math than excessive drill and memorization. Today's students are learning algebra, geometry and statistics as early as kindergarten.

Mathematics is more than just counting. It also includes classifying objects, identifying shapes, interpreting graphs and estimating things such as distances, times and amounts. Here are some simple ways to help your children have fun with math.

Sorting and classifying. Gather four to five each of 12 different things. Mix them up in a bucket, and let your child sort them into the compartments of an egg carton. Try different sizes of bolts, nuts, metal and rubber washers, bobby pins, paper clips of different sizes and colors, buttons, safety pins, cut-up plastic straws, beads and dried beans. Vary the collection to maintain your child's interest.

Counting. Help your preschooler learn numbers the same way she is learning the alphabet—gradually and with a lot of hands-on experience. Write numbers on the bottom of an egg carton and have your child put that number of items in each section.

Supermarket math. When you're shopping, ask your child to get three bars of soap, two packages of cereal or five cartons of yogurt. At the checkout, give your child the pennies from your change to count and put in her penny jar. When she has collected enough pennies, let her count 100 of them to exchange for a dollar bill. Deposit the dollar bill in her savings account and make your trip to the bank a field trip.

Supermarket classification. You can classify what you buy at the supermarket in many different ways: whether you eat it for breakfast, lunch, dinner, snacks or at any meal; whether you eat it hot or cold; whether it is sweet or sour, smooth or crunchy, healthy or junk food, liquid or solid; whether it belongs in the fruit and vegetable, dairy, grain, meat or bread group; whether it is packaged in paper, plastic, cardboard, aluminum or tin; whether it costs less than or more than a dollar; and whether it weighs less than or more than a pound. Classify your purchases a different way each time you shop. Before long, your child will think of new ways to categorize.

Jar jumble. Save different-sized jars and lids for your child to work with. Have her match the covers to the jars and put the jars in order from tallest to shortest or from fattest to thinnest. Using the lids, she can trace different-sized circles with pencil and paper. Have her fill each jar with a specified amount of different objects.

Ordering. Help your child understand this concept by playing ordering games from time to time. Have her line up blocks from shortest to tallest. She can draw pictures of your family members from tallest to shortest. Fill several plastic glasses with water and have her arrange them from most full to least full.

Helping your preschooler become mathematically literate isn't really a daunting task. With a little creativity and commitment, your preschooler will be enjoying and developing math skills before she enters school.

~

Growing in God

Chapter Seventeen ————————————

How to Be a Spiritual Nurturer

by Mary Manz Simon

Toilet training, temper tantrums, and "No!" situations often end up with parents and toddlers on opposite sides. But activities in one area of growth—spiritual nurture—can bring parents and children together. Even during that challenging year between the ages of 2 and 3, you and your young one can grow with Jesus.

Here are three avenues of potential growth. As you read, keep in mind the importance of timing (your child's) and flexibility (yours).

Going to church. Some young ones do best in the church nursery. Others enjoy time with a parent in the church pew—really! Don't automatically assume your toddler will never sit in church; give her a chance next Sunday.

Pack a bag with crayons, paper and a few Christian books for the church service. Think ahead of ways to involve your child in worship. For example, young children can place an offering envelope in the plate and be shown how to hold and open a hymnal. Consider buying a children's Bible as a gift for your child's next birthday so she has a Bible to carry, "just like my dad."

As the mother of three, I looked after young ones alone in church for years (my pastor-husband was always up front). I remember often saying to myself, "I'm not perfect, but most days I do my best. It feels so good to bring my children to church. That's one thing I'm doing right."

Praying. Your child is finally in the booster seat and reaching for the

Even during that challenging year between the ages of 2 and 3, you and your young one can grow with Jesus.

Dr. Mary Manz Simon

365

hot dog. Today's mealtime prayer might be, "Thanks, Jesus, for lunch." Or, while pushing the stroller, you and your child might stop for a moment to fold hands together and pray, "Thanks, God, for that chirping robin." Bedtime prayers might be just as simple. Prayer that's heartfelt and directed to God is perfect for any age.

Prayer can be built into so many times of the day—some planned, some spontaneous. You'll benefit from the "Jesus times," too.

Sharing devotions. Devotions should be short and simple. Take an event from your day, perhaps something you've done with your child, and talk about how it relates to the Lord. Or ask a question that will lead naturally into a discussion about God's caring, his creation, or his gift of salvation.

I jot down devotion-starters on scraps of paper, napkins or shopping lists as events happen during the day. For example, after a spring rain you might ask, "What do you see outside that God made?" Or, if you made a trip to the grocery store that day, ask, "What food did God make that's orange? Green? Red? While I put away the groceries, draw a picture of something God made that you like to eat." Another option is to use a devotional book designed especially for very young children.

As parents, we don't need to make the spiritual nurture of children into a complicated issue. We just need to *do* it: to help them grow up with Jesus. And when we do that, we grow, too.

Teaching Big Truths to Little Persons

by Debra Evans

What do caterpillars, marigold seeds and cake batter have in common? Judging by outward appearances, nothing. But to a young child, each of these wonders can reveal important lessons about the miracles of Christian rebirth and Jesus' resurrection. Caterpillars enter cocoons and emerge as butterflies; a small, striped shoot springs up above the ground and blooms into a flower; specific amounts of flour and water mixed with a few eggs, some sugar and other dry ingredients are transformed into a billowy birthday cake. Our environment teaches us a great deal about the magnitude of God's love for his children.

Parents are a big part of this learning process. From the moment a child is born, she is suddenly surrounded by expressions of what it means to be cared for and loved. A mother and father instantly acquire an identity as the Lord's earthly representatives—personal spiritual consultants and advisors, if you will—to their child. No one will play a more important role in introducing this tiny new person to the sights and sounds of creation.

In the first months outside the womb, a child's understanding of God is largely limited to physical experiences: the comfort of being rocked in Daddy's arms, a soft kiss on the cheek, warm milk flowing from the breast, snuggling up close next to Mommy's heartbeat.

In other words, how parents touch, speak to and nurture their infants *matters*. Your actions offer life's introductory lessons about how Jesus provides for all who depend upon him for daily sustenance and strength.

As the months go by, your child develops new skills. While physical nurturing remains vitally important to a child's sense of security and self-worth, the avenues of communication between parents and their child expand. When Jesus is honored at the center of the home, a child grows up seeing and hearing all about what it means to be a Christian.

This is an awesome responsibility. Because we parents aren't perfect, opportunities for instruction in grace, humility and forgiveness abound. It often helps to remember Paul's words to the Colossians regarding these essentials of Christian life: "Therefore, as God's chosen people, holy and dearly loved, clothe yourselves with compassion, kindness, humility, gentleness and patience. Bear with each other and forgive whatever grievances you may have against one another. Forgive as the Lord forgave you. And over all these virtues put on love, which binds them all together in perfect unity" (Col. 3:12-14).

Has anyone ever written a more excellent set of instructions for sharing Jesus within our families? More than anything else, sharing Jesus with our sons and daughters requires our own obedience to God's Word.

By their third year of life, children have already had many experiences that tell them about who Jesus is and what it means to be a Christian. In addition to parental role models, however, 2- and 3-year-olds are especially eager to learn about the Lord's character through common, colorful examples. It's an adventure you won't want to miss.

That's where the bugs and flowers and cupcakes come in—simple things that children can touch, taste, smell and feel. Small things that brightly reflect the wonder of God's truth. Everyday things that enable even the youngest child to marvel at the Gospel message before they can grasp the meaning of words like *sin* or *redemption*.

Prayer and Praise for Every Day

by Laurie Winslow Sargent

It's never too soon for a child to learn to talk with and trust God. When we experience joy in our relationship with Jesus Christ, we want our children to experience that same joy.

To begin building your toddler's faith and prayer capacity:

Don't underestimate your child's abilities. Toddlers have been known to remember—and describe in sentences—things which happened to them a year before (when they were still learning first words). They absorb a lot. Tell your child stories about how God has helped you. Pray with him. Sing worship songs containing Scripture and spiritual truths. You'll be amazed at what your toddler recalls.

Praising God together can turn into a gift to yourself. One day when we sang praise songs in the car, I was enjoying the fellowship so much that when I looked over at my son I was startled; I'd forgotten that my fellow-worshipper was strapped into a toddler car seat, holding a sipper cup!

Consider your child's level of understanding. When my son was still unaware of death and its implications, he saw a picture of Jesus in burial clothes. "Jesus go night-night," he said. I simply nodded. Too soon he would understand the finality and sometimes cruelty of death. Then he would also begin to understand Christ's awesome resurrection.

Sure enough, within a few short years, after seeing an Easter play, my son's understanding caught me off guard. "Jesus didn't have to let those bad men do that to him, huh, Mom? He did it to save us."

Look for tiny opportunities to praise or pray with your toddler. One day Tyler sat in his high chair watching me as I ran around our living room, muttering crazily. For hours I'd been searching for my scuba certification card. Finally, I approached him in his high chair and grasped his tiny hands.

"Sweetie, if God wants us to find that card, he'll show us where it is."

After we prayed, I walked to the couch. I tore all the cushions off, reached way back behind the springs—and pulled out the card. Tyler immediately yelled out, "Yay, Jesus!"

Allow God to teach you through your child. Parenthood is full of surprises. While attempting to pass on my faith to my child, I've found my child passing faith back to me.

One day I overheard my son again cry out, "Yay, Jesus!" I peeked through his bedroom doorway. There on the floor, he sat back on his heels, clapping and beaming at a tower of stacked blocks.

Often I forget to praise God for my accomplishments in such a spontaneous, excited way. And I confess that when one of my toddler's prayers for his "Gray-grampa" was answered so quickly, I was amazed. With simple trust, he confidently expected an answer to his prayer. No wonder Jesus said we should all become childlike in our faith (Matt. 18:3, 4)—to which I say, "Yay, Jesus!"

Learning the Word

by V. Gilbert Beers

It's not enough to help kids love Bible stories or Bible pictures or Bible verses. A lifetime of Bible reading depends on loving *the Bible*. Of course, we're not cultivating a love for paper, leather and print; we're cultivating a love for God's Word and the God it reveals to us.

But *can* we help kids love the Bible? After all, the Bible isn't exactly a Disney book. It's about people who lived long ago and far away in cultures that even we adults often don't understand. Most of us struggle to understand the Bible and apply it to our own lives. So how can we expect our children to love the Bible?

Some Christian workers say it can't be done; we shouldn't even try. These people settle for kids who learn to love Bible stories, pictures, memory verses or Sunday school lessons. The Bible itself, they think, is just not for kids.

I think they're wrong. We *must* help our young children learn to love the Bible. As a father of five and a grandfather of seven, I'm convinced that one of our most important jobs as parents, teachers, grandparents and ministers is to help children love the Word of God. Lifelong habits of reading the Bible come from a love for the Bible, not from an obligation to read it. If you don't generate that love, the Bible will remain a closed book.

But how do we build a love for the Bible in the hearts of our preschoolers? Here are a few suggestions:

Loving the Bible begins by having a role model who loves the Bible. You will never generate in your kids a greater love for the Bible than you have in your own life. If they do develop a greater love than yours, chances are they looked to other role models.

Do you genuinely love to read the Bible? Do you convey that attitude to your children when you talk about the Bible? Or do you project the feeling that the Bible is boring—a real chore to read?

Do you ignore the Bible each day? Are you careless in the way you handle the Bible, throwing it on the table or putting coffee cups on it? Does TV take a higher priority in your life? Kids learn to love the Book their mother or father loves.

Loving the Bible begins with Bible-reading times that are easy to love. Do you force your children to listen or do you make Bible reading fun and interesting? How you present the Bible to your kids will make a lifelong difference in the love and respect they have for it. Bible reading should be joyful and delightful—just plain fun.

Loving the Bible begins with a children's Bible that is easy to love. Does the Bible you read to your children have adult text or a text geared toward children? Does it have beautiful illustrations that bring the Bible to life? Does it have interesting Bible-learning material for children?

Your child lives in a visual world of TV and full-color printing. Merely reading the Bible to your child (a verbal presentation) will not generate the interest that a visual presentation will.

Invest in a children's Bible that seeks to present its content with high interest. Look for one with a text for children, which is much more interesting to your kids than an adult text.

Loving the Bible begins with Bible reading that is mingled with family fun times. Some of our most rewarding family Bible times were informal rather than formally structured times. A Bible reading around a family campfire, on a fun trip, sitting at a picnic table, or on a hike in the woods will stir more love for the Bible than an enforced time that prevents kids from having fun.

I believe in consistent, daily Bible time for families, but if you have to force it, or generate unloving feelings toward the Bible, wait a day or do it elsewhere.

Your Child's Developing Conscience

by Bonnidell Clouse

The development of a conscience is essential to being a moral person, and the critical period for conscience development is during the preschool period. By "critical," child psychologists mean the optimal time for learning to take place. Before age 3, children usually obey their parents to avoid punishment. Instead, they need an internal monitor that goes with them wherever they are, so their parents can safely say their children can be trusted to act appropriately, even when an adult is not present. External constraint is not enough; morality must come from within.

An understanding of right and wrong is not inborn; it develops gradually as a child matures. Between the ages of 3 and 5, children begin to understand that there are reasons for rules: Saying "please" and "thank you" makes life more pleasant for everyone. Picking up toys or helping set the table includes a child as a valuable member of the family. Taking turns with a brother or sister is a way of being fair.

Children learn to appreciate that manners are good, helping is good, fairness is good.

From age 3 on, children gradually come to adopt *as their own* what their parents expect of them. They have a sense of pride when they do what they know is right, and a sense of guilt when they do what they know is wrong. After the ages of 5 or 6, it is more difficult for normal conscience development to take place. By the time a child starts school, the critical period has passed.

Because of the importance of these early years, parents should be aware of ways to foster moral behaviors and attitudes. Here are a few suggestions:

Teach by example. Telling your child to "do what you say, not what you do" does not coincide with the way learning takes place. Your child learns more by what he sees than by what he is told. Model the behaviors, the speech, and even the tone of voice you want your child to have. All children imitate their parents; your child will imitate you.

Teach by direction. Being a good example is not always enough. We've all known kind and helpful parents of rude and hateful children. Sometimes a parent must explain to her child that such behavior will not be tolerated. State a rule: "Do not hit." Then give reasons for the rule: "Hands are for helping, not for hitting." Then state the consequences if your child breaks the rule: "If you hit, you must be by yourself without toys for 15 minutes." Have your child repeat back to you all three elements of the rule.

Follow through every time. Consequences must be both fair to the child and enforceable. Never give in to fussing, crying, or begging for "one more chance." Each time you give in, your child learns that rules don't matter much, that he (rather than the parent) is in charge, and that being obnoxious will get him what he wants. Out-of-control children have parents who give in.

Encourage reasoning. As parents, we favor autonomy in our children as well as obedience, self-reliance and independence. We want them to learn to make decisions and feel a growing responsibility for the consequences of those decisions. We need to balance control on our part with decision-making on their part. By providing guidelines, we remain in charge while our child develops decision-making competencies that will carry him through life.

Praise your child. Preschoolers can do many things to make life pleasant for the rest of the family. "You were a big help to Mommy" will make your child want to do the same thing again. Find opportunities to let your child know you're proud of her when she strives to be good.

Your Child's Picture of God

by Richard Dobbins

Several years ago a woman came to me suffering from severe depression. I did not talk to her long before I discovered she had a horrible image of herself. She had carried these thoughts and feelings about herself all her life. They were reinforced by her frightening and judgmental view of God.

So I asked, "How do you picture God in your mind?"

"I've never particularly thought about that," she replied, "but I can tell you I'm very frightened of him."

"What makes you frightened of him?" I inquired.

"Well, I've been afraid of him all my life—ever since I got saved," she said. "As best as I can recall," she began, "I was 3 years old when this evangelist came to our church and preached a sermon on hell. I was so scared when he finished that I ran to the altar like the world's greatest sinner and got saved. I can remember everybody making a fuss over me because I had gone to the altar. I know I was relieved at the time, but evidently it didn't make any lasting difference in the way I felt about myself. And I'm still scared of God."

Immediately I felt myself angered by a religion that would put a load of guilt and fear like that on a 3-year-old child.

Jesus felt the same way about adults giving children wrong ideas about God. Read Matthew 18:1-6. Jesus knew that when you turn a child's mind off to spiritual things you deprive him of life's most important discoveries: how much God loves him and how important he is to God.

You can't always control what takes place at church. However, you can see that your child's church experiences are interpreted for him in a spiritually healthy way.

Preschoolers believe anything an adult says must be true. What a responsibility this places on parents and church leaders! It is cruel to take advantage of this beautiful innocence by teaching children overpowering religious ideas largely designed to control them through fear and guilt.

At this age, your child is not mentally prepared for thoughts about hell, tribulation and judgment. Premature attempts to introduce these concepts can damage his future attitude toward spiritual things.

How can children best be introduced to spiritual concepts? Your preschooler is becoming acquainted with nature. This is an excellent time to teach him how God created the world. Reading an account of creation from a Bible storybook might be a good place to start. Then, broaden this with stories about the sun, moon, stars, trees, grass and weather.

Children love animal stories. The Bible is full of them. Genesis tells us God created the animals and allowed Adam to name them. Noah and the ark furnish enough material for many inspirational and instructive times with your youngster. Jonah and the whale make another exciting story, especially since it has such a happy ending. Think of the many times the Gospels mention fish and fishing. And don't forget Jesus' stories about sheep and shepherds.

Children also like to hear about other children. Moses and the bulrushes, Samuel in the temple, baby Jesus, the lad who let Jesus feed a multitude with his lunch—these are just a few of the beautiful stories about children in the Bible.

Learning about God's world, discovering Jesus as God's revelation of how much he loves us, being taught how angels watch over little children—these are all wholesome aspects of the preschooler's religious education.

ABOUT THE AUTHORS

Karby Allington, R.D., and contributing editor for *Christian Parenting Today* magazine, speaks, writes and counsels individuals on nutrition-related issues. She lives in Fort Collins, Colo.

V. Gilbert Beers, Ph.D., Th.D., and contributing editor for *Christian Parenting Today,* is president of Scripture Press. He is the author of many children's books, including *Teaching Toddlers the Bible* and *The Toddler's Bible* (Victor).

Chuck Cerling is a free-lance writer living in Tawas City, Mich.

Bonnidell Clouse, Ph.D., is a former contributing editor for *Christian Parenting Today*.

Richard Dobbins, Ph.D., is director of EMERGE Ministries, a mental health care treatment center in Akron, Ohio. Dr. Dobbin's contribution to *Christian Parenting Answers* was adapted from his *Venturing Into a Child's World* (Revell).

Joni Eareckson Tada is founder and director of the Christian Fund for the Disabled (Joni and Friends) and author of several books, including the Darcy series (David C. Cook).

Debra Evans,ICCE, is a contributing editor for *Christian Parenting Today*. She is author of *The Complete Book on Childbirth* (Tyndale).

Susan Gilliland (formerly Susan Zitzman) was *Christian Parenting Today's* first Single Parenting columnist.

Heather Harpham, columnist for *Virtue* magazine, lives in Springfield, Ore., with her two sons. Her latest book is *I Stole God from Goody Two-Shoes* (Harvest House).

Audrey Hingley is a free-lance writer who often addresses health and medical topics.She has had articles published in *The Saturday Evening Post, Woman's World, FDA Consumer* and *The Christian Reader*. She lives near Richmond, Va.

Allen Johnson, Ph.D., is a licensed marriage and family therapist, author of numerous articles on children with disabilities, and a contributing editor to *Christian Parenting Today.* He and his wife, Lori, live in Auburn, Mass.

James Judge, M.D., and contributing editor for *Christian Parenting Today,* is a family medicine physician in private practice in Wheaton, Ill.

Grace Ketterman, M.D., and contributing editor for *Christian Parenting Today,* is medical director of Crittenton Center in Kansas City, Mo. She is author of *Mothering: The Complete Guide for Mothers of All Ages* (Thomas Nelson).

Kay Kuzma, Ed.D., and contributing editor for *Christian Parenting Today,* is a child development specialist and author of more than a dozen books, including *When You're Serious About Love* (Thomas Nelson).

Vicky Lansky is a columnist for *Family Circle magazine.* Her contribution to *Christian Parenting Answers* was adapted from her *Childproof Your Home* (Safety 1st).

Kevin Leman, Ed.D., and contributing editor for *Christian Parenting Today,* has a private practice in Tucson, Ariz. His contribution to *Christian Parenting Answers* was adapted from his *Getting the Best Out of Your Kids* (Harvest House).

Mary Manz Simon, Ed.D., is *Christian Parenting Today's* "Q & A" columnist. She has written 36 books, and received the "Distin-guished Service Award" in 1994 from the Illinois State University Alumni Association.

Elaine McEwan-Adkins, Ed.D., and contributing editor for *Christian Parenting Today,* is a school administrator and author of *The Parent's Guide to Solving School Problems* (Harold Shaw).

David Peters, M.S.W., and contributing editor for *Christian Parenting Today,* is a professional counselor in Sonora, Calif.

Patricia Rushford, R.N., and contributing editor for *Christian Parenting Today,* holds a master's degree in Christian counseling. She is the author of several books, including *What Kids Need Most in a Mom* (Revell).

William Sears, M.D., columnist for *Christian Parenting Today,* is a pediatrician in San Clemente, Calif., and assistant clinical professor of pediatrics at the University of Southern California. He and his wife, Martha, are co-authors of *The Baby Book* and *The Birth Book* (Little, Brown). The Sears have eight children.

Clara Shaw Schuster, Ph.D., R.N., was a contributing editor for *Christian Parenting Today* and family development specialist on the faculty of Kent State University, Kent, Ohio. Dr. Schuster passed away in 1991.

Pamela Smith, R.D., author of *Eat Well Live Well* (Creation House), is a nationally known nutritionist.

Faith Tibbets McDonald, M.Ed., and contributing editor for *Christian Parenting To-*

day, is a newspaper columnist and former elementary school teacher.

David Veerman, M.Div., and contributing editor for *Christian Parenting Today,* has written more than 25 books, including the *Life Application Bible for Students* (Tyndale).

Laurie Winslow Sargent is a certified occupational therapy assitant and contributing editor for *Christian Parenting Today.*

Christine Yount is a free-lance writer and editor of *Children's Ministry* magazine.

Jeanne Zornes is a free-lance writer living in Wenatchee, Wash.

Most of the material in this book appeared originally in *Christian Parenting Today* magazine. Additional pieces were written by Debra Evans, general editor. For *Christian Parenting Today* subscription information, call 1-800-238-2221.

I N D E X